STAGECRAFT

THE COMPLETE GUIDE TO THEATRICAL PRACTICE

STAGECRAFT

THE COMPLETE GUIDE TO THEATRICAL PRACTICE
CONSULTANT EDITOR: **TREVOR R. GRIFFITHS**

Consultant editor
Trevor R. Griffiths is Director of Media and Interdisciplinary Studies at the
Polytechnic of North London. He has worked in many areas of theatre
since the age of 12. He is chairman of London's Foco Novo Theatre Group,
a leading British fringe company.

CONTRIBUTING EDITORS
Jason Barnes
Lizzi Becker
Richard Harris
Iona McLeish
Alastair Moffat
Alan O'Toole
Philippe Perottet
John Philips
Jennie Stoller

A QUARTO BOOK

Published by Phaidon Press Limited,
Regent's Wharf, All Saints Street,
London N1 9PA

First published 1982
Second impression (paperback) 1990
Reprinted 1992, 1994, 1996, 1998
© Copyright 1982 Quarto Publishing plc

A CIP catalogue for this book is available from the British Library

ISBN 0 7148 2644 8

20 00001 439

This book was designed and produced by Quarto Publishing plc
6 Blundell Street
London N7 9BH.
Art Director: Bob Morley
Editorial Director: Jeremy Harwood
Art Editor: Moira Clinch
Senior Editor: Kathy Rooney
Project Editor: Hilary Arnold
Art Assistants: Nick Clark, Tony Paine, Annie Collenette, Bill Robertson
Illustrators: Simon Roulstone, Sotos Achilleos, Marilyn Clark
Photographers: Ian House, Simon de Courcy-Wheeler, Peter Cogran,
Jon Wyand

Printed in China by Leefung-Asco Printers Ltd.

We would like to thank all those who have helped in the creation of this
book. Particular thanks go to the members of Strathclyde Theatre
Group, Glasgow, from 1974 to 1981, and especially the late Hugo
Gifford for his inspiration. Special thanks also go to Roland Rees and
Ann Louise Wirgman of Loco Novo; Adrian Vaux; Ace McCarron;
Diane Borger; Mark Fletcher; Nina Edwards; the staff and students of
Wimbledon School of Art, Theatre Design Department, especially
David Burrows, Ronald Brown, Josh Thomas, Alan Sherlock, Sean
Barrett, Dick Davey, Peter Whiteman, Rank Strand Ltd, especially Mr
Crisp and Brian Legge for technical advice on lighting; Riverside Studios
and James Dillon; the National Theatre of Great Britain for permission
to use stage management material; Charles H. Fox Ltd, especially Mary
Topping for advice on make-up; Donald Cooper for his assistance.

CONTENTS

Previous page
Theater today involves
actors, production crew and
audience alike. This promenade
production of a medieval cycle
play had the cast and crew
mingling with the audience, in a
modern interpretation of a
traditional theater experience.

FOREWORD

There are no simple formulas for achieving successful theater. The visual impact and finely tuned co-ordination of this chorus (**left**) involved months of hard work from everybody involved in the production. *The Oresteia* was one of the National Theatre's presentations in London in 1981. Amateur companies may not hope to accomplish the masterly control of the great professionals. Yet with careful planning, creative energy, close liaison and enthusiastic dedication, any production can both entertain and impress its audience.

Creating good theater is a rewarding but arduous activity. Anyone who has been involved in theater for a while, whether professional or amateur, works out principles and practices which enable the production to be handled in a better and more convincing way. For this book we have gathered together experts who have formulated their own hard-won experience into a set of guidelines. They show how to achieve the best possible production with the least number of pitfalls. In the theater, problems often occur because the original idea – in any of the many areas of theatrical activity – has not been fully thought through. This book is about the reasons for doing things as well as how to do them. It does not solve every conceivable problem that a company may face, but it does provide a set of principles for each aspect of a production which offer ways for solving problems.

Anyone who puts on a performance for others, whether it be a children's play or a professional opera, owes it to their audience to make the show as good as it can be, given the resources and budget available. This book contains an incredible amount of practical information and advice, both in the text and many illustrations, to help smooth the path of the simplest or most complex production.

The impulse to perform is deep seated in the human race. To be involved in making a performance is exciting in itself, but it is much more exciting if that performance is really well organized. Then it reaches the widest possible audience and impresses them with the quality of all aspects of the production—acting, directing, set, costumes, stage management, lighting, sound, make-up and even administration and publicity. This book helps make that a goal attainable by the experienced and inexperienced alike.

CHAPTER ONE

DIRECTING

CHOOSING AND READING THE PLAY

CASTING · AUDITIONING · PUBLICITY

REHEARSING · BLOCKING

THE OPENING NIGHT

Directing a show is one of the great challenges in the theater. Although it is impossible to stipulate exactly what makes a good director, the director needs the ability to choose the play, select a cast who will work well together and, no matter how many shows the director has done, an ability to approach material completely freshly. However, another main requirement for directors is for them to be able to get the very best out of the play, cast, crew and facilities available. Directing also requires an eye for space and spatial relationships, and ideas about how to translate the play from the page to the stage. Before starting to direct, it would be useful to have experience in some other areas of theater—perhaps stage management or acting.

APPROACHES TO DIRECTING

The role of the director and the role of the critic are diametrically opposite. Where it is the task of the critic to assess the production and point out faults and weaknesses, it is the director's job to find all that is laudable and praiseworthy in a play, to camouflage and justify the inconsistencies and more difficult transitions in the piece, to make certain that the production and the actors serve the intentions of the playwright, and put over the argument and ideas of the play. Obviously, individual directors vary considerably in their working methods and in how they approach their role.

General approaches to directing have changed markedly in recent years. Before then the director tended to be rather autocratic. For example, Laurence Olivier, British actor and director, stated in an interview in the *New York Times* (7 February 1960): 'I expect my actors to do exactly what I tell them to do and do it quickly, so I can see my own mistakes immediately if I have gone wrong. I believe the director must know the play so well that he grasps every important moment of every scene. He knows—and he alone—when the actor should rise and fall. He knows where to place the accents. An individual actor may not see the logic of an action.... An actor gets the right thing by doing it over and over. Arguing about motivation and so forth is a lot of rot.'

However, in recent years the 'I want...' director in the Olivier mold has been slightly outmoded by a new kind of 'let's try this...' director. As the collective company has come about, so the director's role has been changed to allow a more democratic actor-director working relationship. When Olivier says that it is the director and 'he alone' who knows when the action should rise and fall, he may be right that, as an outside eye on the production, it is possible that the director can at times see things that are not as clear to the actor. But often the

Noel Coward's play *Semi-Monde* would make an excellent choice of play for a non-professional company. Coward's name is always a good draw to audiences and, since it was never performed during his lifetime, *Semi-Monde* had an added attraction when premiered by The Citizens Theatre, Glasgow (**left**). The very large cast would have been a hindrance to many professional companies because of budget, but this company took full advantage of it. With careful directing and an elegant, effective set, the production created an impressively bustling and fashionable world.

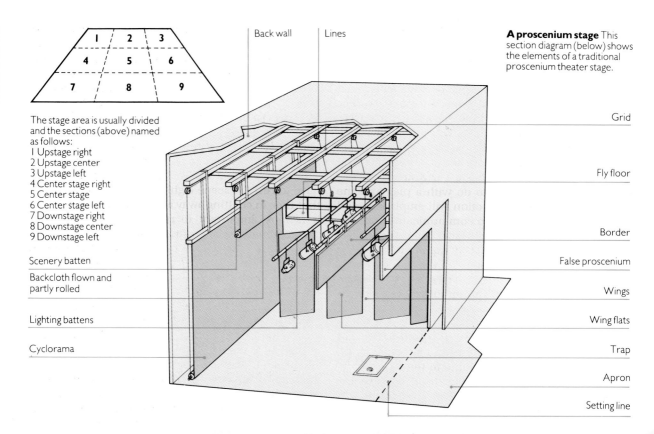

The stage area is usually divided and the sections (above) named as follows:
1 Upstage right
2 Upstage center
3 Upstage left
4 Center stage right
5 Center stage
6 Center stage left
7 Downstage right
8 Downstage center
9 Downstage left

Scenery batten

Backcloth flown and partly rolled

Lighting battens

Cyclorama

Back wall

Lines

A proscenium stage This section diagram (below) shows the elements of a traditional proscenium theater stage.

Grid

Fly floor

Border

False proscenium

Wings

Wing flats

Trap

Apron

Setting line

PRODUCTION FLOW CHART

FUNCTIONS	PRE-REHEARSAL PERIOD
DIRECTING	Choose play • clear performing rights • discuss production with set, costume, lighting designers auditions • casting • discuss publicity and program • visit rehearsal space • organize rehearsal schedule
STAGE MANAGEMENT	Discuss show with director • buy or copy scripts • find rehearsal space • organize crew • set tasks mark out rehearsal space • do crew and cast lists • availability chart • prop plan
ACTING	Prepare for audition • read play and note response • research for the part • give address, details to stage manager
SET DESIGN	Read the play • work out basic ideas • discuss production with director • study theater space research for the play • do sketches • make model • discuss model with director, stage manager make required changes to model • do prop and furniture list
COSTUME DESIGN	Read the play • discuss the production with director • research the play • do planning chart do character charts for each actor • sketch designs • get fabric samples
SET BUILDING	Meet with the designer • discuss proposed set • consider difficulties of set • discuss and obtain materials • buy tools if needed • work out schedule
ADMINISTRATION	Draw up budget for production • check all regulations for theater space • discuss box office consider refreshments at theater • discuss publicity with director
LIGHTING DESIGN	Read the play • study theater space • plan basic lighting requirements

director should take account of the intuition of the actors playing the parts and respect their opinions. Of course, there are many psychological games that can be played by directors so that they give the actors the impression that they are being allowed to follow their instincts but then, by subtlety and stealth, the director can still manage to get the actor to do what the director wants without resorting to direct instructions.

It is, of course, imperative that, at the start of a production, the director has a fairly strong idea of what he or she is going to do with a play and the kind of themes the production will emphasize and what the director wants to communicate about the play to the audience. It is too facile, however, merely to tell the actors that the aim of *Hamlet* is to show a profligate mother in conflict with a son who deeply loves his father. This is insufficient and trivializes the play. Although this is an important aspect, it is superseded by exploring and finding other minor aims, namely the objectives of each character in each scene. If the truth is discovered and rationalized, then the thoughts and actions of individual characters will contribute to the rendition of the whole play. It is vital that the director allows the actors to work this way round.

Actors must act first with thoughts and then with words. It is also important that the words are understood and not just learnt by rote. Acting is a process of discovery in which the honesty of the actor's response is an essential element. It is the job of the director to help the actors find the roots and truth of the characters they are playing. It was the German playwright Bertolt Brecht who said that in theater, copying is not a shame but an art—the theater is a copy of human behavior. The director should help actors to look inside themselves.

In the same interview, Olivier stated 'I'd rather have to run the scene eight times than have wasted that time in chatting away about abstractions'. While it is most important to run sections of the play several times, the stage in rehearsal at which this is done is also a major consideration for the director. If the actor has not sorted out the objectives and thoughts in the scene, the more it is run, the more mistakes are cemented, making it harder for the actor to correct these errors later. Much time may seem to be wasted by working in a more democratic way and talking about 'abstractions' and motivations, but, depending on the temperament and intelligence of the cast, this process may also be invaluable. Directors should never be afraid of stating what seems obvious, because often what to them seems obvious may have been overlooked by an

REHEARSAL	PRODUCTION WEEK	RUN
Workshop and exercise activities · read and block play · liaise with stage management and designers	Technical rehearsal · dress rehearsals · check all elements · make and present notes	Attend performances · note problems have post mortem · cast party
Organize props · make prompt book · mark cues, calls and effects	Ensure all elements ready · do A.S.M.'s running order · do cue sheets · do lighting and sound synopsis · technical rehearsal · finalize prompt book · dress rehearsals · synchronize production	Check all elements · reset stage · check all crew and cast · calls
Arrive on time · learn lines · get to know cast · exercise · attend costume fittings	Technical rehearsals · dress rehearsals · finalize costumes, make-up	Prepare for opening · stay fit
Present model to cast · supervize set building · organize props	Attend load (get) in and fit up · technical rehearsal · note problems · dress rehearsals · last minute alterations	Supervize any repairs · watch for wear and tear · return props
Supervize costume making · hire costumes · find trimmings · do fittings	Complete costumes and fittings · get final accessories · dress rehearsals · make final alterations	Supervize any repairs · return costumes and accessories
Build difficult sections · build practical sections · keep to schedule	Attend load (get) in and fit up · check set on stage · check angles · technical rehearsal · make final alterations	Do any necessary repairs
Organize poster · advance sales · do advance publicity · print programs · organize house staff	Dress rehearsal · organize box office, refreshments · programs	Organize theater · box office
Attend rehearsals · note details · plot lighting plan	Rig and focus lighting · technical rehearsal · final alterations	Do repairs and alterations

Variations on theater design Most people are familiar with traditional proscenium arch theaters but there are many other types of theater and stage space. Theaters-in-the round vary enormously. This Ancient Greek amphitheater (**1**) is at Epidaurus and is still in use today. It seats many thousands of people. A much smaller, but highly flexible, studio theater (**2**) also places the audience round the acting area. This one is at Wanstead High School in London, England.

The Mitzi E. Newhouse Theater (**3**) is an impressive modern design and forms part of the Lincoln Center in New York. A simple thrust stage is an effective feature of the Downstage Theater (**4**) in Wellington, New Zealand. Given a large floor area, even a proscenium theater can be adapted to provide an alternative shape of acting area (**5**).

A theater space can be used in various ways. The simplest is the thrust stage (**6**) which can be backed by a screen (**7**) but allows for little scenery. An end stage (**8**) with a screen can create the impression of a closed space. Curtain sets with borders (**9**) are common in proscenium theaters but can also be created on an end stage. Sets with cut-out cloths and wings (**10**) are now mainly used for pantomime and revues. The box set (**11**) is for creating realistic interiors, and a box within a box (**12**) provides two interiors. It is often possible to use sets with permanent scenery to which pieces can be added or taken away (**13**,**14**,**15**)

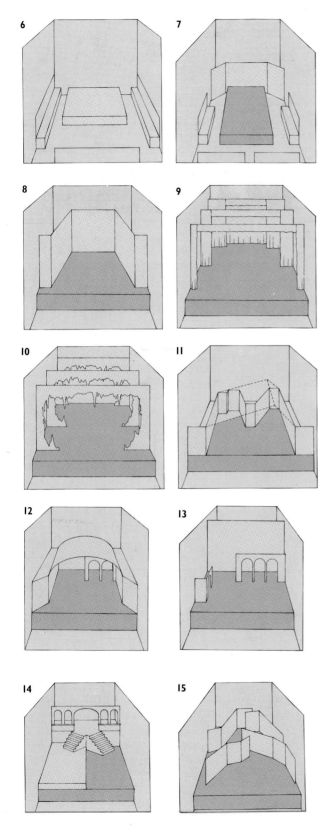

6

7

8

9

10

11

12

13

14

15

actor, and it is important that all knowledge and discoveries about the text are shared.

The temperament of the director is very important too. As a director, you should not try to hide possible weaknesses in the play, but should suggest ways in which the actors can camouflage or get around bad writing, but without necessarily letting them know your real opinions. Often directors resort to using gimmicks to attempt to minimize problems in the play. Do this with great caution, as it may draw even more attention to inconsistencies in the piece. Using tricks or gimmicks is not necessarily a bad thing if their use can be justified within the terms of the piece or if they are in the style and convention of the production. For example, the production of *Richard III* by the Rustaveli Company from Georgia in Russia used many gimmicky devices, but they were all justified by imagery within the play. One example was the final fight between Richard and Richmond which was fought on a huge map, which was visually exciting, but not out of place. An example of less relevant 'business' was the inclusion of Petruchio riding a powerful motorcycle and the presence of a brass band in Michael Bogdanov's controversial 1977 production of *The Taming of the Shrew* at Stratford upon Avon. This was only justified by the fact that the director had chosen to set the play in modern dress. Whilst it proved to be a lot of fun for many people who saw the production, it was not justified by the text itself.

A general change in recent years which has run hand in hand with the decline of the director as autocrat has been the role of the company working together as an ensemble, and even working with the author of the play. Some companies, both professional and amateur, may work for several weeks on a series of workshop sessions, both related and not related to the play that they will finally present. This work is often done in the presence of a writer who will then script their work. Some directors have even assembled a company of actors and allowed them the opportunity to cast themselves. The important British director Peter Brook also believes strongly in this kind of company ethic; his production of *The Ik*, seen in Paris and London in 1975 and 1976, was a good example of this kind of work. The piece was derived from a book about the decline of an African tribe which was worked into a play by Brook's multi-national company of actors.

All directors work differently, and their reasons for wishing to work in the medium of the theater will influence their method. These reasons can range from the totally egocentric to a desire to inform and communicate or, simply, to entertain. Although certain factors are common, methods do vary.

CHOOSING A PLAY

In both the professional and amateur theater, a number of criteria govern the choice of play, some being common to both. For most companies, one of the first considerations and, often, restrictions, is financial—the budget for the production. For example, some musicals may be too expensive to stage because of set and costume changes, as well as the cost of an orchestra, especially in the professional theater. There are, of course, imaginative ways of staging in a simple way what may, at first, seem a far too ambitious choice of play in terms of the physical resources of cast, set and props. For instance, versions of Shakespeare's *Cymbeline* and *Bleak House* by Charles Dickens using only five actors have both been produced with minimal props and no costumes, and yet managed to provide exciting and imaginative theater.

Another important consideration when choosing a play is the space in which you are to perform. The days of being restricted to a proscenium arch stage are long gone, and many new municipal or civic theaters are built now with more flexible performing areas. Community or local halls can be adapted to have greater depth of staging, for instance, by increasing the platform thrust out into the auditorium to improve the actor-audience relationship. It is even possible to perform in the round in such halls, although this may perhaps prove detrimental to the audience possibilities. Many current theaters-in-the-round are conversions of buildings which were originally used for purposes other than theater, including cinemas and schools. Even the recent purpose-built Royal Exchange Theatre in Manchester, England, was built within the shell of an older Corn Exchange. One of the first major purpose-built theaters-in-the-round was Tyrone Guthrie's at Stratford, Ontario, built in the 1950s. This has served as a model for many other theaters.

The director should not be restricted by discounting a play that, at first, does not fit the specifications of the group or company. An imaginative director, who has the enthusiasm to put on a play, can usually overcome at least some of the problems that may arise in casting. If more women than men are available, certain male characters may not need to be played by men. For example, Brecht's male characters do not always have to be played by a man because it is the function, rather than the appearance, of the character that is important in his plays. So, in the case of, for example, a policeman or a trader, a woman may be able to play the part equally well. The same can apply to a Shakespeare play. The style which the director adopts for the production

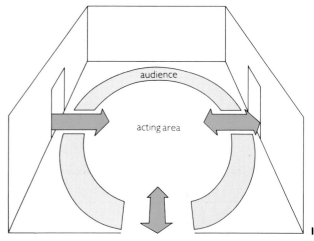

Creating an acting area
Performing in an open space, with no fixed stage or seating, provides an opportunity for creating precisely the acting area suited to a production. The acting area will be defined by the seating. A theater in the round is simply constructed (**1**) by curved seating rostra. Two tier seating is preferable if an end stage is created (**2**). Using the floor and rostra, the audience will have good visibility. Access to the stage and gangways will depend upon the doors into the hall and on the placing of rostra. If a company regularly uses one hall, permanent seating rostra should be built, but in separate units and in various shapes for flexibility. In this hall, a large theater in the round (**3**) or a more intimate one (**4**) can be created, depending on the arrangement of rostra. Alternatively, all the seating can be placed in a horseshoe with the acting area defined by the cyclorama behind (**5**). Gangways can be narrow or wide, depending on the show.

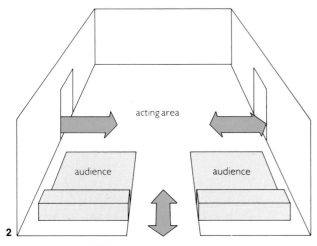

acting area

audience

audience

2

5

may make the audience accept unusual casting, and this can even help to bring out points a director wishes to emphasize, and still serve the play.

IMPROVISED PLAYS

If it is impossible to find a play that suits the needs of the group, and if there is enough enthusiasm, consider the idea of creating a play from improvisation. In fact, an improvised play, whilst it presents a new set of challenges, can be a very refreshing experience for a group.

It is important that the directors reassess their function when working with improvisation. The director's role becomes more one of editor and initiator. It is important to know when to develop something which comes out of an improvisation and when to discard information. Some of the best improvised plays have evolved from the director establishing a strong situation in his or her mind prior to rehearsals.

The director may frequently not even tell the actors at the start of rehearsals the situation which is to be used. The director may work individually with the actors on establishing a character, which can be a very rewarding experience for actors. Instead of having to recreate a character that has been visualized by a writer, actors have the opportunity to create a consistent characterization for themselves. The burden is on the actor to make the character real and theatrically exciting.

The director may then bring the characters/actors together in small groups to do a variety of exercises or scenes which may or may not relate directly to the situation which is to be used in the play. It is important to give the characters a chance to establish themselves in a variety of different scenes, to build up their characteristics and to allow exploration of how the character thinks and functions.

It must be emphasized that working in this way requires a great deal of commitment and concentration from all those involved, as well as, possibly, a longer rehearsal period than a relatively straightforward scripted play. It is possible that time may seem to be wasted in working on scenes which may not appear in the final presentation, but it should help to provide a more complete whole. Another potential pitfall is that the mix of characters created by the actors may not work theatrically. For example, an encounter between two depressed people can make for a dull scene, and it is up to the director to decide whether it is worth radically altering a character for the sake of interest, however well observed the characterization may be.

Although it can be a gamble to improvise a play of

this nature, it can be an extremely enjoyable and exciting experience for both audience and actors. Improvisation can be useful too, if the group wishes to produce a kind of documentary play, about a local issue for instance, or the life of a famous local personality. In this case, the role of director is as researcher, collator of material and, again, as editor. In any kind of improvised project, the way that the group works is much more collective in nature. Improvisation is a group exercise, and it is important to assemble the right personalities for this kind of project, to try to make the right decisions at the right times and to ensure you have enough time to carry the project through.

It may be worth obtaining the services of a writer to write or script a play from a series of improvisations. The influence of a writer can help counter a frequent criticism of improvised work, namely that it suffers from a surfeit of indulgence and can be long-winded. A fine example of this type of cooperation is the Royal Shakespeare Company's *Nicholas Nickleby*, which started out by a series of improvisations, was then scripted by David Edgar, the British playwright, and had great success in both London and New York.

The improvised play seems to work especially well with young people—it can help avoid casting problems and give everyone a sense of involvement because it is an ensemble effort. Nevertheless, the director should still direct an improvised play and must take care not to allow the actors to become too self-indulgent. An improvised piece needs discipline both in its development and in performance. The director must guide the actors and make them look critically at what they have developed, and, if necessary, persuade them to discard elements which do not seem in keeping with the play.

READING THE PLAY

When the play has been chosen, one of the most important first tasks for the director is to read and become familiar with the play. Directors make notes on the play in many different ways, depending on their own preferences and on the play itself. The function of this reading is to work out more fully some of the ideas which sparked the director's enthusiasm first. The director should be enthusiastic and have ideas about the play and be prepared to guide and help the cast. Do not feel that, at this stage, every element of the direction needs to be firmly established. One of the functions of rehearsals is to let ideas emerge and develop.

Another purpose of the initial reading is to establish broadly what resources the play requires, in terms of personnel, equipment and facilities. This should include the numbers needed for the cast. If the play seems to require more actors than are available, work out whether any parts can be 'doubled' or, in other words, played by the same actor. To establish whether doubling is possible, first work out whether the two characters are on stage at the same time. Then consider whether the production will allow time for any costume changes which may be required. Doubling is often more suitable for minor rather than major roles. Doubling can also add greatly to the resonances of the play. For instance, Peter Brook's famous 1970 production of *A Midsummer Night's Dream* doubled the roles of Theseus/Oberon and Hippolyta/Titania, enhancing the relationship between mortals and fairies in the play. However, in the amateur theater, extensive doubling of small roles in plays which seem to require large casts may be possible.

CUTTING A PLAY

Many people may throw up their hands in horror at the thought of cutting a play, but it is worth considering a few things before deciding to perform an uncut play. Firstly, would the argument of the play be streamlined by some cutting? Secondly, would it be possible to perform a large cast play by combining characters? Thirdly, how long does the play run? Another important factor to consider is the audience. When contemplating a long play, bear in mind that the audience may not be able to concentrate for lengthy periods, no matter how good the production is, especially if they have to sit on uncomfortable seats. Also think about local transportation—for example, at what time does the last bus or subway run?

However, it is not advisable to make cuts without careful consideration. For example, a common error in productions of Shakespeare plays is to cut the first few lines of a scene, which often implicitly set the place and context of the scene in an economical and concise way. Whatever cuts are made, it is preferable for this to be done before rehearsals begin. If an actor believes that certain lines should not be lost, then this can be discussed with the director during rehearsals. It is certainly not advisable to introduce cuts and alterations some weeks into rehearsal, as this will only confuse and unsettle the cast. However, cuts may often have to be made towards the end of rehearsals because of the running time of the play, which can only be established when rehearsals are almost complete.

It is worth knowing that many new plays are published to coincide with their premieres. This means that the version that is prepared for publication does not contain the cuts, rewrites and changes that may have been made and approved by the writer during the rehearsal period. This may mean that the performed version of the play may be quite different from the published script.

A play should not be treated with too much reverence. A writer will often agree to changes for theatrical reasons. If a director wishes to make vast changes to the work of a writer whose plays are still under copyright, the alterations should be submitted to the writer's agent for approval. But if you feel that the changes are necessary, do not let yourself be dissuaded too easily.

DIRECTOR'S TASK PLAN

Pre-rehearsal period: choose play considering theater space, cast, type of show to attempt and finance • if show is to be improvised, develop ideas and work out a rough synopsis for the cast • read play and make detailed notes • do any cuts which are necessary • get clearance on performing rights and permission for cuts if necessary • contact writer's agent or dramatist personally if necessary • with stage manager, organize scripts, either copying or buying paperback editions • discuss proposed show with the set, costume and lighting designers • work out details of organization and finance with stage manager and administration • organize auditions • do auditions • do casting • discuss publicity with administration • visit rehearsal space with stage manager • organize rehearsal schedule with stage manager • consider design sketches and models for set, costume sketches and lighting proposals with designers • discuss program with administration • work out production deadlines list with stage manager

Early rehearsals: prepare and do workshop, warm-up and other exercises with cast • discuss play, set, costumes, lighting and all proposals for the production with the cast • read through play with cast • begin to block the play

Later rehearsals: continue to block the play • do detailed work on each scene and with each actor • change blocking as necessary • continue warm-up and workshop activities • discuss set, props, costumes and so on with designers and stage manager in relation to developments in rehearsals • discuss and finalize cues, scene changes, and other details with stage manager, designers and crew

Production week: attend technical rehearsal • check all cues, calls, equipment, scenery, sound and lighting effects with stage manager • make detailed notes of problems and discuss ways of solving them • organize photo call • ensure all props are as required and ready • run dress rehearsal (two if possible) • make notes on dress rehearsal performances and technical details arising from dress rehearsal • present notes to cast and crew • organize curtain call and intermissions

First night and performance run: have final meeting with cast to boost confidence and go over weak points and possible problem areas • check every element in production is ready and working • watch play and note problems • keep morale high • organize cast party • finalize budget • ensure theater is left tidy and undamaged after run • ensure all borrowed and hired items are returned • have a post mortem on the production for future reference • go over production with company • start to prepare for the next production

PRE-REHEARSAL PREPARATIONS

Once the play has been chosen, the director has a good deal of work to do before the play can go into rehearsal. When preparing for a production in the professional theater, one of the first things to happen is that the director and the designer meet and discuss their ideas. Often in amateur companies there may be a team of people who are responsible collectively for producing the set. However, one person should be in overall charge and coordinate the venture. If a designer is available, all the better

Designing for the stage is a specialized skill and a director always has to watch for certain problems in working with the designer. Try to avoid what may be termed a 'designer's set'. This is a set which may be very striking and imposing visually, but may make it impossible for the actors to act. For example, certain areas may become strong positions while anywhere else may be dwarfed by the set. Of course, the kind of set you require depends totally on the kind of style you wish the production to have and the budget available. For example, a very simple production of Shakespeare's *Julius Caesar* may only require an empty space, in other words, one with absolutely minimal props and furniture. This may not seem like an exciting prospect to a designer. If, however, you believe that this best serves your vision of the production, you must convince the designer

The director must always bear in mind the need for great flexibility within the set. Before meeting the designer, the director should have gone through the play to see how many settings will be required, so that the exact location for each scene, can be discussed and decided with the designer. Initial considerations also include how scene changes will be accomplished, whether trucks will be used, where the best position on stage for speeches or soliloquies will be. If a designer wishes the main stage area to taper into a triangular shape at the front, remember that this immediately shifts most of the action upstage and alters the actors' relationship with the audience. If there are fixed settings, such as a store counter or bar, at the back of the stage area, problems may arise with actors always talking with their backs to the audience. The director should also consider problems of sight lines, in other words whether the audience can see the stage. Certain theaters and other spaces may present problems of visibility, and the designer should bear these in mind when working out the set. These matters must be thoroughly discussed.

It is also vital to keep a practical eye on the design

of costumes and props. If an actor has to do anything particularly physical, will the costume accommodate it? Props may be elaborate and decorative, but will they hold up to being used night after night without collapsing? Without dashing cold water on the inventiveness of the designer, the director must be the person who uses common sense and is forward looking enough to keep in mind the practical problems of the designs. The director should be able to clearly communicate his or her vision of the production at the outset, and a good designer will complement a director's ideas and extend the visual side of the production.

When working in the amateur theater, try not to have too elaborate sets and costumes. This applies particularly if the people working on the design are inexperienced. In professional and amateur theater alike, the director must keep a strict eye on practicalities, guiding the designer, encouraging ideas and enthusiasm while tactfully curbing excesses.

CASTING AND AUDITIONING

Directors have many different methods of auditioning. Of course, in the professional theater as in amateur groups, certain actors are known to directors, and their work is familiar enough for it to become unnecessary to audition them. The director will know whether the part coincides with their capabilities. However, it is important always to seek to extend and stretch an actor's capabilities and range. Brecht pointed out the pitfalls of type casting: 'Why cast a haggard, coarse looking woman as a fishwife? There are elegant looking fishwives, young fishwives as well as old fishwives.' Many outstanding performances have come from unlikely casting. Of course, sometimes casting against type is more successful than at others. Nevertheless, it is worth considering, as new light may be shed on a character.

There are various ways of auditioning. Some directors may be satisfied with an informal chat with actors to find out what kind of work they have done and to find out about the actors themselves. A second approach is to ask for two or more audition pieces—a classical and a modern piece, and perhaps a song. In a third type of audition, especially popular with amateurs, the actor may be asked to read a piece from the play being done. Sometimes auditions may be carried out in a workshop style, asking the actors to do a warm-up, then some improvisation and coordination exercises.

It is perhaps best to have both a chat and to see the actors doing something where you can see them

using the whole of their bodies. Many people have mannerisms which may prove undesirable, and it is good to see their coordination. These are important factors, while an audition piece often shows mainly what standard actors can achieve when they have worked on a piece for some time.

Naturally an audition can be a nerve-wracking experience for actors, and it is better if the director can allow them to relax and feel at ease before they do their pieces. As well as taking into account the actual skills of actors, it is important to check what kinds of personalities they have. In auditioning and casting, it is imperative that the director uses his or her psychological judgement to balance the personalities in the cast and avoid obvious clashes of temperament. It is worth remembering that casting the play well is a large percentage of the director's job. Mistakes in assessing the abilities of actors can waste time and be costly. It is important to be sure, and to have faith in your judgement.

PUBLICITY AND PROGRAMS

Before the play goes into rehearsal, it is useful to have got most of the publicity in motion and to have considered what kind of information you want to put into the program. In this area, the director should again guide and supervise those responsible for publicity and programs. Posters should serve two main functions. First of all, they should be eye-catching. However, the director should make sure that the title of the play is displayed boldly and that the image on the poster gives a clue to what the play is about. There is no point in being oversubtle, unless the play has a guaranteed audience.

The type of program may be a fairly personal choice. Apart from obvious information, such as the list of characters and credits, you might consider putting in information about the playwright and the circumstances that surround the play, as well as photographs of previous productions. Some directors even put in a personal statement about why they decided to put on the play. This can often be unnecessary and even embarrassing.

SCHEDULING REHEARSALS

In the professional theater, actors will be available to work during the day. However, with amateur companies, evenings and weekends may be the only times when rehearsals can take place. It is very difficult to make a generalized statement on how best to divide up rehearsal time. Rehearsal periods in the professional theater vary enormously. In weekly repertory, for example, a play would be rehearsed one week and performed the next, so that the cast would rehearse one show during the day and perform another at night. Although this approach has practically died out in many places, it is still a common summer practice in the United States. With the large, non-profit making subsidized or national companies, rehearsals can take months. The recent production of Aeschylus's *The Oresteia* at the National Theatre in London required some six months' rehearsal, but even this is a small period of time in comparison with the Moscow Art Theater which may rehearse a play for more than a year. On average, however, a rehearsal period in the professional theater lasts between three and four weeks. This, in amateur terms, may be equivalent to 10 to 12 weeks of three sessions per week.

Before rehearsals start, the director should work out the dates of the production, making sure that they do not clash with, for instance, other large local productions, holidays and so on. Once the production dates are fixed, work out the rehearsal schedule in conjunction with the stage manager. Cast and stage management will prefer to have a basic detailed schedule rather than arranging rehearsals on an *ad hoc* basis. However, it is wise to ascertain whether certain evenings or times will definitely be difficult for members of the cast. Although actors and stage crew usually accept that rehearsals will be more frequent and take longer as the first night approaches, a wise director will not make excessive demands on a cast from the outset—particularly amateurs giving up free time.

FIRST REHEARSALS

The function of rehearsals is to prepare the play for the production by practice. Rehearsals mainly concern the actors, but the designers, stage management staff and the other members of the technical crew will need to attend at various points.

Certain decisions will have been made by the director before the cast assembles for the first rehearsal. These include, broadly, the style in which the play is going to be played, the kind of settings, costumes, the sound effects and lighting effects that are going to be used. It is important that the director knows the play inside out, so that time is not wasted by lack of homework. The first few weeks of rehearsal are the time when everybody is working toward a shared knowledge of the play. During this period it is up to the director to make certain that everybody

has the same ideas about characters, situations and other aspects of the production.

At the first meeting of cast, director and technicians, it may be worth the cast reading the play through. Some directors think that 'read-throughs' are not such a good idea, as it well may put pressure on the actors to 'perform' the play before they have studied it in much depth. However, it is possible that the advantages outweigh this consideration. It is good for the company to hear each others' voices, to correct any misprints or omissions in the text, and to get an approximate idea of the running time of the play at the outset, for plays rarely run shorter in final production than at a read-through.

APPROACHING THE TEXT

There are still some professional directors who feel that it is a good idea to begin to place or 'block' the play straightaway. Before rehearsals begin, they have already worked out at home, using a model or diagram of the set, where the furniture will be placed and where they want the actors to move around it. This kind of approach, however, is now considered rather old fashioned by many professional directors. It is obviously a good idea if the director has a rough outline of the physical shape of the scenes in the play, but it is equally good to allow an actor to move instinctively in a given scene and, if there are problems, other ways can be tried out.

In a naturalistic play where the director and designer have already decided the positions of furniture and room divisions for best theatrical effect, then it is often more successful if the actors follow their natural instincts. Sight-lines are also a tremendously important consideration, and during the blocking the director should not remain seated in the middle of the room but should view the action from a variety of places to make sure the majority of the audience will be able to see the action.

Other directors may not wish to work directly on the play at the start of rehearsals. When time allows, some directors prefer to prepare their companies by a series of workshop activities or some unrelated improvisational exercises, so that the actors get to know one another better and break down inhibitions, both physical and social. There are many improvisational games for this purpose. Often professional directors may use the assistance of a movement specialist who may do a warm-up with the company. This may include gymnastic and vocal exercises. This can produce good results, depending on the physical nature of the play. For example, it would be important in a play like Peter Shaffer's *Equus* or Tom Stoppard's *Jumpers* where the nature

Blocking positions on stage
In rehearsal (**1**) the director must work with the actors to find the most effective physical relationships between the characters. William Congreve's eighteenth century play, *The Double Dealer*, describes a highly artificial society. To stress this, the actors have been arranged in a line (**2**) and the men carry ornamental walking sticks and handkerchiefs. The relationships between characters is indicated by grouping three of them with a man and a woman separated on each side. The set is always a factor in determining how actors can be placed. These steps (**3**), for Boris Vian's *The Empire Builders*, gave the director great scope which was used to create interesting visual effects.

of the play relies heavily on the strength, stamina and fitness of the company. Often professional actors do a warm-up privately prior to rehearsal or a performance. Most acting or drama school trainings nowadays place a strong emphasis on voice and movement training—it is important to build up an actor's strength for what is a hard and tiring profession.

It is a good idea for amateur companies to consider the advantages of a half-hour warm-up prior to an evening rehearsal. The purpose of this is to allow people who have been working in a variety of different environments to meet before doing work on the text, in order to clear their heads of their daily work, to shift their concentration and shed tensions. There are several breathing and relaxing exercises which can be used to good effect in helping the company begin to work together well as a group and ensemble. A warm-up can repay the time spent on it because it will help the actors to cohere as a group more quickly. This is obviously an

advantage for amateur companies where rehearsal time may be limited and when the cast may only meet once or twice a week.

Certain professional directors who have the luxury of, say, an eight-week full-time rehearsal period, may not approach the text of the play they are to work on for maybe 10 days or two weeks. If they are doing a period play, where the language is unfamiliar or somewhat archaic, they may consider it worthwhile working on pieces of writing, such as novels or philosophical and political tracts written in the same period, so that the actors become familiar with the language and the presentation of complicated ideas. For example, this type of work might be particularly worthwhile when working on a Renaissance or Shakespearean play. With this type of play, too, it is a good idea also if the director does not actually follow the actors' reading in the text, but listens to the play like a member of the audience to see how much the actors understand and how well they are putting over the argument to someone

The set for a production of Shakespeare's *Twelfth Night* raised the acting area to various levels. This enabled the director to situate Olivia in a higher, dominant position over Viola, in male disguise (**4**). Maria carefully places a letter for Malvolio on the lower level (**5**), and when he comes to retrieve the letter, Malvolio is positioned on the higher level (**6**). A situation has been created whereby Malvolio is forced to unbend from his stiffly dignified pose and the extra distance he has to reach makes his stooping even more ridiculous.

who may be hearing the play for the first time. In this way, anything that is unclear or tedious can be clarified quickly and discussed as it arises, and then it becomes clear whether the actors understand what is being said. It is possible for the director to help the actor to communicate words and phrases in the text which are unfamiliar to present day audiences. Try suggesting a gesture or a piece of business which clarifies the meaning.

Another popular way to approach a text is for the director and actors to sit round and discuss the play and read it through scene by scene, stopping to clarify information and points which are not immediately consistent in the piece, such as meanings of words and information about characters. This helps the cast create a whole character from the glimpses that the writer reveals in the course of the play. Nowadays discussions in rehearsals about the motivations of the character and the objectives in the scene are almost taken for granted. Such questions were first worked out by the Russian actor and director Constantin Stanislavsky (1863–1938). Stanislavsky's work at the Moscow Art Theater stressed the importance of a character's motivations and of building a picture of a solid character from what is gleaned in the play. Stanislavsky's theories and his 'method' were influential and controversial, although many of his ideas are now generally accepted and used. Most good actors extend for themselves their information on the character that they are playing. It can be a worthwhile exercise for less experienced actors to be given a scene to improvise, where the characters that they are playing meet in a scene which, although related, is not depicted in the play. This will enable them to explore for themselves through their imagination how their character would react in such a scene. This helps to free the actors from the confines of the text. Then, when they come back to the text, they may have gained a clearer view of their scenes.

Improvisation can be a useful device, too, if actors are finding it difficult to make a particular scene

1

4

2

5

3

6

Edward II by Bertolt Brecht

The open stage area of the Round House in London was used for the Foco Novo company's production of Brecht's play. In a stark set, the director Roland Rees and the designer Adrian Vaux used simple combinations of actors and props to stress important themes in the script. The scholarly Mortimer is urged by a priest (**1**) to leave the comfort of his desk and enter the harsher world of politics. Later the priest offers the imprisoned King Edward a table to rest at (**2**). It is the same prop, the desk of the earlier scene, and so provides a physical link between Mortimer and the King. The desk is important again as a unifying background when the priest and King change positions (**3**). The priest's red costume is another strong and constant link between scenes and characters.

Unusual and contrasting stage positions were used throughout the play. The close relationship between Edward and his favorite, Gaveston, is clearly indicated in this scene (**4**). The two are together, downstage and face to face. In contrast, a straight line of soldiers is placed upstage and stand face to back. It remains unusual to direct actors to turn their backs on an audience so, when this is used in the coronation scene (**5**), the audience's attention is drawn to the characters with their backs turned. The contrast between those kneeling and those standing emphasizes the apparently submissive relationship of the King to the priests. This has changed radically in a later scene (**6**) where the defeated rebel priests are kneeling, heads lowered, while the King's gesture is confident, expansive and dominant behind them.

7

8

9

10

11

12

The throne, like the desk, was another important and significant prop. When the King initiates trouble, he invites Gaveston to join him at the throne (**7**), while the Queen, whose power is threatened, stands isolated with her back to the audience. When the Queen manages to move up near the throne, the King continues to face Gaveston (**8**) and the nobles stand in defiance of the King's actions. Their backs are toward him and they spread out away from the throne. When the throne is vacant (**9**), and the struggle for power has begun, the royal rostrum becomes a convenient place to write petitions.

When the Queen occupies the throne (**10**), she is balanced between the conflicting pressures of her lover Mortimer and her son Edward. Mortimer stands closer to the throne and the Queen turns to him, indicating young Edward's disadvantage. The King regains his position on the throne, but now as a captive of Mortimer (**11**). The two men are apart and isolated, which reflects their struggle for power and is in contrast to previous scenes when their positions on stage showed them in a different relationship. When Mortimer and young Edward confront each other again (**12**), with the Queen once more between them on the throne, Edward is now in the dominant position. He is closer to his mother and standing while Mortimer's stance is a submissive kneel.

work, when they are still using their texts or 'on the book'. It can be a good idea to tell them to do the scene in their own words without their scripts, so that they can get the right mix of emotion and find the pivotal points of the scene. It can help to broaden their understanding of where the shifts in emotion and character take place. The director may find it helpful to act as a kind of arbiter or inquisitor to question the other actors in the scene so as to see what they read from each other's performances. This approach can be particularly useful in love scenes, as freeing actors of their books allows them to be more physical and to elaborate what may be rather economically written by the playwright.

In the initial period of rehearsals, too, it can be a good idea to talk about the usual routines that the characters follow. For example, if you were working on a play in a domestic setting such as one by J. B. Priestley, Simon Gray or Neil Simon, it may be worth discussing in detail how the characters usually spent their days, so that any detail incorporated into the production would be truthfully conceived. For example, how many times does a table appear on stage with exactly the right number of chairs for the characters who are going to sit on them—and how many times does this happen in life?

USING THE SET

Blocking is the positioning of actors on the stage in relation to the set and plotting their movements. By the time you wish to 'block' the play, it is important that the stage management staff have marked out the rehearsal space to the precise measurements of the stage. It really is no good to be approximate, as the actors must get the right feeling of the space in which they will have to perform. They should know where the windows and doors are, and which way they open, they should also know of any steps. If the set is on different levels, then, as soon as possible, they should have a model of the set.

From the start of rehearsals, it is important that the furniture on the set is as similar to that which will be used in performance as possible. This is because, for instance, it can be very alarming for an actor to have a much lower chair in performance to the one used in rehearsals. This may seem fussy, but the director should insist on having the actual furniture and properties as soon as possible because the more the actors can get used to them, the more secure their performances will be.

In a way, it is part of the director's role to protect the actors from enormous changes at the last minute. Acting can be a harrowing experience, and the safer the actors feel, the greater the chances that

the production can really come together successfully when it is before an audience. Rehearsal is a fancy word for practice—it is wise not just to work on the play itself but to spend a great deal of time practising mechanics and technical aspects as well.

The way in which the rehearsal time is utilized will depend on a number of different factors. If you are doing a musical, it may be a good idea for the musical director to do some preliminary work with the company in order to teach them the melodies of the songs, or for the movement director to begin work on choreography. Then during the main rehearsals you already have a framework which can be improved on. Some parts may demand particular actions or pieces of 'business' as they are termed. Some plays may require the actors to dance, play the piano, have sword fights or even do magic tricks. Actors should start to learn these things at the earliest possible time to avoid pressure and running out of time in later weeks.

WORKING THROUGH THE PLAY IN DETAIL

Most of the observations made so far are fairly general and may not vary greatly from director to director. However, the bulk of rehearsal time is taken up with working through the play in detail with the actors, and these methods can be very individual, according to the director. The director who blocks the show on the first day of rehearsal is, as has already been said, a thing of the past in the majority of professional companies, but this is often the approach used by amateur companies. To set the action of the play rigidly too early in rehearsals can be a very misguided approach, for, as the actors become better acquainted with their characters, they learn how and where their character would move, how they would sit, and so on. In this way of working actors are told, for instance, to enter upstage center, walk down left and finish up down right to allow the next two characters to enter left, leaving them space for their entrance. This unimaginative approach is unfortunately all too common in the non-professional theater.

If all the elements of the play are fixed too soon, stupid errors can be made and not enough detail may be paid to the characters. For example, at the start of Chekhov's *The Seagull*, Masha and Medvedenko enter onto the stage. Certain considerations should be taken into account—they have been walking for some time before the play opens so they might be ready to sit down. Who should come on first? Medvedenko is in love with Masha, a love that is unrequited for she is in love with Constantin, so it is Medvedenko who is following Masha around. Her answers to his questions in the first scene are terse and somewhat rhetorical, his speeches are long, so that it is almost a scene between two people who are talking to themselves. It is the director's most important task to bring such points to the actors' attention to make sure that the actors understand them, and perhaps suggest physical ways to help the actors tell the audience something about the characters' relationship immediately. This type of approach should be applied to every scene in the play. If these matters are discussed and resolved at the time of blocking the play, character analysis can emerge at the same time.

Directors have many different points of view on the merits of following stage directions. Many amateur companies use published acting editions of plays in which stage directions appear, and this can be rather limiting. It may be perverse purposely to disregard stage directions, but not every writer has a strong sense of what is theatrically possible or the most effective way to play a scene. George Bernard Shaw's stage directions are usually very reliable, but if directors think that it is worth trying another way they should not fear to do so. The modern British dramatist Harold Pinter is very deliberate in his stage directions. They are economical and seem to be conceived as strongly as the words his characters use. He is precise with timings, with pauses and silences, and his directions contribute strongly to the stylistic conception of his plays. This precision should not be ignored. Pinter has a strong instinct for what kind of atmosphere he wants his plays to have and his directions are aids to this end, adding to the poetic quality of his work.

When directing Shakespeare, bear in mind that very few stage directions which appear in published editions are the author's. So be wary about adhering to them, especially if they seem to make little sense.

Going through each scene individually blocking it, and examining characterization and motivation in detail may be a slow process and mean that the broad framework for rehearsal takes longer to arrive. However, in the majority of cases this approach provides a strong foundation on which to build. It may take the first 10 rehearsals, but it does mean a lot of discoveries are made early on, and probably fewer changes will have to be made at later stages.

Having established the initial framework, more detailed work on individual scenes can begin. If a play is not written with scene divisions, it will help if the director splits the act into more convenient sections, so that some actors do not have to hang around for hours whilst others are being rehearsed.

During this work-through, more time can be spent in experiment. It is sometimes worth trying to play a scene in exactly the opposite way to how it might usually be played. For instance, if you are working on a sad, emotional scene, consider the places where the scene can lighten. Think how many times people say 'I'm really depressed', and then laugh at themselves. It is, in some ways, a perverse way to work, but often it is worth trying to avoid the expected, and this can make for a more original production. Also, try to forget all previous knowledge of the play and try to get the actors to do the same, so that no-one is influenced by preconceptions about the play.

This work-through is also the time for actors to experiment both physically and vocally. May an accent be useful to the character? Often less experienced actors can be overenthusiastic in their use of accents other than their own, and this kind of indulgence needs a firm hand from the director. Make sure that actors only use accents which they can sustain throughout the play. When accents are used by several actors, they should be consistent. For instance, a play set in an isolated community should not have some characters with northern accents and others with southern tones. Bad use of accents can make the production suffer by a lack of unity. However, it may not be a bad idea to agree to set a play with an unspecified setting somewhere specific in order to make a point of some sort.

Physical experiment should also be tried at this stage. Actors need to be aware of the physical presence of the character they are playing. For instance, extroverted people tend not to sit hunched with arms folded across their chests, but to be more expansive and open. It is worth doing some exercises with the company which can help bring these sides of their characters into the open. An easy and popular game is to ask the actors to imitate the physical movements of each others' characters silently and allow the others to guess who it is. Another physical game of this sort is the 'adverb game'. One person goes out of the room whilst the group decides on an adverb describing the actions of their character in the play—for instance sensuously, venomously, intensely. Then the outsider comes back and is given instructions of actions to do and has to guess the adverb in question. This helps actors perceive how others see their performance. It is important for actors to get the physical measure as well as the mental state of the characters they are to play. For example, some actors consider it important to know the kind of shoes their character would wear, fairly early on.

Often at this second work-through stage, actors

1

2

4

3

Production styles There are many different types of play and many ways of producing and directing them. Every show, whether a classic drama, an improvised original or a modern documentary, requires an overall style of presentation. Anton Chekhov's modern classic, *The Cherry Orchard*, usually has a realistic setting. This production (**1**) used a bare stage so the visual impact came simply from the floor texture and costumes. The contrasting colors of the clothes play up the differences between the sexes which is heightened by their alternating positions in the dance. Costumes are also of central importance in this Restoration comedy (**2**). The clothes, accessories and wigs indicate the status and personalities of characters. A completely different style of show was devised by the Strathclyde Theatre Group. *The Golden City* (**3**) was about the fifteenth century Anabaptist rising in Germany and was performed in St Mary's Cathedral, Edinburgh. British dramatist David Hare created *Fanshen* with the Joint Stock Theatre Company (**4**). It was based on an account of revolution in a Chinese village. In the same way, Colin Turnbull's account of life in an African tribe was the basis for *The Ik* (**5**), which Peter Brook devised with a company of actors. Many written works, such as diaries and memoirs, can provide a basis for good theater. *Galileo* is Bertolt Brecht's modern interpretation of events which took place in seventeenth century Italy. The play demands a detached, scientific atmosphere created here (**6**) by a back projection of Florence which is labeled and dated. *The Massacre at Paris* is a little known play by Elizabethan playwright Christopher Marlowe. This full-blooded production (**7**), perhaps in an attempt to disguise some of the play's weaknesses, was presented as a performance for Queen Elizabeth I. She can be seen through the smoke presiding over events.

5

6

7

have problems in establishing the consistency of their characters. They may feel that in one scene their character is acting totally 'out of character'. Something that is impressed strongly on student actors at many acting or drama classes is that there must be a consistency in their characterization. To a large extent this is true, but often it can get in the way of allowing for the surprises in a performance. In real life, people are not always consistent in their actions, they often act out of character because of the kind of situations in which they find themselves. In the theater, the director should give the actors the confidence to do this in a play. As long as the change can be justified in some way, there is no need for too rigid an emphasis to be placed on consistency of characterization.

During rehearsals, too, a director should try and prevent the actors from overacting and projecting too much. By projecting their performance too early on in rehearsals, actors can falsify the truth of their characterization and become rhetorical and phony. Actors need to learn to pace their performance, and the director should guide them in this where necessary.

The individual inventiveness of actor and director are the factors that influence the success of a production most strongly, and, out of context, it is not possible to teach people about flair or charisma. But, in an ideal actor-director relationship, it should be possible for the actor to show the director something which can be added to, developed or tempered according to the needs of the production. It is not possible to teach anyone this, it is something that comes from doing!

The director should watch out for and curb the tendency of some actors to signal the character they are playing too strongly. This results in a very limited performance, only showing narrow facets of the character. If an actor is playing a despicable, unpleasant character, a director might find it useful to suggest reasons why the actor should like the character, including what justifies his or her behavior and what circumstances have contrived to make up the character. If actors prejudge the part they are playing and simply comment on it throughout the action, this tends to mean that the performance lacks scope, and the actor has no way of finding out more about the character. Similarly, the members of the audience will quickly make up their minds about the character and lose interest. A scheming character may be more effectively depicted by being played charmingly than by their acting suspiciously. It is often worth reminding the actors that they should forget the outcome of a play, and act the part moment by moment. It is extremely

bad to let the final denouement of the play influence the preceding scenes. It is also important to prevent actors who enter after an argument or a disclosure of a shocking nature from catching the mood of the preceding scene. They must confine themselves to the character's own knowledge in the play, not their personal knowledge of the play.

A director should be able to create an atmosphere where it is pleasant to work and where everyone feels that their contribution is important. All too often people playing small parts can be ignored and their contribution underestimated. However, if the playing of a small part is overlooked and the performance undisciplined, it can jeopardize the whole production. Actors in small parts should be encouraged to be inventive and detailed in what they do, and their importance should be acknowledged. It is sometimes necessary to set a deadline for when actors should have learned their words, because one particularly slow actor can hold up the development of other actors' performances. If possible, make this deadline at least two weeks before the final week of rehearsal, so that runs of the play towards the end of rehearsals are not protracted by a lot of prompts. Run-throughs of the play should be built up gradually so that the actors get a sense of continuity and can pace themselves scene by scene, act by act, until they can run the whole play. Time permitting, try to have a speed run-through to make sure that cues get picked up quickly and that the moments built into the production are clearly established.

One of the most difficult parts of directing a play is at what stage to make which decision. It is impossible to make general rules about this. Knowing when to fix things, when to make drastic changes, final cuts, reworking scenes and so on, is a question of practice, instinct and, finally, an arbitrary gamble. Directors have to rely on their knowledge of the text, the period of the play and their own taste, and the extent to which this manages to coincide with an audience's enjoyment.

FINAL PREPARATIONS FOR THE OPENING NIGHT

Working back from the production's first performance, it is possible to plan the final stages of the production at the beginning of rehearsals so that everyone concerned knows what deadlines they have to meet. It is a good idea to have two full dress rehearsals prior to the opening, as well as a full technical rehearsal. To save time, a director should try to run the technical rehearsal as quickly as possible by cutting from one cue to the next without including the text. This is called running the show 'cue to cue'. However, if actors have quick changes, it is always worth running the appropriate text to make sure that there is time for the changes. However, it should be possible to cut from entrance to sound cue, to lighting change. It is vital that everything technical should be gone through thoroughly at the technical rehearsal.

In professional theater, the final production stages may take three or four days and may mean working through the night. In amateur theater, technical rehearsals often take place at weekends. It is a good idea for the director and lighting designer, who have talked about the lighting prior to rehearsals starting, to work together when the lights are being focused so that levels of light can be fixed approximately. This applies to sound levels as well. It can save time and energy if the director does this without the actors present. Obviously a lighting designer will have come to at least one run-through of the play and will have worked out the areas that have to be lit and any special effects that are required.

It is quite important to leave enough time for two dress rehearsals so that there is a chance for changes and adjustments to be rehearsed again and seen by the director before the production goes before an audience. If the play is a comedy, it may be worth doing the second dress rehearsal before an invited audience so that the actors can get used to timing their lines with the laughs. This is often a problem with inexperienced actors who are not confident enough to wait for laughter to subside before continuing the speech, and so they go on with their lines with the result that the audience lose the sense of what is being said. Obviously, the degree of laughter depends on the audience and it can vary enormously. But it is a good idea for the actors to get a rough idea of where the laughs will come.

Intermissions Consider carefully when the intermission or interval should be. It is important that the action ends at some kind of climax, on a high point. If the act divisions are not specified by the playwright, the director should look for such a point and work the play up to that climax. It is usual for the first half of a play to be longer than the second half, and, in some ways, it is important to acknowledge this kind of tradition. The concentration span and psychological as well as physical needs of the audience should be thought about. In most cases, it is somewhat unfair on an audience not to have an intermission, even if inserting one may seem to break the action of the play. This applies especially if the play runs for more than one-and-a-half hours or the seats are uncomfortable.

Curtain calls A curtain call should be organized prior to the first public performance. In the late 1960s and early 1970s it became rather unfashionable for companies to take curtain calls. However, the type of call depends on the final effect achieved in the production. If the play is a musical or a comedy, then the curtain call can be quite amusing and elaborate. If the play is a tragedy or a profoundly serious play, it may be best to keep the call simple. At all costs, it is important not to underestimate the vanities of the cast and to make the call fair and democratic according to merit, otherwise fits of pique could well occur.

Notes The director should give the actors comments on their performances after the first performance. But the kind of comment, usually known as 'notes', should be well thought out and aimed at helping the cast achieve better results. Everything should be couched in a positive tone. It is important not to discourage or throw an actor who has to perform again by giving them spurious or too drastic notes. Notes should be constructive. It is extremely unhelpful to say simply 'I don't know why, but I think it's not quite right'. It is important to make the actor feel secure and confident, so changes that are made must be carefully explained taking into account the condition of the actor's ego.

Audibility is something that a director should always keep in mind both in rehearsals and performance. It is, perhaps, difficult for directors to judge how audible a play is because they know the play very well. It can be worth getting somebody who is not so familiar with the text to watch the dress rehearsal. Remember that the presence of the audience actually absorbs sound, so it should be pitched up when the audience is there.

It can be good psychology for the director to give the company a confidence-boosting chat before the first performance and to give them a voice and physical warm-up and suggest this continues before every performance. The director's enthusiasm to get the production on can be a vital asset. It is crucial that the director keeps this enthusiasm growing and flowing within the company. It follows often that, if a company enjoys performing the show, the audience will share in their enjoyment. Communicating, after all, is what the theater is about.

Finally, it is up to the director to make sure that all the facets of the production of the play—cast, set, lighting, costumes, props, and so on—come together. Only if this happens can the performance match the aims of all those involved, and the audience see the production at its very best.

CHAPTER TWO

STAGE MANAGEMENT

PRODUCTION MEETINGS

TECHNICAL AND DRESS REHEARSALS

MAKING THE BOOK · PROPS

CUES · CALLS · FIRST NIGHT

Stage management is not one of the obviously glamorous areas of theatrical activity. However, the role of the stage manager is vitally important as the smooth running of the whole show depends on it. Stage management can be easily summed up as a flair for the management of people, things and events. The qualities needed by a stage manager include a detailed knowledge of the functions of *all* those who contribute towards a production and the ability to carry on undaunted in a crisis. The ability to communicate clearly is vital for any stage manager, who also requires an actor's voice, a scholar's brain and a sense of humor at rehearsal each day, together with the script, pencils and paraphernalia of the stage manager's table.

The stage manager must be nursemaid, confessor, caterer, librarian, stationer, mechanic, actor, mediator, judge, clairvoyant, historian, carpenter, chauffeur and linguist—all rolled into one. Any required skill not possessed, any unanswered question, in short any demand or request at all, should be met with total confidence and flair! Actors will arrive late with nowhere to park, will damage themselves (and others), get hungry, drunk, sick, electrocuted, depressed—and it is up to the stage management to get them on stage right on cue! The stage management will be expected to share the experiences of director and designer too.

However few of the back-up departments or people examined here are available to the average non-professional theatrical company, an examination of the way in which a professional production is mounted will be useful because most major aspects of the production remain the same regardless of its size or scale. The stage manager must continually monitor the progress of the production for weakness or failure and must know how to keep the process moving ahead towards that immovable deadline—the opening night. The first element in a production is the choice of play. Next come the director, designer, lighting designer and the cast.

AUDITIONS

Many companies, amateur and professional, hold auditions, and careful planning by the stage manager can make sure that they run smoothly. The room in which auditions are held must be large enough to allow the director space to sit back from the artist and to make discreet comments to those around without distracting the auditioning actor. There should be comfortable adjoining space in which the actors can wait, and entrances should allow discreet movement to and fro by the stage manager. The artists should be called at intervals agreed with the director, say 10 minutes apart, and should never be kept waiting.

The theater in which the play is subsequently to be presented is ideal for casting. Artists who are nervous will be comforted by a smiling, efficient

Left With a hand on the controls, the stage manager guides the production from behind the scenes. The audience will not notice his or her work unless something goes wrong. Yet the responsibilities of the job are wide ranging and crucial to the production. This calm, confident and decisive figure may well have recently faced a multitude of disasters. But a successful show depends upon the stage manager's ability not to panic when everyone else does.

STAGE MANAGER'S TASK PLAN

Pre-rehearsal period: discuss show with the director, designers and administration • read the play • organize script copies • attend casting • organize production team and crew • allocate tasks • do crew and cast list • do availability chart • find rehearsal space • do rehearsal schedule and circulate • discuss the set design with designer and set builders referring to sketches and models • discuss costumes with designer, costume makers and lighting designer • discuss lighting with designers • do props list • do furniture list • organize rehearsal props and furniture • circulate script copies • mark out rehearsal space • do preliminary call sheet and distribute • write and distribute deadlines list and preliminary running order chart • do furniture and prop plan

During rehearsal period: attend rehearsals and note all changes which will affect props, sets, costumes, and lists • organize props and furniture • make prompt book • start to mark in cues

Production week: ensure all set building, lighting equipment, props, costumes, furniture and equipment ready • do cue sheets, prop settings and running order • prepare assistant stage manager's running plot • do lighting and sound synopses • load (get) in and fit up set for technical rehearsal and dress set • at technical rehearsal, make all final checks and study all effects with director • time cues and calls in prompt book • finalize all elements of prompt book • attend dress rehearsal and note any problems

First night and performance run: check everything • remain calm • reset play after performances • give calls and check all actors and crew present • liaise with front of house staff • note any alterations or repairs necessary

stage manager politely asking for their names and addresses and telephone numbers and, for a professional, their agent's number. After auditioning, each actor should be thanked for coming and told how and when they will hear the result. The old cliché 'Don't call us, we'll call you' may be true, but do not let artists think you will not contact them.

PRELIMINARIES

When the basic elements of the production have been agreed, the stage manager should set up the team to work on the show. The size of the team will depend on the scale of the play and its cast, as well as the resources of the company in terms of both personnel and finances. It is wise to work out as far in advance as possible who will take responsibility for props, set construction, costumes, make-up, publicity, lights and working the lighting board during the show, as well as the sound and running the sound during the show. If the production has a complicated set, think how many people will be needed to put the set up before the production and, similarly, to take it down—or 'strike' it—at the end of the production. In a non-professional company, many of these jobs will be done by a single person,

but it is important to sort out both how many stage management and technical people the production requires and who will be responsible for what.

Having engaged or agreed on your team, send them a neatly typed schedule of deadlines for the stages of the production, rehearsal and performance. Work out the schedule in conjunction with the director. Calculate back from the date of the opening night, allowing time for dress and technical rehearsals, as well as for an appropriate number of ordinary rehearsals.

Include in the information a distribution list showing who has received it, together with useful addresses and telephone numbers. This is common office practice, but a good one for the stage manager to adopt also.

It is important for the stage manager to be involved in all aspects of the production, so try to attend as many early discussions as possible. These include, for instance, meetings between the director and set, costume and lighting designers. Only by being accepted by them as a part of the team from the very beginning can the stage manager build up the firm foundation of a working relationship that will stand for the weeks up to the opening.

THE PRODUCTION MEETING

Call those other than the cast to a meeting to discuss the play and designs. A ground plan of the settings and a model showing the way they will appear should be available. After the director and the designer, the most important person at the meeting is the lighting designer. His or her ideas and early involvement are crucial if the production is to be seen at its best. Others who should attend the initial production meeting include sound personnel (to discuss placing of speakers and discussion of any ideas the director may have of the way in which sound effects may be produced), costume makers (to see the designer's sketches), as well as the set builder, property maker, and the assistant stage manager. The person responsible for publicity should also attend to catch the first flavor of the project in order to write imaginatively about the event as a whole, and to encourage the audience to attend the show. Whether the team is one person or many, everyone should be encouraged and enthused at this first information session.

When setting up this meeting, plan for it to last between two and three hours. If possible, provide refreshments. If the set model is available, small spotlights and a darkened room will help to show it

at its best. Models and drawings are made as accurately as possible for only with correct scaling down can the production team estimate and assess the appearance, size, color, position, weight and maneuverability of the items they are being asked to prepare or subsequently manage.

Most models and ground plans are usually made to ¹⁄₂₄th or ¹⁄₂₅th of actual size. Use the first with the traditional Imperial scale. This means models and plans are prepared to the half-inch scale (¹⁄₂in to 1ft). Expressed as a ratio, this is 1:24. In this case half an inch on the drawing or model represents one foot (12in) at full scale. When working in metric measurements, 1:25 is more convenient. In this scale 1cm on the drawing represents 25cm in reality. An easy way of visualizing this is to say that 4cm (¹⁄₂₅ meter) represents one meter. It is therefore useful to have a scale rule which is marked at 4cm intervals, so that sizes and distances at full scale can be read off drawings of the model. It is helpful if everyone works in the same scale and establishes how measurements are referred to. This prevents the all too frequent event of something being made 10 times too big or 10 times too small.

At the production meeting, have some spare information sheets available, and go over them to

Equipment checklist The stage manager must be a model of efficiency. When something is urgently needed, be it a paper clip or a bandage, the stage manager should have it to hand. A well-equipped office is essential but since so much of the job entails work outside that office – in the rehearsal rooms or backstage – it is also essential to have a briefcase containing a wide range of equipment and to carry it at all times. Here is a checklist of those essentials:

Clipboard – for paperwork
Plenty of pencils and ballpoints
Pencil erasers and sharpeners
Chalk – for marking floors
Felt tip pens in many colors
Note pads and paper
Hole puncher – for file paper
Rubber bands and staplers
Notice board pins and paper clips
Glue and adhesive tape
Tape measure
Colored tapes – for marking floors
Craft knife – for cutting tape
Screwdriver and pliers
Flashlight – for blackouts
Stopwatch – for accurate timing
Emergency medical kit – bandages; sticking plasters;

pain killers; cough syrup; throat lozenges; antiseptic; and indigestion tablets
Soap and towel
Instant camera – a useful luxury
Padlock – for valuables
Corkscrew and bottle opener

Certain checklists, schedules and other paper work should be kept in the briefcase since they need to be referred to at all times:
Cast and crew list
Set drawings
Ground plans
Deadlines' list
Prompt list
Cue sheets

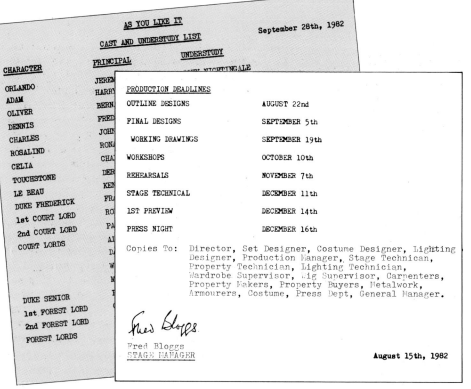

AS YOU LIKE IT

CAST AND UNDERSTUDY LIST   September 28th, 1982

PRINCIPAL   UNDERSTUDY

CHARACTER		
ORLANDO	JEREM	
ADAM	HARRY	
OLIVER	BERN	
DENNIS	FRED	
CHARLES	JOHN	
ROSALIND	RON	
CELIA	CHA	
TOUCHSTONE	DER	
LE BEAU	KEN	
DUKE FREDERICK	FR	
1st COURT LORD	RO	
2nd COURT LORD	PA	
COURT LORDS	Al	
	D	
	W	
	M	
DUKE SENIOR		
1st FOREST LORD		
2nd FOREST LORD		
FOREST LORDS		

PRODUCTION DEADLINES

OUTLINE DESIGNS	AUGUST 22nd
FINAL DESIGNS	SEPTEMBER 5th
WORKING DRAWINGS	SEPTEMBER 19th
WORKSHOPS	OCTOBER 10th
REHEARSALS	NOVEMBER 7th
STAGE TECHNICAL	DECEMBER 11th
1ST PREVIEW	DECEMBER 14th
PRESS NIGHT	DECEMBER 16th

Copies To: Director, Set Designer, Costume Designer, Lighting
Designer, Production Manager, Stage Technican,
Property Technician, Lighting Technician,
Wardrobe Supervisor, Wig Supervisor, Carpenters,
Property Makers, Property Buyers, Metalwork,
Armourers, Costume, Press Dept, General Manager.

Fred Bloggs
Fred Bloggs
STAGE MANAGER   August 15th, 1982

Lists and schedules There will be endless lists, timetables, schedules, notes and checklists written, copied and amended during each production. They are all important, but the two most crucial will be the crew and cast list and the deadlines' list. Make sure these are always up to date and to hand. The crew and cast list (**far left**) should not only show the name, address and telephone number of everyone involved in the production but also the function of each person, times when people are not available and places where they can be reached when not at home or in the theater. The deadlines' list (**left**) must indicate all important production deadlines and the rehearsal schedule. The deadlines' list should be distributed to all concerned. These lists show the detail required in a professional company, the circulation lists especially may be simpler for amateurs.

iron out problems. Check both work and home addresses and telephone numbers of everyone concerned and provide the director and designer with a list of all personnel at the meeting. Do not forget a copy for yourself to enable you to introduce everyone at the production meeting with accurate names and functions.

MARKING UP THE REHEARSAL SPACE

If possible, reserve the hall early enough to settle in, even a full day ahead. The outline of the set should be accurately represented on the floor with distinct colored tape. Use as many colors as there are different settings. Waterproof cloth tape, about ½ inch (1.25cm) or 1 inch (2.5cm) wide is best, as it will tear accurately without scissors and will not stretch, unlike electricians' or PVC tape. Follow the main pattern of the set according to the designer's ground plan. Add helpful labels, such as 'No Exit', 'Steps', to help the actors learn about the set, with which you should already be familiar.

The set should be marked out making the best use of the features of the rehearsal room. Keep the main door of the room behind the director and to one side to minimize distraction for all. Cover mirrors as they may distract the cast.

A series of marks on the floor cannot give a full picture for the cast. Try to get platforms or rostra of up to 3 feet (1 meter) in height to represent the levels of the set. For example, rehearsals of Juliet's balcony scene will be so much easier if she is standing even only slightly above the floor. Steps can be represented by a set of 'rehearsal treads'. This is simply a wooden section of about four treads, enough to allow actors to start moving up a staircase even if they have to jump off the end once they are 'off stage'. Doorways or arches may be shown with vertical markers simply made of scrap timber, with a weight to keep them upright. Such devices help give the cast the feel of the set from the start and will make the transition to using the real set easier.

Before moving into the rehearsal room, the stage manager should have read the script carefully and prepared a list of *every* prop that is clearly mentioned or implied in the text. This list should be typed out and discussed at the end of the production meeting and then amended with additions and changes. Beware of starting preparations for rehearsals or obtaining substitute props without reference to the director and designer, as they may easily decide to set *Hamlet* in Tokyo in the 1920s, and medieval furniture, carefully secured in advance, will look most out of place at the first read-through.

Chairs, sofas and sets of all kinds may be substituted by ordinary, readily available chairs. Tables should, if possible, be of accurate size within about 6in (15cm) in each dimension. This is important for

THE REHEARSAL SPACE

When finding a rehearsal space, there are a number of factors to be considered. Solve problems about the rehearsal room well before rehearsals start.

Recommendations
Undoubtedly the best way to find a rehearsal space is to ask around and find out which places are used by other groups, or if any, member of the group knows a suitable space. But never rely on the opinions of others. Always visit the place first and take the director with you. The stage manager may be delighted with the decor of a hotel's mirrored ballroom, but the director will not appreciate blocking multiple casts all round the room. Also take this checklist to ensure that the facilities are adequate.

Contact Find out who to ask for by name. It is friendlier to use a person's name when calling. It also helps to establish good relations with the caretaker or janitor concerned which is essential to the smooth running of rehearsals.

Rent Check whether the sum is for a day or a week and if power bills are included. The group treasurer will not be pleased to get a bill for five times as much as was expected.

Dimensions Get the exact measurements of the space. It must be large enough for: plotting the whole set on the floor; allowing exits and entrances from the stage area; allowing the director to sit away from the stage area and out of earshot of the actors. The director will need to see the rehearsal as if from a seat in the audience and to discuss things or pass notes without interrupting the actors.

Access Do not arrange rehearsal times or book the space until you are certain exactly when it will be available to you. Also check who else may be using the space and when they are expecting access. This will affect your time there since it may or may not be necessary to clear everything away or set up anew each time.

Storage It will save an enormous amount of time and trouble if props can be stored at the rehearsal space – even the strongest stage manager cannot take all the rehearsal furniture home on the bus.

Lighting and power Make sure that the power points are adequate for any equipment needed, and that the plugs fit the sockets. Do not forget things such as tape recorders. Also ensure that the lighting is sufficient.

Noise The local police band may be rehearsing above your space so find out if this, or any other possible interference, is likely.

Heating This can be crucial and expensive so check that there is some, that it works, and if the cost is included in the rent.

Washing and lavatory facilities Another crucial factor.

Green room This is the traditional name for the place in which actors wait between cues. It is a great advantage to have somewhere separate and quiet so that actors can relax and, perhaps, learn lines.

Dressing rooms Costumes will probably become a feature of rehearsals so a space will be needed for changing and fitting.

Moving in Check that any props or equipment will get through the entrance.

Furniture Find out exactly what is provided. Adequate seating is essential for director, stage manager and actors. Other furniture will help with props and creating substitute sets.

Parking Find out how much is available at the hall and if it is not adequate, see what can be found nearby. Inform those who travel by car.

Refreshments It will save time and money if basic refreshments can be made on the premises.

Shopping Check what is available in the area – everyone needs to shop and last minute props may be required.

Name and location Everyone concerned must be given the exact name, address, and telephone number of the place. There may be another hall with a similar name. Also give instructions on how to reach it by car and public transport.

Rehearsing at home The club member who unwittingly volunteers his or her home should certainly read this checklist before committing a family dining room to the rigors of rehearsals.

the director to begin moving the cast around the set.

Before the rehearsal is due to start, two tables should be set about 10 feet (3 meters) from the front of the set for director and stage manager. Each person will require a chair. Rehearsal furniture should be set for the opening of the play. The designer's model should be set on a table and lit imaginatively with two model lights in a position where the cast may gather round to view it. Prepare tea, coffee, and use disposable plastic cups which saves washing dishes.

Before the first read-through, make sure that cast and others receive their scripts well in advance. Have spare copies available. Allow half as many again as the number of the cast. Provide pencils, ideally those with a small eraser at one end.

All the people required for the first rehearsal should be notified, probably by telephone. Put up a confirmatory notice at the company's office or base and in the rehearsal room. All details of location, times and expected duration should be included. Make sure you have a definite and positive reply to your call.

THE FIRST REHEARSAL

Before the first—and subsequent—rehearsals, arrive early. Punctuality is a vital, basic discipline. The stage management staff must set an example in order to maintain this discipline with the artists throughout the production. Lack of punctuality creates bad feelings and a bad working atmosphere.

The first rehearsal will often begin with an informal half hour to allow the cast and staff to meet, some, of course, for the first time. The stage manager should first settle the cast in a circle of chairs with the director centrally positioned to introduce the cast. The stage manager should then introduce all the production team and any other technicians, the designer, author and others attending the first rehearsal. The designer should then show the model, the arrangement of different sets if applicable, as well as perhaps other drawings of major props that will be built to designs. Costume designs may be shown or displayed attractively on boards around the room. At this moment the stage manager must assist in communicating the designer's ideas to the cast, to help prevent later unnecessary upsets over details of costume and so on. The director, after all, should have approved the designs well in advance.

The cast should now read the play through. The director may speak about his or her interpretation and fill in any historical, geographical, political or cultural background to the work.

MARKING THE REHEARSAL SPACE

LONG DAY'S JOURNEY INTO NIGHT

FURNITURE FOR REHEARSALS

CARVER ARMCHAIR

PIANO STOOL (Square)

SMALL TABLE (Occ)

ROUND PEDESTAL TABLE 5'6" by 3'0"

CHAISE WITH HALF BACK.

CANE ARMCHAIR

SWIVEL CHAIR WITH ARMS ?

3 WICKER ARMCHAIRS

SOFA

3 WICKER CHAIRS

ROCKING CHAIR

13.10.71.

Before rehearsals begin the stage manager should draw up a list of any furniture or large props to be used in the production (**1**). Rehearsal furniture must be found which is as close as possible in size to the actual furniture to be used in the sets. This is important so that blocking in rehearsal can be accurate. The stage area and set has to be marked out on the floor of the rehearsal room. Using scale plans of the set and theater (**2**) for measurements and positions, the area is first marked on the floor in chalk and then in colored tape (**3**). The furniture and set props are marked (**4**) using a different color tape for each scene so that the actors and stage hands get a clear idea of scene changes. If there are varying levels or steps these should be indicated clearly (**5**) so that actors are aware of them. A door frame can be indicated by two simple battens (**6**) as a replica of the set is arranged. Exit directions should also be marked in different colors (**7**) depending on the scene. It is essential that everyone concerned is aware of the color coding for each scene so it should be written up on a board in the rehearsal room.

2

4

5

6

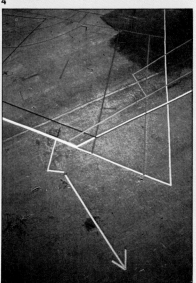

7

THE STAGE MANAGER'S ROLE IN REHEARSALS

Whether a production has one stage manager or half a dozen, the main stage management duties remain broadly the same. This outline shows the main responsibilities of each member of the production team serving performance and production in a large professional repertory company. The jobs can be adapted and divided between whatever number of staff is available. The exact titles used may also vary from company to company.

Production manager In a large professional repertory company, the production manager works mainly in a supervisory capacity, having no specific tasks during the show. However, the production manager does bear the ultimate responsibility for the performance as a whole and so must make sure it is all running smoothly.

Stage manager He or she should be fully capable of acting as the production manager's replacement, if required. The primary responsibility is to cue or 'call' the show from the prompt side or the prompt position in the front of the house.

Assistant stage manager 1 The first assistant stage manager is responsible for prompting and monitoring the shape of the scene. This means making sure that the actors' moves are accurately reproduced at performance according to the director's original requirements. The position should have a good view.

Assistant stage manager 2 In the case of the stage manager giving cues for the show from the front of the house, the second assistant stage manager will run the prompt side, but will not actually be prompting or giving cues. He or she will be calling actors and technicians to the stage for entrances or cues. No-one is encouraged to hang around backstage between cues as this can promote noise. In some larger theaters, calls are made on a public address system. It is vital that actors and crew specifically acknowledge that they have heard their call. This member of the team will also control backstage working lights which may be used throughout to illuminate prop tables, quick-change areas, narrow passages at the side of the stage, positions for operating flying scenery, and other stage lights for scene changes when the stage production lighting is not on. This may be either between cues or at intermissions to save electricity.

Assistant stage manager 3 A third assistant stage manager is responsible for setting all property and furniture both on the stage and presetting off stage in the wings. This includes complete responsibility for 'personal props'. These are small items such as

cigarettes, lighters, or wallets, which may be kept in an actor's dressing room when not in use. Such props should not be left lying around or forgotten.

Even in many professional theaters, the work outlined for this team of five will be carried out by only three people, and some straightforward plays with few props can be looked after by a single stage manager. However, the ability to service director, cast and rehearsal properly should determine the team's composition.

During rehearsals the key figure is the person whose job is to look after 'the book'. The 'book' is the vital main copy of the script which contains details of all moves, cues and props.

MAKING THE BOOK

In the past, some professional managements have rented scripts for the actors, particularly if they are undertaking a play a week. However, the stage management must be allowed a new copy. There are three ways of making up the book assuming that prompting and all cues are to be combined.

Try to obtain paperback rather than expensive or valuable copies of the script so that you can cut it up and make notes on it. Cut the spine of the script, punch the left-hand side and fit it into a loose-leaf notebook with a hard, washable cover. Use a reasonably large size regardless of the size of the script, as you are bound to accumulate larger notes and papers, including perhaps rewrites of the text and, subsequently, cue sheets for lighting and sound. Intersperse the text pages with sheets of fairly substantial lined paper. Divide the lined paper into three vertical columns. On each page label the column nearest the text 'Cues', the next 'Moves', and the furthest from the text 'Calls'. Reinforce the holes in both text and paper as they will have to withstand constant turning in rehearsal and performance.

The second way of making the book requires two printed texts. Paste pages from alternate scripts onto lined file paper so that every text page appears on the right, faced on the left by a clear page of lined paper which is the back of the previous page. Write down moves and notes on this empty page.

If the production is using professionally typed scripts, these should only be printed on one side of a page, and so are ideal for prompt books. They should still be taken apart and punched, as the book must be loose-leaf and extremely flexible.

MOVES

When the director starts to block the play, every entrance, exit, move, turn will be worked out, as

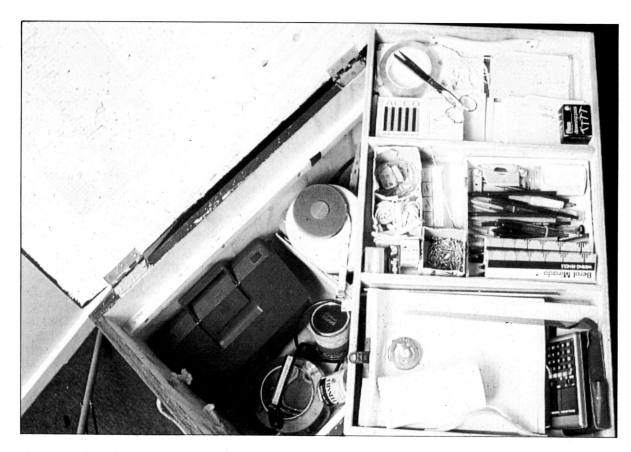

often will the motives within the text that will subsequently lead to the actors' gestures. Sitting and standing should also be indicated. All these moves must be recorded accurately by means of small numbers within a circle at the precise word at which the move occurs, with the same number and a shorthand description in the move column.

A simple outline diagram of the set, about 4in (10cm) wide and 3in (7.5cm) deep is often reproduced three times on the blank left-hand page of the book to make it easier to note down complicated multiple moves or groupings at any particular moment. These should be annotated with the initial letters of the character in the text and *not* the actor's name. This is because actors may change, and replacements will need to be rehearsed.

The book must be written in accepted and legible notations in case someone else takes over a rehearsal or there is a change of stage management. All these notes should be made in pencil as they will change constantly before the first night. It is helpful to number similar articles, such as doors or chairs, but make sure to agree these with the director first.

In order to anticipate actors' entrances, write the character names in pencil on the left of the text

Touring box Whenever a company is performing away from home – whether on tour or doing a show for schools or other groups – the stage manager will need an office. In many places this will not be provided and even if it is it may not contain essential equipment. A touring box provides a portable office to be taken wherever it is needed. If rehearsal rooms are some distance from the theater, it will also be needed there. The box should contain a portable typewriter with carbon paper and correcting fluid. Headed notepaper is always needed for official correspondence. Since the stage manager will probably be in charge of budgets and the box office, a calculator is important. The stage manager's briefcase will contain many essentials, but it is important to duplicate some of these in the touring box such as pencils, scissors and colored tapes. Copies of ground plans and elevations, photographs of set models, important lists and schedules, notes and budgets should also be included. Keep a checklist of everything which should be contained in the box on

the lid for easy reference and make a note when supplies run low. Experience and practice will soon make clear what other essentials need to be added to the box. It is wise to label all objects as property of the stage manager and to take note of things which are lent to others. The box itself should be sturdy and spacious and preferably custom made out of wood. Make sure it is fitted with practical handles for easy moving.

about five minutes before the character should appear. This will serve as a reminder to look round to check that an actor is present. Actors will often make good use of the time when they are not on by learning their lines, generally in another room, and may therefore need to be called. As the play is blocked, information will come thick and fast, all of which must be documented in pencil. Position in the text likely sound cues, lighting cues and special effects cues. Use clear abbreviations which have been agreed so as to minimize possible confusion. Note down new or amended requirements for props or furniture. You should detail any slight changes to the construction of the set required by the director, such as a door or window which needs to open off stage and not on.

Always check the way doors are to open and *confirm* these with whoever is building the set. Later see for yourself that the construction is correct before the set is in the theater and precious time is wasted in alterations and reconstruction.

One of stage management's basic rules is to confirm and check everything for yourself. This is of paramount importance. Adopting this rule is taking responsibility, although it may mean a lot of extra work. No actor—let alone director—appreciates a stage manager who rushes round at the last minute dealing with problems that could have and should have been prevented by a little foresight or intuition. The wardrobe staff, too, will appreciate being informed about the need for an inside pocket on the *left* because it is easier for a right-handed actor to cope with business with a wallet or gun, or that the reverse applies if the actor is left-handed.

Once the play has been blocked completely, the director will probably work slowly through each scene or act, dealing with questions of interpretation and moving towards the final interpretation from each actor. New plays and, especially, new translations of foreign plays may often involve extended discussion of a particular choice of words or detailed examination of the author's real meaning which the actors must share before they can give a convincing delivery. When using a translation from a foreign language, it is valuable for the director and stage manager to share a copy of a literal or word-by-word translation. However incoherently it reads as a whole, this will often serve to explain the translator's meaning.

After the play has been worked right through, it will usually be run through, and the actors should learn their words and the moves given to them as soon as possible. The stage manager with the book should quickly point out any divergence from the text, even by a word, especially for classical work, and also from the moves agreed on, as a scene will go very wrong if actors find themselves incorrectly placed. Lines are easier to remember when actors have the same relationship with their fellow actors, furniture and set each time the lines occur.

Once a play has been run through two or three times, the stage manager should make sure that the other departments attend rehearsal and are given a list of suggested cues with page numbers. This is not to be regarded as doing their work for them, but as saving the director from having to go laboriously through the whole play and produce the same list from memory. Clearly, further cues may be added later, even at the dress rehearsal stage.

CUES AND CALLS

One extremely important job of the stage manager is to work out when all the cues should be given to actors and crew. It is vital to warn all members of the cast and production staff *before* any entrance or cue so that all aspects of the production will occur at the correct time. Late entrances or slow lighting or sound cues make the production seem slipshod and careless.

The second time the play is run through, keep a stopwatch running in front of you, and every 30 seconds make a small pencil cross in the left-hand margin near the text. This will produce a time grid for the whole production which will be invaluable for timing all cues. Note especially where actors need to be called for their entrances. This usually happens five minutes before the entrance. If possible, write these calls at the top of a new page, where they will be more obvious. Technicians' calls may be made in the same way. Stage managers with the book may also need to warn themselves of cues they will perform themselves—these include live effects, such as door or telephone bells or checking that certain equipment is switched on.

Other calls to be in the prompt book before the dress rehearsal will be the half hour call (given precisely 35 minutes before curtain-up); the quarter hour call (given precisely 20 minutes before curtain-up); the five minute call (given precisely 10 minutes before curtain-up); the final call (given precisely five minutes before curtain-up); and 'places' (given precisely one minute before curtain-up). The following should be noted immediately after the first part of the production has started—curtain-up (or lights if there is no curtain) on Act I (Part 1) and, immediately after the end of the first part, curtain down (or lights down) on Act I (Part 1). Another use for your 30-second grid is to provide the likely duration for cues, such as sound, for example background noises, and

The promptbook The script is the basis of a show so any element of the performance must be recorded against the relevant point in the script. A promptbook is made: on one side is the final script and on the facing page all moves, lighting and sound cues and important details are noted. It is a log of the show, a blueprint from which, say, one actor taking over from another could tell precisely what moves to make. These pages are from a promptbook for Eugene O'Neill's *Long Day's Journey Into Night*. In this case the whole script has been retyped but this is not essential. A cheap paperback could be cut up, making sure that the text is identical to the one being used by the actors. The pages shown (**right**) are for the end of an interval and the beginning of Act Four.

Below A sound cue is indicated here. Cue '4' means that Mary crosses upstage of chair 3 and a table, and Tyrone sits in a chair stage right. 'Warn' is always indicated in the same color to show the same kind of instruction. Light and sound cues are each in different colors for easy reference. The type of sound cue required here is described by '(Foghorn)' and a line extends from 'Go' to the point in the script where the cue begins.

The stage manager calls the actors for the beginning of the act, then indicates to the audience that the interval is about to end.

Opening position and actions of Tyrone. Chairs are numbered for precise identification. Standard abbreviations are used to save space.

Drop some cards on the floor downstage of the table.

Stage manager gives advance indication to lighting and sound operators of their next cues, which are numbered.

Sound and light cues are marked in different colors for easy reference. 'Go' indicates the exact moment for operation, but here the cues are based on watching actions rather than words.

U/S or U.S. means upstage.

---

14 MINUTES AFTER CURTAIN DOWN
CALL: ACT 4 BEGINNERS
    TYRONE
    RING THREE MINUTE BELL
15 MINUTES AFTER CURTAIN DOWN
    RING TWO MINUTE BELL
16 MINUTES AFTER CURTAIN DOWN
    RING ONE MINUTE BELL
CHECK | ACT 4 PRE-SET ON
       | WORKING LIGHTS ON
ON F.O.H. CLEAR
       STAND BY BEGINNERS
WARN | LX HOUSE LIGHTS + Q14
      | SOUND Q 11 (FOGHORNS)
      | D.S.O.P.
GO: LX HOUSE OUT
WHEN HOUSE OUT
GO: TABS OUT (7)
WHEN TABS OUT
GO: SOUND Q 11
AS TYRONE KNOCKS CARDS OFF TABLE
GO: D.S.O.P (DOOR SLAM)
AS EDMUND STOPS CURSING
GO: LX Q 14

Tyrone sat Ch3 at end table playing patience. He goes thro' pack in threes – then clears game.
Drops some cards on floor D/S table.
He hears front door bang.

① Ed bangs into something in hall. He turns on hall light.

② Ed appears U/S pass door

3.10

① M Kiss T.

② M + R to Kiss Ed. She leads him to sit in ch 3.

③ Tyr R to R/Ch

④ M + U/S Ch 3 to U/S table
Tyr sit R/Ch

⑤ M pours a small drink for Tyr then one for Edmund. Putting bottle back near Tyr without cork.

⑥ M sits Ch1.

WARN: SOUND Q 8 (FOGHORN)

GO: SOUND Q 8

MARY:
(contd)

ions. But for the moment MARY is un-
conscious of their condemning eyes. She
kisses her husband and then EDMUND. They
Her manner is unnaturally effusive. They
submit shrinkingly.

I'm so happy you've come. I had given up hope. ①
was afraid you wouldn't come home. It's such a
dismal, foggy evening. It must be much more cheer-
ful in the bar-rooms uptown, where there are people
you can talk and joke with. No, don't deny it. I
know how you feel. I don't blame you a bit. I'm all
the more grateful to you for coming home. I was
sitting here so lonely and blue. Come and sit down.

③

(She sits at left rear of table, EDMUND
at left of table, and TYRONE in the
rocker at right of it)

Dinner won't be ready for a minute. You're actually
a little early. Will wonders never cease? Here's
the whiskey, dear. Shall I pour a drink for you? ⑤
(without waiting for a reply she does so) And you,
Edmund? I don't want to encourage you, but one
before dinner, as an appetizer, can't do any harm.

(She pours a drink for him. They make
no move to take the drinks. She talks
on as if unaware of their silence)

⑥

Where's Jamie? But, of course, he'll never come
home so long as he has the price of a drink left.
(she reaches out and clasps her husband's hand –
sadly) I'm afraid Jamie has been lost to us for a
long time, dear. (her face hardens) But we mustn't
allow him to drag Edmund down with him, as he's like
to do. He's jealous because Edmund has always been
the baby - just as he used to be of Eugene. He'll never
be content until he makes Edmund as hopeless a failure
as he is.

EDMUND: (miserably) Stop talking, Mama.

TYRONE: (dully) Yes, Mary, the less you say now – (then
to EDMUND, a bit tipsily) All the same there's truth
in your mother's warning. Beware of that brother of
yours, or he'll poison life for you with his damned
sneering serpent's tongue!

4.1

ACT FOUR

SCENE: The same. It is around midnight. The lamp in the front hall has been turned out, so that now no light shines through the front parlour. In the living-room only the reading-lamp on the table is lighted. Outside the windows the wall of fog appears denser than ever. As the CURTAIN RISES, the foghorn is heard, followed by the ships' bells from the harbour.

TYRONE is seated at the table. He wears his pince-nez, and is playing solitaire. He has taken off his coat and has on an old brown dressing-gown. The whiskey bottle on the tray is three-quarters empty. There is a fresh full bottle on the table, which he has brought from the cellar so there will be an ample reserve at hand. He is drunk and shows it by the owlish, deliberate manner in which he peers at each card to make certain of its identity, and then plays it as if he wasn't certain of his aim. His eyes have a misted, oily look and his mouth is slack. But despite all the whiskey in him, he has not escaped, and he looks as he appeared at the close of the preceding act, a sad, defeated old man, possessed by hopeless resignation.

As the CURTAIN RISES, he finishes a game and sweeps the cards together. He shuffles them clumsily, dropping a couple on the floor. He retrieves them with difficulty, and starts to shuffle again, when he hears someone entering the front door. He peers over his pince-nez through the front parlour.

TYRONE: (his voice thick) Who's that? Is it you, Edmund?

(EDMUND's voice answers curtly, "Yes." ①) Then he evidently collides with something in the dark hall and can be heard cursing. A moment later the hall lamp is turned on. TYRONE ~~frowns and calls~~:

② Turn that light out before you come in.

---

15 minute interval, but 17 minutes allowed.

Front of house.

When the audience is in, standby for the beginning of the act.

D.S.O.P. means Down Stage Opposite Prompt which is down stage right for this British production but usually means down stage left in the United States. Here it indicates the assistant who is to do the door slam effect.

Numbers refer to the actions described on the facing page.

Tyrone screws in bulbs to a chandelier (**above**) and the prompt book (**below**) records his various actions. The stage manager warns the board operator that a light cue '(LX)' is imminent. '(15)' refers to a preplotted combination of lights and dimmers to be used. '(ABCD)' indicates that the cue has four components. Opposite the exact point in the script, 'GO' is marked. The individual components of the cue match Tyrone's actions of screwing in the bulbs. Each light coming on is a separate mini-cue within cue 15, based on watching the actor's actions.

WARN: Lx Q15 ABCD

① Tyr half rise from chair sits back again

② Ed rise

③ Tyr rise to climb on table. He turns on four lamps

④ Tyr backs on to D/S L edge table he remains poised then backs off table + round Ch 3

AS TYRONE SCREWS IN 4 LIGHTS
GO Lx Q15 A B C D

TYRONE: I never said he was a good one. He was a renegade, but a Catholic just the same.

4.3

EDMUND: Well, he wasn't. You just want to believe no one but an Irish Catholic general could beat Napoleon.

TYRONE: I'm not going to argue with you. I asked you to turn out that light in the hall.

EDMUND: I heard you, and as far as I'm concerned it stays on.

TYRONE: None of your damned insolence! Are you going to obey me or not?

EDMUND: Not! If you want to be a crazy miser put it out yourself!

TYRONE: (with threatening anger) Listen to me! I've put up with a lot from you because from the mad things you've done at times I've thought you weren't quite right in your head. I've excused you and never lifted my hand to you. But there's a straw that breaks the camel's back. You'll obey me and put out that light or, big as you are, I'll give you a thrashing that'll teach you —!

(Suddenly he remembers EDMUND's illness and instantly becomes guilty and shamefaced)

① Forgive me, lad. I forgot - You shouldn't goad me into losing my temper.

EDMUND: (ashamed himself now) Forget it, Papa. I apologize, too. I had no right being nasty about nothing. I am a bit soused, I guess. I'll put out the damned light. ②(he starts to get up)

TYRONE: No, stay where you are. Let it burn.

(He stands up abruptly - and a bit drunkenly - and begins turning on the three bulbs in the chandelier, with a childish, bitterly dramatic self-pity)

③ We'll have them all on! Let them burn! To hell with them! The poorhouse is the end of the road, and it might as well be sooner as later. ④(he finishes turning on the lights)

lighting, for long fades such as sunset or dawn. Stage technicians will also appreciate knowing the time between their cues. Lighting switchboard operators, too, require to be told how long they will have to prepare for the next cue.

Actors will need to be fitted for costumes during the rehearsals and may need several fittings if clothes are being made specially. Stage management can assist greatly by arranging fittings, so as not to clash with the director's requirements. A fitting call should be written down and notified in the same way as a rehearsal call.

At the end of each day, preferably before any artist has left the rehearsal, the stage manager should confirm with the director exactly what is to be rehearsed the following day or, preferably, for several days ahead. This may depend on the director. This information, if possible, should be typed immediately and displayed. Draw up a scene division to enable the stage manager to discover quickly who is required for any particular scene. This applies especially to plays with large casts and many scenes.

PROPS

After the provision of rehearsal or substitute props at the beginning of rehearsals, as soon as final requirements become clearer, the person responsible for props will start to replace these with actual props. Breakables, such as china and glass, will only be provided after the actors no longer need to use their scripts, as an actor struggling with script and cut glass at an early stage will lead to disaster! Liquids will not be needed until later, perhaps not until the dress rehearsal. The basic rule, however, is 'something for everything'. In other words, never leave an actor without a prop which is central to the business being rehearsed.

Food and drink For domestic plays with food, provide full props for china, glass, knives, forks and so on. Setting and clearing tables requires considerable rehearsal for the actor, so make sure that the table is the correct size. Setting everything on a different sized table, plus the strain of a dress rehearsal, can have more effect on the floor than on the table, with amusing but undesirable results. Make sure that trays are the correct size. If possible, obtain the real one very early.

If hot food is required, decide with the actors what they prefer. If real meat is problematic or expensive, try brown bread with hot gravy. Ham can substitute for bacon. Frozen vegetables are easy to prepare in hot water. Coffee and tea may be real, but alcoholic beverages should not be consumed in any quantity on stage. Cold tea is a good substitute for sherry, whisky, dark rum and so on, while water will serve for gin and vodka.

Spend some time getting quantities right, as everyone will have their own opinion as to the colors. More exotic colors may be prepared with vegetable food colorings. A set of these small bottles is essential for any modest prop room. Fresh milk is preferable, but keep a can of the powdered variety which can be useful in emergencies.

Telephones Decide early how bell effects are to be achieved and put into rehearsal so that assistant stage manager and actor can rehearse timing together. Check on the length of wire required to run from the wall to the instrument and the instrument to the handset. Sophisticated telephones are available for purchase or rental, but confirm availability early. This goes for all unusual items. Solve the problem as early as possible. Decide how to get the wire for the bell effect to the telephone; a trailing wire upstage of the sofa is dangerous. Fasten to the floor with wide marking tape or feed beneath a carpet or rug.

Armor and weapons Swords are best used under the supervision of an experienced fight arranger, and rehearsals for fights should be started early, as stage fights must be slick and safe.

Guns Basic safety rules must be applied by the stage manager. Check legal restrictions on the use of guns. In Britain, for instance, certain guns require a police certificate or licence, and this may take several weeks to secure. Check local legal requirements carefully. It should be the responsibility of a specific member of staff to supervise the use of the guns, and take responsibility for storage. In case the shot does not sound, arrange an alternative sound effect, such as a starting pistol offstage. A crude but effective alternative is a plank of wood with a cord holding one end up, so that heavy pressure with the foot will slam the plank onto the floor.

SET DRESSING

Some items will be chosen by the designer to dress or decorate the set and will not arise from rehearsal. The designer's model and impression drawings, however, should indicate many of these. They will become the direct responsibility of the property manager once the show is running.

When plotting the set dressing, remember the following points. Mark positions for furniture carefully on the stage surface and, if similar pieces differ at all, mark these with numbers or positions which cannot be seen by the audience. Plot carefully all cushions, antimacassars, extra stuffing or boards

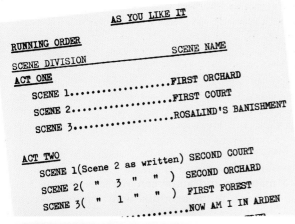

Rehearsal lists and charts
Some of the most important of
the stage manager's many lists
concern rehearsals. A running
order chart (**top**) is essential if the
production's breakdown of
scenes does not correspond
exactly with the original script.
Giving each scene a working title
ensures that everyone knows

which scene is referred to. An
availability chart (**below**) shows
at a glance when actors are
needed by dividing the script into
pages and marking the actors next
to the pages in which they appear.
Display all important charts on a
prominent noticeboard (**above**)
and see that everyone consults it.

ACT 1	4–7	9–14	14–16	16–24	24–26	26–30
JAMES	X	X	X	X	X	
MARY	X	X	X		X	X
JAMIE	OFF	X	X	X	X	
EDMUND	OFF	X				X
CATHLEEN						

ACT 2 SC 1	1–2	3–6	7–10	10	11–12	12–14	14–16	16–17
JAMES						X	X	X
MARY			X	X	X		X	X
JAMIE		X	X	X	X	X	X	
EDMUND	X	X	X	X	X	X	X	
CATHLEEN	X		X					

required to keep actors firmly upright. Make sure
that trick furniture, such as chairs with breakable
sections, which have to be replaced for each performance is correctly and carefully set. Check the
positions of drawers in tables and desks. Do not use
locks for furniture or doors, mime if possible, or
provide a spare key on stage. Carpets and rugs
should be securely fixed to the stage, particularly on
steps. If an interior 'box' set is to be carpeted from
wall to wall, it is economical and neat to lay the
carpet before setting the scenery. This enables
carpets to be rented without them having to be cut
to size.

Pictures Secure pictures to scenery either by tack-
ing through flats from behind, alternatively with
glass plates or small clips. To enable pictures to be
repositioned quickly and accurately, especially on
tour, or when in repertory which involves setting
and striking regularly, pop-rivet one half of the
fitting to the flat, screw the other to the picture, and
number the pictures. Any wall decoration near a
'practical' door—one which opens—may draw attention to the movement of the flat. This can be
avoided by using transparent nylon fishing line
drawn tight across the object and through the flat.
When not used in the action, china and bottles on
shelves may be glued down to avoid movement or
resetting.

Fabrics and drapes Soft fabric materials may have
to be flameproofed. Check with the local fire department. Thin materials may be dipped in a special
chemical salt solution readily available from theatrical suppliers, and hung to dry. Heavier fabrics may
be sprayed. Regulations vary from one area to
another, but, as a general rule, no material used on
stage should start to burn for at least 10 seconds
after exposure to a naked flame.

Make sure that curtain fittings are of good quality,
beware of the plastic sort that come undone, leaving
the actor enveloped. Never expect actors to listen
carefully about the precise way in which they must
cope with operating stage effects—they have much
more to cope with.

Light fittings Never wire up a switch so that it
actually operates a prop fitting, as the switchboard
may not synchronize. Feed it from the switchboard.
Fittings that are to be 'struck'—or taken off—in a
scene change, on tour or in repertory, should be
fitted with a small connecting plug, which can pass
through a hole in the flat. Use the clips suggested for
pictures to connect the parts.

Centrally hung chandeliers tend to spin, especially when encouraged by currents of air once
the curtain is up. Avoid using rope as a suspension,
as this increases the problem. An invisible nylon

```
LONG DAY'S JOURNEY INTO NIGHT
PROPS AND FURNITURE

FURNITURE
3 WICKER CHAIRS ✓
UPRIGHT PIANO
ROUND SWIVEL PIANO STOOL
SOFA ✓
SMALL TABLE ✓
ARMCHAIR
2 CHANDELIERS ✓✓
WINDOW SEAT
OVAL TABLE
2 ROCKING CHAIRS
4 CANE ARMCHAIRS
CHAISE ✓
DESK
BOOK CUPBOARD ✓
SWIVEL DESK CHAIR
UMBRELLA STAND
2 CARPETS

PROPS
2 VASES ✓✓
7 PICTURES - INCLUDING ONE
   OF EDMUND BOOTH ✓
SMALL STATUE  ?
2 ASHTRAYS
10 CUSHIONS
1 BOLSTER
MATCHSTAND/ASHTRAY
MATCHES
BLOTTER
PENCIL POT ✓
PENCILS AND PENS
CORKSCREW
INKSTAND ✓
TABLE LAMP ✓
SMALL BLACK BOOK ✓
WHITE ENVELOPES ✓
BROWN ENVELOPES
ASSORTED BILLS
4 BIRTH CERTIFICATES
WASTEPAPER BASKET
TELEPHONE ✓        CONTINUED...
```

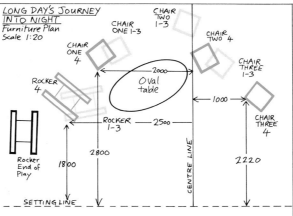

Furniture and prop plans This complicated set (**above**) was for a production of Eugene O'Neill's *Long Day's Journey Into Night*. Particularly for such complicated sets, a full props list (**far left**) should be made and a record should be kept of precisely where the props and furniture should be at the beginning of each scene. This is written out in a preset for each act (**right**) which lists the furniture which should be on stage and indicates the precise positions of props. On a ground plan (**left**) the furniture positions must be in a different color for each scene and these should correspond with the tapes used to mark the stage floor.

fishing line tied to one arm of the chandelier and led upstage to a convenient fixing point will prevent unwanted movement.

PREPARING FOR THE DRESS REHEARSAL

The stage manager responsible for props should continue through rehearsals preparing and updating the setting and dressing list. This will contain all items which need to be preset both on and off stage for all items, and indicate their position, subsequent changes made offstage in readiness for further cues, and details of scene changes or intermission changes. If many props are to be struck or removed quickly for a complete change of setting, start working out who will be responsible for what during rehearsals and, if necessary, invest in a supermarket cart or trolley to fill up and wheel away. Do not panic about *learning* the changes too early, as things will change, but commit all the information to paper

accurately and legibly. Dress rehearsals are extremely important for the stage crew as well as for the cast.

During the last rehearsals, prepare packing for all props: boxes, crates, plenty of newspaper for breakables, and tick off what is where. Backstage in a darkened theater is not the best place to find an urgently needed prop in a hurry.

The stage manager should take time to neaten up (in pencil only) the prompt book, cues, calls and warnings. These will be given about three to five minutes before each cue, and will have as clear a moment to be given as the cue itself. Make sure that character names in the margin are rewritten as actors' names at the top of the page, still as near five minutes away from the cue as possible. Type out sound and light cues synopses, as there will often be changes in plotting sessions, and the stage manager will be required to know what comes next.

The stage manager should make suitable arrangements for moving all equipment and effects from the rehearsal space to the theater, when they are re-

```
LONG DAY'S JOURNEY INTO NIGHT          PROPS SETTING LIST
PRESET FOR ACT ONE

PORCH       3 WICKER CHAIRS

FRONT PARLOR
UPRIGHT PIANO - LID CLOSED             ON IT: CLOTH/PAIR OF VASES
ROUND SWIVEL PIANO STOOL
SOFA                                   ON FLAT ABOVE: 3 PICTURES
SMALL TABLE                            ON IT: TABLECLOTH/3PICTURES/STATUE/ASHTRAY
ARMCHAIR
CARPET
CHANDELIER
WINDOWS CLOSED
BLINDS DOWN AS MARKED
PORCH DOORS OPEN
R. FOLDING DOOR ON 1ST MARK
L. FOLDING DOOR OPEN

PARLOR
WINDOW SEAT                            ON IT: MAGAZINES/NEWSPAPERS/4 CUSHIONS/1 BOLSTER
                                       UNDER IT: BOOKS
OVAL TABLE SCREWED TO FLOOR            ON IT: TABLECLOTH
                                              BOX OF MATCHES IN STAND
                                              WITH ASHTRAY(CHECK CATCH IS OPEN)
ROCKING CHAIR                          IN IT: CUSHION
CANE ARMCHAIR 1                        IN IT: CUSHION
CANE ARMCHAIR 2                        IN IT: CUSHION
CANE ARMCHAIR 3                        IN IT: CUSHION
CHANDELIER ABOVE TABLE - BULB (US TYPE) OUT
CANE ARMCHAIR 4                        IN IT: CUSHION
CHAISE                                 ON IT: CUSHION
DESK                                   ON IT: ASHTRAY/BOX OF MATCHES/
                                              BLOTTER/ASSORTED PAPERS/
                                              POT WITH PENCILS INSIDE
                                       ON TOP: PICTURE OF EDMUND BOOTH/
                                               CORKSCREW/INKSTAND WITH
                                               PENS AND PENCILS/TABLE LAMP
                                       IN 1ST HOLE: WHITE ENVELOPES
                                       IN 2ND HOLE: BROWN ENVELOPES
                                       IN 3RD HOLE: SMALL BLACK BOOK
                                       IN 4TH HOLE: ASSORTED BILLS
                                       IN MIDDLE DRAWER D.S.: 4 BIRTH CERTIFICATES
WASTE PAPER BASKET L. OF DESK
CUPBOARD ABOVE DESK                    IN IT: BOOKS
SWIVEL DESK CHAIR SET FACING U.S. PARALLEL WITH DESK
CARPET
```

quired. Leave enough time to clear and tidy the room thoroughly, not only out of common courtesy, but in case the company wishes to rehearse there again.

TECHNICAL REHEARSALS

The stage manager should give early thought to the planning of the time available and the work to be achieved during the production period. A stage schedule showing starting and finishing times, breaks and specific work should be finalized at least a week before the load-in or get-in, distributed to all concerned, and posted at the theater. A distribution list on the schedule itself will serve as a reminder as to whom it has been sent.

If the production is to be photographed, check who should be called for the photographer and when. This is termed the picture or photo call. Schedule these calls so that actors, director, wardrobe and, if necessary, wig and make-up departments know that full costume and make-up will be required. Other dress rehearsals might possibly take place without these.

Discuss the arrangements with director and crew. Allow sufficient time for getting all the equipment and props, including the set, into the theater and into their final positions. Lighting and sound rigging also takes time. This is when the lights and sound equipment are positioned correctly. Pieces of scenery which are to be 'flown' or lowered into place need to be secured carefully. Check the counterweight or hoist system thoroughly. Focusing lights and plotting lights can also be time consuming, as each light has to be focused individually and plotted on the cue sheet. Time should be allowed for setting levels on the sound equipment too and the sound cues should be finally plotted. The technical rehearsal (or 'tech') with the actors will vary in length depending on the type and complexity of the play. However, good preparation and organization by production staff can help this often hectic rehearsal run smoothly. The number of dress rehearsals will depend on time and the facilities available. Make sure there is time for dress rehearsals.

In the professional theater the stage management may not be particularly involved when the set is put into position. However, in the amateur theater this task will probably fall to the stage manager. When the set is in position, the assistant stage manager should set out prop tables conveniently to accommodate all props set off stage, and start unpacking.

The stage manager should set up the prompt position and become familiar with the available controls. Ideally, from the prompt position the stage manager should be able to contact all the technical staff and cast. Some sophisticated theaters have a cue light system, which links the prompt position to other parts of the theater including, possibly, lighting booth and dressing rooms. When using such a system, carry out a thorough pre-show check by flashing all cue lights in use to make sure they are working. Another sophisticated aid to giving cues is a headset system which enables the stage manager to cue actors and technicians verbally.

Other equipment in a sophisticated stage management control panel might include a loudspeaker to dressing and staff rooms, a public address system to the stage, which with a large theater and cast can allow the director and stage manager to be heard easily without losing their voices; safety curtain controls, if appropriate; electric house curtain controls; an in-house and an outside telephone; and a switchboard to operate the lights. However, most non-professional theaters will not have such extensive equipment. During rehearsals, work out the best way to cue both actors and technicians. For example, do you need an assistant to go to the dressing room to call the actors?

Once the set is dressed, the furniture needs positioning, and for critical areas of the stage involving important action, get agreement from director, designer and even main actors. The lighting designer who is about to focus all the lamps will not appreciate subsequent changes. A member of the stage crew should be available throughout focusing to reposition furniture as required and walk through the actors' moves.

For the lighting rehearsal, the stage manager should sit with the lighting designer and director to remind them of changes of light agreed, note alterations and additions, and record the cue numbers allotted in the prompt book. Subsequent extra cues may be given, mark these with suffixes, such as a, b, c and so on, as required. Lighting rehearsals usually take longer than expected, allow *at least* twice the duration of the full running-time of the production as a whole, and, preferably, a one or two hour session after an overnight break, to tidy up final details when everyone feels fresh.

The stage manager with the first technical dress rehearsal when the show is being cued for the first time, should make a pencil note of the nature of all cues being given. For example, specify 'practical table lamps off' or 'blackout'. Abbreviations such as BO (blackout) or DBO (dead blackout) can be used.

The sound rehearsal should also be attended by the stage manager in the same way, to begin the process of understanding why a cue is to be given at a precise moment. For those giving cues from backstage, this may be their only opportunity to see and hear the desired effect from the front. Finally, check all working parts of the set, doors, windows, special effects, prop settings, clear and tidy up the stage area. The dress rehearsal can now begin.

The stage manager is responsible for allocating dressing rooms, and should look these over a week or so before the production. If any artists are to share, check that they get along well together. It is traditional not to mix sexes in the dressing room, although company practice may vary. Bear in mind that some actors may need to be close to the stage for quick changes, and that those with body make-up may need to shower or at least wash. The position of the bathrooms may affect allocation. Check too that dressing room lights work. Important items for the dressing room include tissues or toilet paper, and cleanser for removing make-up. The dressing room should be equipped with wastepaper baskets for used tissues and so on.

If the cast are expected to tidy up the dressing room after the show, make sure that they know what you want them to do, and also make sure that they do it. Encourage the technicians to be tidy also. An untidy theater, particularly backstage, could lead to accidents. Try to sort out such matters before the dress rehearsal. Type out the dressing room list and post a copy on the call board at the stage door, so that the actors can find their rooms. Keep a copy in the prompt position—if a costume or prop is needed urgently, it is useful to know where to look.

THE DRESS REHEARSAL

The first technical dress rehearsal is less for acting than for running through all physical events in the production—actors' entrances, moves, exits, timing all cues, lighting, sound and other effects, as well as all scene changes. No cue whatsoever should be glossed over without sufficient rehearsal, except where lack of props or scenery makes it impossible. At the same time, the production manager should not let the director or cast dwell overlong on any section. Use your judgement to time when to suggest politely that they move on.

In order to make good use of time, the director may decide to 'top and tail' or run through the show 'cue to cue'. This involves cutting long dialogue not involving physical cues. Sections which present no difficulties to the cast may also be omitted, but, for all others in the crew, it is probably the first time they will have run the play, and they must be allowed their rehearsal. Schedule three times the duration of the play for this rehearsal, except for plays with very few cues.

Find out before the dress rehearsal starts how the director wishes to 'give notes'. This is when the director makes comments, criticisms or changes and can take place after each act or at the end of the rehearsal. Check whether notes will be given to actors and technicians separately, or all together. The latter is often more efficient, however boring it may be for those who have little to do, or get it all right anyway. When taking their own notes, the production team should write them down carefully, as a tired mind will not remember details.

During the dress rehearsal, the stage manager should sit with the director and lighting designer out front, unless the production involves scene changes. This view will enable the production manager to advise the crew during and after the rehearsal, to share the director's point of view and quickly translate need into action. Much tension may be avoided by having this important technical coordinator working closely with the director. The second stage manager in the prompt position, apart from giving cues from the carefully prepared

PRODUCTION WEEK

The week before the opening night is an exhausting succession of technicals, dress rehearsals and last minute problems.

Everything has to be tried, tested and made good. The following schedule would be typical:

SATURDAY: Get in scenery, costumes, lighting, props, etc.
9.00am	Rig lighting and sound, load (get) in set
	Crew call: all lighting, props, stage management, stage crew and design staff required.
1.00pm	Lunch break
2.00pm	Continue setting and focusing lights
6.00pm	Supper break (sound checks)
7.00pm	Continue lighting and prop setting (to 1.00am)

SUNDAY: Technical work on stage, complete prop setting
9.00am	Continue focusing lights—crew as Saturday
11.00am	Lighting rehearsal
1.00pm	Lunch
2.00pm	Start technical dress rehearsal with actors
6.00pm	Supper break (sound checks)
7.00pm	Continue technical dress rehearsal (to 1.00am)

MONDAY: Stage available for technical work from 9.00am if crew available
6.30pm	Dress rehearsal Act I
8.30pm	Supper break
9.00pm	Dress rehearsal Act II

Dress rehearsal may finish late

TUESDAY: Stage available during day as Monday
6.30pm	Dress rehearsal Act III
8.30pm	Supper break
9.00pm	Dress rehearsal Act IV

Dress rehearsal may finish late

WEDNESDAY: Stage available during day as Monday
6.00pm	Notes with the director in auditorium
7.00pm	Second dress rehearsal (15 minute interval)
10.30pm	Finish rehearsal and start notes

THURSDAY: Opening night
5.30pm	All crew required
6.30pm	All cast required: make-up, dressing
7.30pm	Curtain up

Anyone involved in the production will be giving every spare moment of their time to the production during this week and there is no point in joining a theater company if you are not willing to do so.

The director's notes When these are given, the entire cast should be listening, but the crew can often work on.

prompt book, and noting changes, should be readily available to talk to the director or main stage manager the moment the rehearsal comes to a halt. If it is decided to go back over a sequence, the stage manager on the book should state clearly how far back to go in order to pick up the sequence of cues for actors and technicians. The technicians should then be told what condition they should be in, for example 'Back to cue 34' or 'Standing by for cue 35', and only when those technicians reply that they are ready to continue will the actor who is to speak next be asked to 'Go from . . .', the relevant line.

However domineering this approach may seem it is the accepted and efficient way of proceeding. The 'book' stage manager should also make notes of revised blocking or moves agreed on. During the rehearsal, he or she should become familiar with the appearance of lighting cues from the prompt position and the way sound cues are heard, so that errors in subsequent performances may be spotted.

The props person should note changes to properties required in the light of rehearsal, and amend the prop setting list accordingly, noting in the script particular cues or preparations to be made. Small props may be collected by the actor from the prop table. However, bear the convenience and safety of the actor and props in mind: actors will appreciate being handed a full tray or lighted candle not too far from the entrance, for example.

Subsequent dress rehearsals provide an opportunity for cast and director to work on interpretation and acting. A good technical dress rehearsal with proper attention to detail should prevent physical details worrying the company any further. Remember, though, that the performer has to suffer problems in public, and the stage manager is there to reduce these to a minimum.

At the end of an exhausting dress rehearsal day, remember that the company need calling for the following day. Try to elicit the detail for the following day from the director before the end of rehearsal, as the cast and technicians will be eager to get away, and will appreciate a firm statement of the work to be achieved on the next occasion.

THE OPENING NIGHT

The old adage of a bad dress rehearsal preceding a good first night is famous. Phrases like 'It'll be all right on the night' have an element of truth, but underlying the tension, excitement and celebration of the first night must run the basic discipline that the stage management firmly intends to prevail for the run of the production, however brief.

Good organization, thorough preparation and

Running plot and synopses
Stage management require detailed plots of precisely what happens and when during a performance. The Assistant Stage Manager's Running Plot and the light and sound synopses (**right**) are the most important of these.

Curtain up.

All practical lamps must be checked in good time before each performance.

Stage management are responsible for offstage sound effects. A door slam apparatus, made of a small portable door with a solid casing is often used for such effects.

Some props are stored offstage or are taken off by actors and have to be replaced by stage management.

Number doors and windows to avoid confusion.

Stage right.

Stage left.

Actors should not be allowed to wander about offstage with naked lights.

Actors can be forgetful, so stage management check that they have personal props for each scene.

LONG DAY'S JOURNEY INTO NIGHT
A.S.M. RUNNING PLOT 22.12.71

PAGE		
6.30 pm	CHECK CHANDELIER AND TABLE LAMP WITH ELECTRICS	
ON C.U.	CHECK DOOR 1 CLOSED	
	HAND NEWSPAPER TO TYRONE	S.R.
	FLUTTER WINDOW 1 BLIND ON C.U.	S.L.
1 - 26	CHECK PROPS STANDBY TO COLLECT CIGAR	S.L.
	CHECK EDMUND HAS BOOK	S.R.
1-2 Sc 1	CHECK SCENE CHANGE	
2.1 - 17	CHECK PROPS STANDBY TO COLLECT TRAY	S.R.
2.2 - 37	FOOTSTEPS TYRONE DOWNSTAIRS	
	CUE: MARY "GO ON EDMUND"	S.R.
	DOOR OPEN	
	CUE: AS EDMUND CLOSES DOOR 1	S.R.
2.2 - 38	DOOR SLAM	
	CUE: MARY "GOODBYE" PAUSE	S.R.
3	CHECK ACT CHANGE	
3 - 9	DOOR OPEN	
	CUE LIGHT	S.R.
	DOOR CLOSE	
	CUE LIGHT	S.R.
	COLLECT TYRONE'S PINZ NEZ CASE AND	
	BIRTH CERTIFICATE FROM DRESSING ROOM	
	COLLECT WEDDING DRESS FROM DRESSING ROOM 2	
3 - 17	DOOR SLAM	
	CUE: MARY "SO THE SERVANTS WON'T SEE HIM"	S.R.
3 - 20	CHECK PROPS STANDBY TO HAND BOTTLE TO	
	TYRONE	S.R.
	DOOR SLAM	
	CUE: EDMUND "I DON'T WANT ANY DINNER"	S.R.

A snap fade on the dimmer mimics switching off a light. Here it is the hall light which is practical.

Follow on means that the effect comes in as a related part of the previous cue.

Increase the light on a specific area, occupied by the rocking chair down right.

Build means increase the intensity of light.

The actor screws the light bulb into the chandelier. As he does so, the lighting operator snaps on lighting to match each bulb being illuminated. ABCD indicate the four parts of the cue.

A different practical chandelier is now brought into use, indicated by the position Up Stage Left.

Two tape recorders (A and B) are used with two speakers (Up Left and Up Right). Sound is channeled to the appropriate speaker.

PAGE 4   LIGHTING SYNOPSIS CONTINUED...
                              ACT III CONTINUED...   12-1-72

PRESET TIMING
Q13 SNAP   HALL PRACTICAL OUT

                    15 Minute Interval

                        ACT IV

CU		MIDNIGHT PRAC LIT TIGHT TO TABLE
Q14	SNAP	PRAC ON EXT. USR (THRO' DOOR US)
Q15	ABCD	SNAP VISUAL. BUILD AS 4 LAMPS ON
		C CHANDELIER ARE LIT
FO	30 sec	FOG THRO' WINDOWS
Q16	ABCD	VISUAL. REVERSE Q15
Q17	SNAP	USR PRAC OUT
Q18	AB	2 LAMPS IN CHANDELIER ON
Q19	30 sec	BUILD L
Q20	SNAP	USL CHANDELIER ON
FO	15 sec	ADD TO ARCH
Q21		BUILD CHAIR DR (ROCKER)

                        CURTAIN

Volume starts at 7 on a scale of 0-10, and diminishes to O.

Effects.

The car is on one tape, the hedge clipping on another. Each is played through a separate speaker.

SOUND SYNOPSIS

CUE NO.	PAGE	EFFECT	TAPE	VOL.	SPKRS
1	1.4	Cicadas	A	3-2	U.L. & U.R.
2	1.4	Cicadas out	A	2	
3	1.14	Cicadas	A	1½	U.L. & U.R.
4	1.14	Cicadas out	A	1½	
5	1.20	Cicadas	A	1½	U.L. & U.R.
6	1.20	Cicadas out	A	1½	
7	1.27	Hedge clipping	A	2½	U.L.
8	1.27	Car passing &	B	7-0	U.R.
		clipping out		4-5-0	U.L.
		Tape snapped out as car FX starts			
10	3.1	Fog horn & ship bells	A	9	U.L. & U.R.
			B	9	As above
11	3.1	Fog horn & ship bells	A	9	As above
			B	9	As above
12	3.2	Fog horn & ship bells	A	3½	As above
			B	3½	As above
14	3.2	Bells out	B	3½-0	
15	3.7	Fog horn	A	2	U.L. & U.R.
16	3.10	Fog horn	A	3	U.L. & U.R.
17	3.16	Fog horn	A	3	U.L. & U.R.
18	3.20	Fog horn & ship bells	A	3½	U.L. & U.R.

calm attention to detail are important at all stages of a production, but they are particularly vital before the opening night. These will help to make sure the show can run without hitches. Attend to all details, the precise functioning of the performance, and the discipline of checking before the show and clearing up after the show before relaxing.

Preshow checks must include the following. Make sure that set and doors, windows, curtains and so on are in position and working; that props are correctly placed on and off stage; that consumables, smoking materials, food, water and so on, are correctly located; that cue lights are working; that the light switches are working; that any special effects are prepared; that scripts and cue sheets are in position; and—importantly—that all actors and stage staff are present.

At the 'half'—35 minutes before curtain-up—a member of the team should tour the dressing rooms until they have actually *seen* each member of the cast. Never rely on report that an actor is 'around'. At the same time say a polite good evening, but tactfully avoid interrupting an actor's preparation,

or getting involved in a domestic crisis. There are other important priorities.

After the performance, the stage manager should prepare a stage manager's report showing the precise duration of each act to the minute, and of the intermissions, and then comments should be added about the running of the performance. These should be confined to occurrences which clearly, to the audience, were unintentional and events which were not prescribed by the director. Timings will be important to the director, as these will enable him or her to understand whether a section of the production is going astray and how to put it right. Comments about the physical elements of the production will serve as a reminder for repairs to be made, and those about cues may deem that further rehearsal is necessary.

The production is now open. Store the prompt book carefully and, in case of loss, make a fair copy at the earliest opportunity, or photocopy the original, together with prop plots and other documentation. Finally, remind the cast of their call for the next day. Now even the stage manager can relax.

Each member of the team will need a breakdown of their exact tasks on the night. This one (**right**) is for an assistant stage manager whose duties include laying out a complicated patience game in the same way for each performance. The stage manager's report sheets (**below**) are a useful record of each performance and can be used for future productions of the same show.

Specify such things as whether a bottle should be open or not, to avoid confusion.

LONG DAY'S JOURNEY INTO NIGHT
PROPS SETTING AND RUNNING ORDER
PROPERTY STAFF

1. COLLECT CIGAR FROM TYRONE
2. DURING LATECOMERS BREAK
   TAKE CUSHION FROM ROCKER AND RESET ON WINDOW SEAT
   CLOSE DOOR 1
3. RECEIVE TRAY FROM CATHLEEN D.S.R.
   SET TRAY OFF R. WITH - UNSEALED WHISKY BOTTLE WITH
   CORK ON TRAY, 6 GLASSES, 2 PITCHERS OF WATER
4. SCENE CHANGE ACT 2 - ACT 3
   STRIKE BOOK FROM CHAIR 3 AND RESET IN WINDOW SEAT BOOKSHELF
   ASHTRAY ON C. TABLE
   SET - ON TABLE - TRAY - ON IT - UNSEALED WHISKY BOTTLE WITH
   CORK ON TRAY, 6 GLASSES, 2 PITCHERS OF WATER
   CLOSE PORCH DOORS TO CLOSE ALL WINDOWS
   OPEN DOOR 1
   RESET ASHTRAY AS IN PRESET
   DESK CHAIR, ARMCHAIRS 1,2,3 ON PRESET MARKS
5. HAND FULL SEALED WHISKY BOTTLE TO TYRONE S.R.
6. RECEIVE TRAY FROM CATHLEEN S.R.

CARD ORDER FOR PATIENCE
TOP LAY OUT LEFT TO RIGHT   ACE, 2 DIAMONDS
                                   ACE, 2 SPADES
                                   ACE CLUBS

LAY OUT LEFT TO RIGHT   6 CLUBS TO 10 CLUBS.......4 DOWN
                                   10 HEARTS................4 DOWN
                                   6 SPADES.................3 DOWN
                                   7 SPADES TO KING CLUBS...2 DOWN
                                   4 CLUBS
                                   ....2 DOWN
                                   KING HEARTS
                                   QUEEN DIAMONDS TO KING SPADES

DECK FROM TOP FACE DOWN   10 SPADES, 5 HEARTS, 9 HEARTS,
                                   5 SPADES, 7 CLUBS, QUEEN SPADES,
                                   7 DIAMONDS, KING DIAMONDS,
                                   8 CLUBS, QUEEN CLUBS

DECK FACE UP   8 DOWN WITH 8 HEARTS ON TOP

When card games are featured the pack should be arranged in the right order. This detailed plot ensures that the correct pattern will emerge at each performance if the props staff have followed the procedure.

DATE	Wed			
	UP	DOWN	PLAYING TIME	INTERVAL
ACT 1	7·30	7·58	28	
INTERVAL				2
ACT 2	8·00	8·20	20	
INTERVAL				17
ACT 3	8·37	9·11	34	
INTERVAL				2
ACT 4	9·13	9·44	31	
		TOTALS	113	21
		TOTAL RUNNING	2 hrs 14 mins	

REMARKS / PROBLEMS / PROPS
ACT 3 - 2 mins over time
Handbag clasp (Jenny) broken.

MAKING SOUND EFFECTS

Most theatrical productions require occasional background noises. Sound effects can either be created by the stage crew behind the scenes or by using a tape recording. In some productions, particularly musicals, microphones may be required to strengthen weak voices or to project one voice above others. If electrical sound equipment is necessary, amateur groups may have to make do with equipment they can borrow rather then buy. Since sound equipment is both complicated and expensive if a company is aiming at professional standards, it is wise to make sure it can be used well, since the poor application of electrical equipment could spoil rather than enhance a performance.

Producing sound effects requires imagination and practice. Some dried peas or beans rolled around in a metal drum, for example, can be used for the effect of rain, applause or the sea, depending on the number of beans and the speed at which they are rolled around. For the sea, a few seagull calls will add to the general effect. Crowd noises can be recorded on to a tape but can also be supplemented by live sound from the actors on stage or behind the scenes. Similarly, for battle sounds, shouting voices could be supplemented by the occasional crash or the sound of a gong. Gun shots can, of course, be created by using a starting pistol and blanks, but often this effect will be overpowering and bending a plank of wood up and releasing it on cue could sound more authentic.

There are endless possibilities for such effects and using bits and pieces found in kitchens and garages, an imaginative stage manager can usually come up with what is required.

If it is decided that electrical equipment is necessary for producing effects in a production, try to make sure that your equipment matches your requirements. Many domestic tape recorders are the cassette type, but these are not easy to use in the theater, since it is difficult to start them at a very precise point. However, this may not be necessary. Reel-to-reel recorders produce the best sound, but can be noisy to switch on and off. If used in a small theater this could distract the audience. Cartridge tape recorders are probably the best to use but they may be difficult to find. Tapes should be made with great care and a sound should be practiced and tried out in the theater before it is committed to the final tape. Careful planning is vital if a number of sounds are to be put on one tape, which will be turned on and off as those sounds are required through a performance. Cues for the particular sounds should be noted and then colored leader tapes can be spliced on to the tape to correspond with these cues. Often noises are required when there are many changes and the stage manager will indicate a cue for lights, sound and maybe scenery change all at once.

Special effects equipment
Most of these sound machines could be easily constructed in the theater workshop.
1 Double bell box. This is run on batteries and has a socket for inserting an extension push.
2 Door slam box. This is simply a sturdy wooden box with a hinged door. The door is fitted with latches, bolts, chains and so on, to enable a variety of effects.
3 Glass crash. This wooden box is padded inside. In order to create the sound of shattering glass, a pane of glass is placed across the top of the box and smashed with a wooden mallet.
4 Thunder sheet. A piece of galvanized iron, suspended in this way, is banged to create a crash of thunder.
5 Wind machine. A revolving drum of wooden slats has a strip of canvas weighted over it. Turning the handle makes the wind sound.
6 Gravel tray. Walking across this try provides the sound of feet on a loose surface.
7 Clatter crash. By releasing the rope, the suspended pieces of wood fall to the ground.
8 Door or ship creak. A small barrel, with both ends removed and the bottom replaced with plywood, has a length of cord pulled through it. A piece of leather is rubbed along the cord.
9 Rain or sea drum. Dried peas, or lead shot, are swished around a wooden drum or sieve.

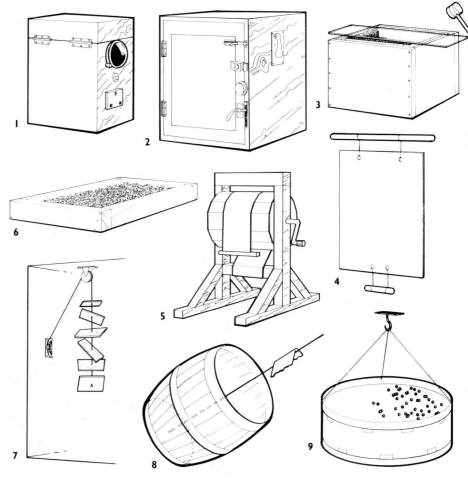

Taping The most important piece of sound equipment for most companies will be a tape recorder. It offers the most flexibility for a range of sounds which can be cued in and turned on as required. As with all electrical equipment, the more expensive products will be more reliable and provide a better sound, both in terms of quality and pitch. Since recorded sound can be disastrous if not properly recorded, or if played back on inadequate equipment, it is perhaps only worthwhile using a good tape recorder, amplifier and speakers.

Reel to reel tape recorders offer the best quality sound because they run at a faster speed than either cassettes or cartridges. One of the popular stereo tape recorders is the Revox B77. It has built-in facilities for sound-on-sound recording. This means that layers of sound can be built up and played either separately or together. If a play requires that a storm is raging outside a window and that a car drives past and skids during it, the sound of the storm can be recorded on one track and the sound of the car on another.

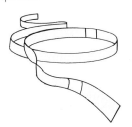

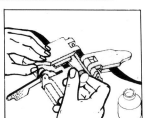

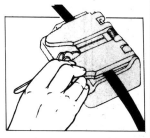

Splicing a tape 1. In order to attach colored leaders to aid accuracy and timing of sound cues, the tape is separated between recordings and the leaders are attached. Either an adhesive or a sticky tape is used.

2. This simple machine both cuts the tape and, using an adhesive, connects the colored leaders to the sections of tape. The tape is first carefully aligned in the machine at the precise point to be cut.

3. Adhesive is then applied to the end of the colored leader when it has been placed in the machine.

4. The tape and the coloured leader are then brought into firm contact under pressure for 30 seconds to bind them. The coloured leaders should be numbered to correspond with sound cue numbers.

Other electrical equipment
Loudspeakers should be carefully chosen to correspond with the level of sound required. For example, it is pointless to try and use one small domestic speaker to produce high level battle noises. Always use two speakers, place them where they are most effective, and test them carefully.

Microphones come in an enormous range of sizes and designs. If they are to be purchased, it is best to find the most flexible and the most simple to use. Seek professional advice to make sure that the microphones are suited to your needs.

Modern technology has created the most versatile of all electrical sound machines: the synthesizer. They are now widely used and are definitely worth investing in. A synthesizer can produce an enormous range of sound effects. They can also be used for almost any musical instrument sound required.

CHAPTER THREE
ACTING

An actor's task, said the American James Dean, is to interpret life. To do that, actors have to be open to the widest possible range of experiences which life has to offer. They must seize on pieces of information about people, store them away, ready to bring them out and use them when necessary. Actors rely on concentration and imagination. Performing in front of an audience can be extremely lonely, and actors must be able to call on the reserves they have within themselves.

In short, acting is a combination of intuition, intelligence, observation, memory and skill. At the very beginning, though, there is the play. The actor's job, and that of the director, is to create the world of the playwright on stage by making the characters come to life.

Acting is subjective and no two actors will approach or play a scene in the same way. It is important to approach every single part as openly as possible and without prejudice. A useful aid to achieving this is to carefully record your initial response to a play. The first time actors read a play, they will discover their own intuitive response to the play, and it will be the only time this happens. As soon as actors begin to rehearse with the rest of the cast and the director their minds are influenced by their thoughts and ideas, as the performance is shaped and guided. However, it is often from this first intuitive response gained on an initial reading that actors feel instinctively how they want to play their part. If they have kept notes of their first impressions, they can later compare how they first felt and thought with the knowledge they have gained of their characters during rehearsals.

It is a terrible mistake for actors to look at a play purely from their characters' point of view. Actors should never count the lines they have to say or just read the scenes they appear in. That first instinctive response must be to the play as a whole. When taking notes, actors should try to write intuitively and spontaneously, jotting down first impressions as they read. They should respond to characters in terms of color and texture and try not to make intellectual judgements. Obviously it is impossible to eliminate the intellect and of course the intellect is important, but actors' primary concerns are with their instincts and how to develop them.

MOVEMENT AND VOICE

Actors have two valuable tools—their bodies and their voices. Both must be flexible and both should work on stage through relaxation rather than through tension. To achieve this, both must be physically exercised. Activities, such as swimming, which are obviously good exercise for the body, can also help the voice by developing breathing. A wide range of special exercises have been worked out to meet an actor's specific needs.

Voice exercises The following exercises can be

After all the physical exertion and mental concentration of the rehearsal period, comes the exhilaration and rewards of a performance. The curtain call (**left**) is a moment of mutual appreciation between actors and audience. There was a tendency to abandon curtain calls in the 1960s but most audiences feel there should be an opportunity to express recognition of the actors' efforts. This call for a production of *Hamlet* has the actors in order of importance, with the stars at the front. Such elaborate calls can be effective but it is often more appropriate for the whole company to take a joint bow.

done alone or with a group. It is most important in voice exercises to develop both high and low vocal register. The first exercise is to develop a capacity for vocal power by extending breathing capacity.

For the first exercise, kneel on the floor with your hands clasped loosely behind your back and place your forehead on the floor. Your bottom should rest on your heels, and you should feel completely relaxed. Close your eyes and breathe in very slowly as you raise your body to an upright position. Work from the base of your spine up, so that your head is lifted last. As you raise your head begin to let your breath out to the sound of an 'oh'. Then release down to your original position lowering your forehead back to the floor. As you do this let the 'oh' change into a hum forming an 'mm' sound. Repeat the whole exercise 10 times and do not break the rhythm. Breathe in as you go up and let your voice out going down to an 'ohhmmm'.

This will, in time, develop your breathing, and you will note an improvement very rapidly within the exercise as you find you can hold the sound for longer and longer. Remember to move very slowly and count the 'ohhmmms' off on your fingers.

The next exercise is to make you aware of bringing your voice forward. If you hum and your lips vibrate, your voice is forward, as it should be at the end of this exercise. It is good to do before rehearsals.

Sit cross-legged on the floor and gently pat your face with your hands. First pat your cheeks, then pat the back of your head with one hand and your forehead with the other. Do this until you feel quite tingly. Then squeeze and tense your face and hands very tightly. Release this by opening your hands, eyes and mouth wide, and sticking out your tongue. Then squeeze hands and face very tight again. Release in the same way. Do this whole exercise six times. As you are tensing and releasing, you should begin to feel very lively. Now breathe in and let your breath out on a hum using an 'mm' sound and producing a vibration on your lips. By concentrating, you should be able to switch the humming vibration to a different part of your face. If you think of producing the sound in your nose or forehead, you will soon find that you can do it. Put your hand on your cheek, nose or forehead and feel the vibration. With practice, this will become easier.

The warm-up Actors differ in their methods of preparation for a performance. Some actors will run through their lines. Others prefer to lie on their backs and do nothing before a show. Some will have a drink in a local bar, and many will do what is called a warm-up.

A warm-up is also useful if done by the whole company before rehearsals. It serves as a way of helping concentration, gives the actors a focus, and wakes them up. The voice exercises can certainly be used as a warm-up. There are also the following physical exercises which are as useful before a performance as they are for rehearsals.

For the first exercise, stand with your legs about 18in (45cm) apart. Raise your arms above your head and stretch up, dropping your shoulders as you begin. Stretch through your legs so that you are standing on tiptoe and on up through your arms, hands, fingers. Feel the energy streaming out of you in an upward direction. Now release forward. First let your wrists relax, then your elbows, head and neck. Bending forward with your knees bent and spine dropped, hang over your knees and breathe. You should feel completely relaxed. Hold this position and lift yourself up a little from the base of your spine. Then drop back. Continue lifting and dropping until you build up some momentum. Be careful not to strain.

Next, come to rest in the original position of release, hanging over your knees, and take the movement sideways, raising an inch (2.5 cm) or so, swing your body from the waist and swing your arms, then drop to the side. Come back to the original center position, then swing and drop again. Repeat this six times coming to rest in the original hanging position. Then straighten up very slowly working through the spine vertebra by vertebra. Make sure that your neck and shoulders are free from tension, and that your head is raised last. You are now upright with your legs straight and feet apart. It is vital to do this slowly.

Releasing the neck, drop just the head forward. Make sure that the rest of your back is straight. You are working with only your head and neck. Tilt your left ear toward your shoulder and let your head hang to the side for a moment. Now drop your head behind you, and then bring it round to your right shoulder and, finally, drop it forward again. Do this circle to the left twice more. Then repeat the exercise starting the circle in the opposite direction. Lift your head after completing the movement. This is excellent for getting rid of tension.

The next exercise is for the shoulders. First walk your shoulders up to your ears, and then drop them. Walk them up and drop them twice more. Then starting with your left shoulder, make a circle with it, bringing it forward, then lifting it up and taking it back. Press down and release. Do the same movement with the right shoulder and repeat six times with alternate shoulders. Then do the same movement circling both shoulders together. Move forward, up, back, down and then release. Now start the movement backward, taking the shoulders back,

FACIAL EXERCISES

The face is made up of bones, muscles and flesh just as any other part of the body. It requires exercise in the same way too. Before beginning stand or sit comfortably with the spine and neck straight and with the face relaxed Repeat each exercise several times. First purse the lips to make the mouth small (**1**) then expand it to a wide grin (**2**). Combine these two movements as if chewing. Move the tongue (**3**) to feel every area inside the mouth (**4**). Then stick out your tongue and stretch it down to touch your chin (**5**). Force the tongue upward to try and touch the tip of your nose (**6**). Stretch your eyebrows, first raising them high (**7**) then forcing them down (**8**). Now screw up the face contorting the features (**9**) and stretching the skin (**10**). Finally place the palms of the hands on the face moving the skin over the bone structure (**11**). Massage the scalp in the same way (**12**).

lifting them up, bringing them forward and then releasing. Move backward, up, forward, down and release. Repeat this six times.

Now stretch your right arm forward on a diagonal. Then drop it and let gravity take it round behind you as if you were throwing a ball overarm. Try and keep the rest of your body still. Build up the momentum of this movement so you are swinging your arm round very fast. Your hand will feel tingly. Release your right arm and repeat with your left. Move it faster and faster and then release.

The next important part of the body to exercise is the legs. To begin some leg exercises, stand up straight with your feet together. Put your weight and balance on your left leg and concentrate on this. Lift your arms out to the side to aid your balance if necessary. Lift your right leg and bend it at the knee. Keeping it bent, take it behind you and then let gravity swing the leg forward. Swing it backward and forward with the tip of your foot brushing the floor. Repeat the movement eight times. Then change legs. Swing the left leg while balancing on the right leg.

To relax the ankles, lift the right foot off the ground and take it round in a circle from the ankle. Do this circle four times clockwise and then four times counter-clockwise. Repeat the movement with the other foot.

The next exercises are floor exercises for stretching and releasing the spine. Lying on your stomach, stretch out flat on the floor. Let the floor take your weight. Work with the image of a cat which is getting ready to spring. Stretch your arms out and through your whole body. Then place the palms of your hands flat on the floor next to your shoulders. Lift your head slowly and turn it in various directions, stretching your neck. Then slowly raise your chest off the floor, shifting your weight to your hands. When your chest is completely off the floor, straighten your elbows and knees. Tuck your toes under and raise your body as high as it will go. Stretch up into an arch with your buttocks as the apex. Flex the arch by dropping your buttocks and snapping your head up, then immediately raising your buttocks and dropping your head back again.

Slowly bring your knee toward your ear and stretch your head toward it over your shoulder. At the same time push your foot out and away, attempting to stretch the leg. Repeat with the other leg for the other side. Come back to the first push-up position and release back down into the floor.

Remember that the object of this series of stretches is to imitate the movements of a cat. If you find the movements a strain at first, do not try too hard. You will slowly develop more agility.

To complete the exercise, turn over on your back and relax. Lift your legs and buttocks off the floor, supporting your back with your hands. Get as much of your back off the floor as possible, pushing your ribcage toward your chin. Legs are straight, toes pointing to the ceiling. Now take your legs over your head so that your feet touch the floor behind you. Flex your feet and open your legs wide, keeping your feet on the floor. Now drop your knees to the ground on either side of your ears and breathe. Straighten out the legs again and slowly, vertebra by vertebra, bring your spine forward until you are flat on the floor again. On completion sit up and release forward over your knees.

Now sit up straight and open your legs wide. Lift up your arms in the air making sure your shoulders are dropped. Stretch your arms out toward your left leg and grip your left ankle. Try to place your forehead on your left knee. Breathe in and out and count up to 10. Counting aloud will make sure that you are breathing. Come back to the center and stretch over to the right and repeat, gripping your right ankle. Do this exercise twice more. On completion, lie back on the floor and relax completely. In your own time turn over to one side and get up slowly.

Some of these exercises are fairly difficult. It is important not to strain or push yourself too far at the beginning. You will find that your body will become more flexible with practice. It is important to always remember to breathe as the more you concentrate on your breathing, the greater your degree of release and relaxation will become.

AUDITIONS

A general audition, perhaps for a place in a company or when no specific reading is requested, usually involves preparing two pieces. It is normally best to choose one classical piece and one modern and to make sure that they contrast in terms of content. For instance, one piece could be funny and the other more serious.

It is important to choose speeches from plays to which you have a personal response and to select a character in a situation you can identify with. If there are supposed to be other characters on stage, try to imagine the person you are playing opposite and what he or she looks like. If possible, place a chair where that person should be on stage. This will give you a concentration point which is important in auditions since they are nerve-wracking occasions. If you have chosen a piece where your character is alone on stage, such as a Shakespearean soliloquy, try to have the courage to play it directly to the people who are auditioning you. This means

HEAD AND SHOULDER EXERCISES

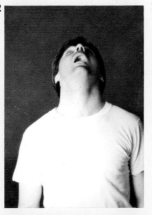

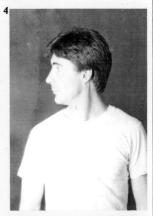

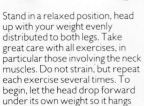

Stand in a relaxed position, head up with your weight evenly distributed to both legs. Take great care with all exercises, in particular those involving the neck muscles. Do not strain, but repeat each exercise several times. To begin, let the head drop forward under its own weight so it hangs against the chest (**1**). Slowly raise it and relax. Now let the head drop back opening your mouth (**2**). Raise it slowly again. Turn just the head to the left (**3**) and then to the right (**4**). Facing forward again, let the head drop to one side (**5**), raise it and then let it drop to the other side. Take great care in doing the next exercise, letting the weight of the head do the work. Drop your head forward (**1**) and slowly rotate it round to one shoulder (**6**), let it drop back (**2**) on round to the other shoulder and to the front again (**1**). Reverse direction of this rotation. Now raise both shoulders high (**7**) then let them fall (**8**) and relax. Lift one shoulder and rotate it back, down, forward (**9**) and then do the same with the other (**10**). Finally, rotate both shoulders first pushing forward (**11**) and then pushing back (**12**).

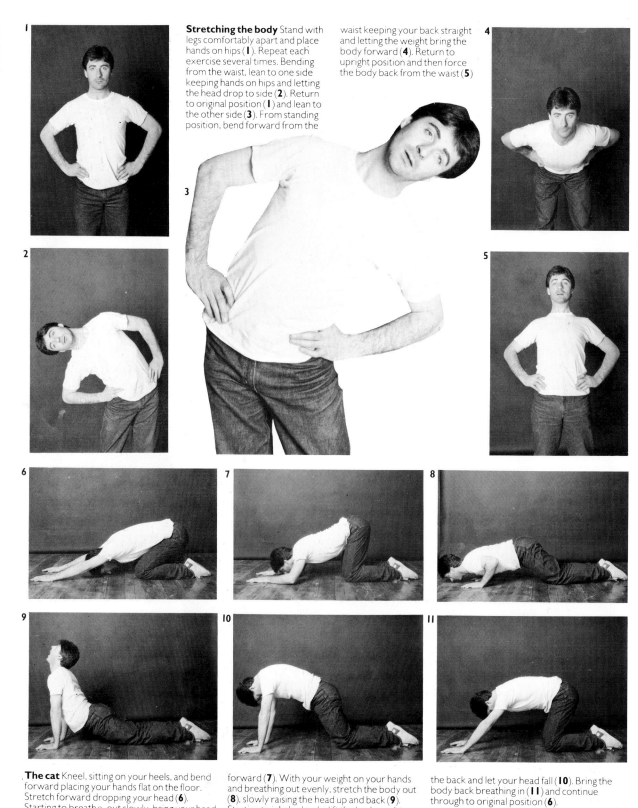

Stretching the body Stand with legs comfortably apart and place hands on hips (**1**). Repeat each exercise several times. Bending from the waist, lean to one side keeping hands on hips and letting the head drop to side (**2**). Return to original position (**1**) and lean to the other side (**3**). From standing position, bend forward from the waist keeping your back straight and letting the weight bring the body forward (**4**). Return to upright position and then force the body back from the waist (**5**)

The cat Kneel, sitting on your heels, and bend forward placing your hands flat on the floor. Stretch forward dropping your head (**6**). Starting to breathe out slowly, bring your head forward (**7**). With your weight on your hands and breathing out evenly, stretch the body out (**8**), slowly raising the head up and back (**9**). Starting to inhale slowly, lift the body, arching the back and let your head fall (**10**). Bring the body back breathing in (**11**) and continue through to original position (**6**).

1

Limbering up Stand upright (**1**). Make a slight jump, bending your knees as you land and drop to a crouching position resting on the balls of the feet and with your hands flat on the ground (**2**). Bounce your rear up and down twenty times, keeping the knees bent and resting your weight on your hands and the balls of the feet.

From a standing position with feet forward about 1 ft (30 cm) apart, drop from the waist allowing the spine and body and arms to hang limp (**3**). Touch the floor twice in front with the palms of the hands if possible (**4**). Moving rhythmically, swing the arms back between the legs and touch the floor behind twice (**5**). Move from the waist and try to reach as far behind and in front as possible as you repeat the movement several times. Return to the drop position (**3**), and slowly straighten the spine, finally raising the head to the original standing position (**6**).

3

4

2

5

6

7

10

9

8

Relaxing the body and standing After a series of exercises, and to relax the body completely, lie on your back in the most comfortable position (**7**). Tense every muscle and then slowly relax each of them from your toes to your head. Concentrate on each part as you relax it.

It is essential to start any standing exercise from the correct position. Most important is the distribution of weight. It must be spread evenly between both legs and *not*, as is shown here (**8**) with the weight on one leg or the other.

11

Shoulder stand Lying flat on your back with your arms by your side and toes pointed, bring your knees up to the chest (**9**). Supporting your hips with your hands, raise them up keeping the back straight and toes pointed. Your weight should be supported by your hands and shoulders (**10**). Slowly let your legs come back as far as possible and keeping them as straight as possible. Continue to support your hips (**11**). Gradually roll forward feeling each vertebra of the spine as it unfolds to the ground. Lowering the legs, return to lying on your back.

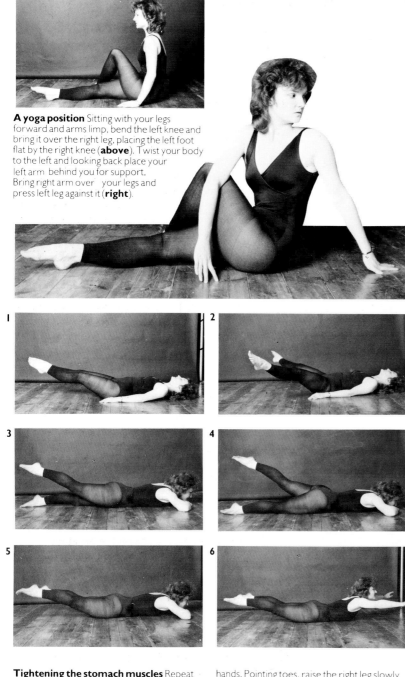

A yoga position Sitting with your legs forward and arms limp, bend the left knee and bring it over the right leg, placing the left foot flat by the right knee (**above**). Twist your body to the left and looking back place your left arm behind you for support, Bring right arm over your legs and press left leg against it (**right**).

Tightening the stomach muscles Repeat these exercises several times. Lie flat on your back, feet together and toes pointed. Raise both legs slowly, keeping them straight, to no more than 1 ft (30 cm) from the ground (**1**). Hold and gradually lower. Raise feet again and hold. Flex the feet back and part your legs widely (**2**). Keeping legs straight, cross them in a swinging scissor movement, left over right, right over left, several times. Bring legs together, point toes and lower slowly. Now lie flat on the stomach resting your chin on your hands. Pointing toes, raise the right leg slowly keeping pelvis on the floor (**3**). Lower slowly and repeat with the other leg (**4**). For the next exercise, raise both legs slowly with feet together and toes pointed (**5**). Part your legs widely and hold. Close legs and lower slowly. Repeat this but with both arms stretched out in front and with the head tilted back to arch the spine, keeping the pelvis on the floor (**6**).

SES FOR TWO

Stand facing partner, making eye to eye contact. With one person taking the lead, make slow movements in unison as if facing a mirror (**left, below**). Build up co-operation by maintaining eye contact.

Sitting upright, hold ankles and bounce the head down to touch your knees. Your partner can aid this by gently placing his or her hands on upper spine (**below**) or by gently sitting against the spine (**bottom**). Great care should be taken with exercises involving the spine. Do not strain or apply too much pressure to your partner.

looking them in the eye. Always take a moment to compose yourself and breathe out before beginning.

In general preparation for an audition, approach the parts you have chosen in the way that you would approach any part. There are five basic questions that you must ask yourself. They are—who am I?; where am I?; what do I want in this scene?; how do I go about getting it?; why do I want it? When you can answer these questions with reasonable confidence, you will have learned some basic elements about the scene. If, for example, your piece involves in answer to question three that you are obtaining money from another character, consider how you can achieve this end. Your approach could vary from goading, shaming or teasing to mocking, taunting or cajoling. These questions can be useful not only for auditions, but also as an initial way of working out some aspects of the character.

You can also be auditioned by doing a reading. This is a common method in amateur theater. You may or may not know the play from which the reading is selected. Often you are told a little about the play and what has happened to the characters prior to the scene you are given to read. You may have only enough time to read the scene through to yourself once before you read it aloud to the director. Do not attempt to act it, but read it as simply and truthfully as possible. Follow the structure of the sentences and let the text work for you.

WORKING ON THE CHARACTER

When approaching a part there are many ways in which an actor can build a character in his or her own mind. This process is important in order that the actor can become that character on stage.

First there is the actor's intuitive response to the play and the particular character he or she is playing. On first reading the play, notes should be made of immediate impressions. Then the character should be studied and researched in as much detail as possible. In doing this, actors must constantly use their imaginations. But actors should never make moral judgements about their characters.

Comb the text for what is said about your character, both by the character him or herself, and by other characters in the play. Decide how true or false this information is and how much you want to reveal of it. Also decide at what point in the play you want to reveal these observations to the audience. Note carefully exactly what happens to the character during the play and how the character changes or develops as a result. Consider how different the character is at the end of the play compared to the beginning. Think about when changes occur.

Build up as much autobiographical detail of the character as possible from the play. Note how he or she spends the day, and in what environment. Try to understand the character's view of him or herself, and how this influences his or her actions. Often when studying a text, you will find that one particular line expresses something which will illuminate your character's personality and life. Use that line as a foundation and decide how much you want to express, what that line says about the character, and how much you want to conceal it.

When probing the text, look for opposites. Find the anguish in joy and the pleasure in sorrow. Think about whether your character actually means what he or she says, or is it a cover-up. Constantly search for aspects of truth about the character, then discard them and start again.

If you are given a part you cannot identify with or easily research, use the 'if' method. This means when faced with a character trait or action of which you have no experience, say a murder, then ask yourself—if I was this murderer how would I behave and feel?

Actors must always be hungry for information and details. Start by reading as much as possible about the period in which the play is set. Do not just rely on your imagination for details but research wherever possible. Whether you are playing a doctor or a tramp, a junkie or a lawyer, an artist or a taxi driver, always go to the places your character would go to. Find people who do what your character does; go to where they work or relax and observe them and talk to them. Something you see or hear can stimulate

your imagination and open a door which can help your performance.

When problems arise because of a particular scene or line in a play, actors can overcome them in a number of ways. First either whispering the passage or alternatively shouting it out loudly. It is often in extremes such as this that the actor can break through a self-conscious barrier.

This ability to overcome difficulties or 'blockages' when approaching a character is important, and it can sometimes be achieved by concentrating on physical activity during a difficult scene. Actors may try approaches as diverse as moving props whilst playing the scene, or even throwing a ball between themselves. Concentrating on the physical activity rather than on acting out the scene may bring a release and they will say the lines in a different way.

Whenever you are on the stage, you should know what you feel about every character that is present.

ACTOR'S TASK PLAN

Pre-rehearsal period: prepare for the audition • choose material carefully or learn set pieces • research characters for audition • when cast, read the play with care for the first time and note intuitive response to it • read the play several times noting all references to your character, take down details of character's past, lifestyle, personality and appearance • research for the part in whatever way possible • get to know the character well and learn to judge how he or she would think, feel and respond to any situation in the play • give your address and other details to the stage manager for cast list and availability chart • start to learn your lines

During rehearsals: check the rehearsal schedule carefully and ensure you are always on time • learn your lines thoroughly • get to know the other members of the cast • build on your character, and other aspects of the part which come out in rehearsal, in your own time • practice any difficult sections • exercise as often as possible to remain fit and relaxed • attend costume fittings • practice make-up

First night and performance run: prepare for the first night to arrive as relaxed as possible and in good time • approach each performance as if it is the first

Learning to observe details
Much of the impact of a
performance comes from the
visual impression an audience
receives of a character.
Observation of people is crucial
to actors so that they understand
how an overall impression is built
up through details. These
characters have been created
through costume, posture, facial
expression, gesture and
movement. The Elizabethan
period is clearly evoked by this
detailed costume (**1**), but the
relaxed feeling of the character
comes from the curved posture
and the way the tankard is held. In
contrast, the tension of a
deformed body (**2**) is expressed
on the face and by gripping a

chair. The splayed legs and a
raised shoulder create awkward,
painful shapes within an ill-fitting
suit while the graceful model
church suggests the character's
aspirations. A black dress (**3**) set
off by a flash of jewelry and a
bold crucifix makes a strong
impression. Crossed legs (**4**) give
an informal air despite the formal
costume. The leftward tilt of the
head indicates sharp attention
because the main angle of the
pose is rightward. An even more
elaborate Elizabethan costume
(**5**) suggests sophistication, but the
pose is open and relaxed. A
cravat implies ease (**6**), but this
character's pursed lips and fixed
eyes indicate perplexity.

Expression through the body

Using obvious, mechanical, gestures does not work on stage. It is only through careful observation of the subtle details of body movement that actors can use them to express emotion to an audience. A neutral, open stance (**1**) shows the figure ready to move in any direction. Hands on the hips (**2**) suggest a degree of defiance and surprise which is echoed in this face. A protective hand to the face (**3**) indicates that something has occurred which may require withdrawal for deep consideration. A lowered head (**4**) is further withdrawal from contact and is reflected by the position of the arms. A relatively open stance, but with the eyes and mouth hidden (**5**), indicates the figure's withdrawal from contact. This angled stance (**6**) with hands and mouth open expresses relaxation. Hands tight to the body coupled with this facial expression (**7**) shows unwillingness to look out. Crossed arms sometimes indicate inwardness (**8**), but the open facial expression here creates a contrasting impression of self-confidence.

6 7 8

2

3

4

5

Early stages of rehearsal
Rehearsal is a process of exploration. A script conference usually takes place early on (**above**). Confusion, introspection and puzzlement are often created when the show is studied for the first time, but as the rehearsals progress the actors gain confidence. Ideas can really begin to be tried out when the company moves into the rehearsal room. At first, the actors continue to work 'on the book' (**right**), blocking in the rehearsal room with the director and the stage manager. The floor has been marked out to represent the size of the stage and the position of scenery so that moves can be accurately worked out as the production takes shape.

Know what you should be thinking at all times and especially when your character is not required to speak. Thinking like your character is as important as saying the lines.

In an extreme situation, actors may feel they are receiving no help from the director and that the scene is going badly and nothing is happening between the characters. In such cases, the individual actors should concentrate on what they want from that scene. Having decided simply what their character wants in the scene, they should play it as boldly as possible. This will produce an energy in the scene and could spark something off.

The text can help an actor decide how a scene is to be played or a line delivered. The playwright will often give a key to the rhythm of the words through punctuation and phrasing. The British writer Harold Pinter is an example of this, as the punctuation, pauses and silences in his texts often provide valuable keys to approaching his characters. Shakespeare can be difficult though, since the punctuation in his plays tends to be the work of successive editors and not Shakespeare's own. So, if you are going to pause anywhere in a Shakespearean verse speech, let it be at the end of a line. Remember that in his comedies there is often no subtext, no hidden thread of meaning, so that the characters tend to say exactly what they think at the moment they speak.

So you should try to believe implicitly in what is said at any one moment.

THE REHEARSAL PROCESS

There are as many ways of working on a play as there are types of play, or types of directors and actors. Each play offers its own challenge and experience, but the basic task of the actor remains the same whoever the director is and whatever the play. That task is to seek out the truth about the play and the character and to bring the playwright's words to life as the character is born on stage.

Working on a play in rehearsal is like undertaking a journey of discovery. A constant stream of ideas, suggestions and impulses about the play will come out during rehearsals and the actor must be open to all these influences. This does not mean that the actor should not think about the play at home, but there is a huge difference between saying lines in peace and quiet by yourself and rehearsing standing with the cast. The difference is contact. The interaction between actors is what gives their characters life. It is during rehearsals that this interaction can be used creatively as the play is explored. All acting is a selection of choices as the actor, consciously or unconsciously, makes decisions about the interpretation of a role. As a play is explored in rehearsal and

65

Touching Simple embraces can create a wide variety of effects. In this scene (**1**) from Shakespeare's *Hamlet*, the mother tries to recreate a maternal bond with her son. Gertrude clasps Hamlet round the shoulder and he behaves like a child, turning away to show his unwillingness to respond to her. The neck is a vulnerable area so in this scene (**2**) from Eugene O'Neill's *Long Day's Journey Into Night*, Mary's embrace expresses a long and intimate relationship with James. Again, the man is avoiding eye contact, preserving his independence. The physical closeness and strong eye contact between Desdemona and Othello in this scene from Shakespeare's *Othello* (**3**) expresses warmth. Dominance is also suggested by the stance through Othello's height and his firm hold of her wrist, creating a sense of conflicting feelings.

Eye contact Direct eye contact can create quite different impressions depending on postures. The angular position of these two figures (**4**), with the man above the woman, suggests the conflict between them. In this scene from Tom Kempinski's *Duet for One* both characters are in an uncomfortable position echoing their feelings. The woman's hand is warning rather than appealing, and the man's arms remain close to him, offering nothing. In contrast, the two figures from Shakespeare's *Twelfth Night* (**5**) are leaning at the same angle in similar positions and suggesting easy intimacy. People tend to match the postures of those they agree with.

an abundance of ideas is brought out through interaction between the actors and through ideas from the director, the actor can begin to make those choices about the role. In responding to those around them, actors should choose ideas and re-create them as truthfully and spontaneously as possible, as the scenes are rehearsed.

This journey of discovery and selection should never stop. If your work as an actor has a strong basis in searching out the truth, then your perform-ance will grow and become rich in rehearsal and on stage during the run of the performance. There are always new things to be discovered and doors to be unlocked, and this is particularly true of a great classical text. The moment an actor thinks 'Ah, I've found it, I am giving a perfect performance' is the moment to stop and give up acting completely. It is always a struggle to become the character, and this is one of the great challenges of acting.

The actor's own personality is, however, still important, because it has its own impact upon the interpretation of the role. If two actors are handed the same poem to read and both are given precise instructions on how to speak it, the results will be different. Even if both actors follow their instruc-tions on the reading, the expression of the poem will be different because they are different people and will bring their own impulses to the poem. All actors therefore must find their own methods of working which can be adapted and used in any situation.

One of the most difficult moments of all will be a first reading of a play at the start of rehearsals. No matter what method of rehearsal is being used—and this will vary depending on the company and the director—the pressure of the first reading is enormous. There is always a feeling of paranoia because actors feel they have to justify why they have been chosen for particular parts. It is impor-tant to remember that everyone, including the director, feels the same way. To help overcome this, actors should try to make contact with each other during that first reading. Simply managing to look at one another reduces the fear and lifts the pressure off individuals to have to 'act'.

Rehearsal methods vary not only depending on who is producing the play but also on how much time there is to rehearse. The best possible situation is that of a company which has worked together on many productions and which has plenty of time to rehearse. It is likely however for a more difficult situation to occur, when a group has come together for one play perhaps, not having worked together before and not having much time for rehearsal.

If a production has to be mounted in only, say, a few weeks by a group who are not familiar with one another, there will be pressure on the actors to make decisions about the play and their own characters more quickly than is ideal. The short period of rehearsal will not allow for the luxury of a deep exploration of the play. After the first reading, the director will often talk about his or her ideas for the production, giving a personal interpretation and opinion of how it will develop. There will also be an immediate consideration of set and costume de-signs so that the actors can have some idea of the physical space they will find themselves in and how they will look.

BLOCKING

The director will then start blocking the play. In its most traditional meaning, blocking a play involves the director giving detailed instructions to the actors concerning their every move on stage, how they should deliver their lines, the timing of their actions and so on. This process creates a basic skeleton for the play, a structure on which the actor can build his or her performance.

Blocking may involve going through the entire text in detail, scene by scene, or it may involve dealing with the whole play quite quickly. This process can take several weeks or just two days, depending on the text and its complexity, but the first blocking period is always undertaken with the actor reading from the script. As a result, it is often difficult for the actor to know whether a move or an intonation is right or wrong. The director may be very specific and strict at this stage, giving line readings, perhaps, and telling the actor precisely how to stress a word and whether to end on an upward or downward inflection. But there may be some discussion where the actors can give their opinions as a scene is read through a few times before it is blocked.

The next period of rehearsal will be quite different because the script will no longer be read but will have been learned. This is the point at which the actor can begin to make decisions about interpret-ing the role. Acting is basically a process of selec-tion, and throughout rehearsal actors are refining and extending the range of choices available.

From the moment you are given a specific role, your imagination will have been engaged in inter-preting that character. As you begin to work with the director and the other actors, you will find them charging your imagination and channeling it in different directions. You will find yourself exploring areas you had not even considered in connection with the role. This inspiration and exchange of ideas is what rehearsals should, ideally, be about. The process really begins to work at the point where the actor knows the lines, has some idea what the scene is about and starts to work directly with the other actors in the cast.

As rehearsals progress, you should find that you lose your self-consciousness and instead become engrossed in what you are feeling and work instinctively from moment to moment. You will often have a strong feeling whether something is working and you may sometimes be able to explain why it is working. Actors can never really fully explain how they work, since there is no foolproof method to producing a brilliant performance. Some actors work from the inside out, and some from the outside in. As you rehearse you will find what is right for you. Rehearsals are about trusting and risking, and you may have to fail before you succeed. It can be like learning to dive. You may produce a belly-flop at first, but by constantly trying you may find the confidence and skill to dive from the top board.

As the performance develops in rehearsal and through learning the part, notice where you stumble and lose the words, especially when memorizing the lines. When this happens, ask yourself if you really know the character's thought process at that moment in the play. In any scene, there are usually moments such as beginning, middle and end which involve changes for the character. Those changes may be slight, or they may be big. Note instinctively and intellectually how your character is at the beginning and end of the scene.

FINAL REHEARSALS

By the last week of rehearsal you will start to do what is called running the play, which means no longer working on particular scenes in detail but rehearsing the whole play. This provides a first opportunity to get a perspective on the whole journey your character travels through in the play. You can then note the high and low points your performance has to reach, you can see the dead moments when things do not work. You can also see more clearly what does work. Working on scenes in isolation can produce certain indulgences in the performance. Moments can get extended when an actor takes longer to say something than is necessary or pauses between cues. Running the play helps the actor realize, with the director, the right pace or tempo for the whole play. Pauses are valuable and the actor must learn this. However, he or she must also 'earn' those pauses, because they must serve the text, be consistent with the character the actor has built up, and not just be self-indulgent.

Running a play can be compared to a competition relay race. As the play builds up momentum, the actor must pass the level of energy achieved onto the next character, so that the momentum is maintained and the play is driven forward.

The jump from rehearsal to the stage with the approach of the opening night is fraught and hazardous. The final stages of rehearsal can produce sheer terror in an actor, but this can be put to good use and produce huge dividends. An enormous amount of energy and adrenalin is released through this terror. It is at this point that the actor can begin really to make the part his or her own. The groundwork done, the actor severs the direct link with the director and takes off for the performance; ready to fly or fall in public.

There will be technical rehearsals which provide valuable experience for the actors in moving around the set, sometimes in costume. These rehearsals can be exhausting and long for the actors, as the stage crew get lighting and music cues and all the other backstage details right. Naturally these rehearsals are not primarily for the actors, but they are important to them because they offer the opportunity to practice exits and entrances and other technical aspects of the performance. Even a simple action, such as opening a door, must be rehearsed carefully, and most important of all the actor must use this time to really get to know the set, for this is where the character lives. If your part involves making an entrance in the dark, close your eyes for a few seconds before you go on as you will then find it easier to adjust to the darkness.

The rehearsal process discussed here would probably apply to a company of people who are not used to working together. It is not ideal for the actors, and working within an established company should be better. Many amateur companies have often worked together several times, and this often can be of benefit to the actors. The main advantage for the actors is that they are more relaxed and confident in trying things out and taking risks. Another advantage is that there will often be a longer rehearsal period. This may mean, for instance, that decisions about costumes can be delayed until the actors have a stronger sense of their characters. Also among the group there will be a commitment to the method of work involved and a language for communicating ideas will have evolved.

There will be shared references to previous productions and a familiarity will exist that is difficult to achieve with an ad hoc company. Trust and respect will have built up not only between the actors and the director, but also with the designers, musicians, stage managers and so on. This caring and sharing comes from every individual understanding that they are contributing to a whole and it

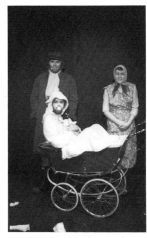

Playing multiple roles Howard Brenton's *The Education of Skinny Spew* is a very short play, but a demanding one for the cast of three. The actors play a variety of roles with costume changes during only 20 minutes on stage. At the birth of Skinny Spew (**left**) the mother is covered by a vast sheet as the doctor delivers the baby. This sheet later becomes a sea in which the monstrous Skinny drowns his parents. But before this the family pose proudly for a group photograph (**right**). The doctor has now become the father and the mother has changed costume. The sheet is again on stage when Skinny is sent to an institution (**below left**). Under the sheet the mother becomes a nurse and the father/doctor becomes the superintendent of the institution. He also plays a car driver and a police dog which is controlled by the mother/nurse, who is then playing a policewoman. The actor playing Skinny has the relatively easy task of growing from a baby to a schoolboy. The characters are caricatures, but such roles must be carefully created with accurate observation. The challenge for the actors is to go not simply for broad effects but to emphasize the truth which lies at the heart of any caricature. In this play with the actors having to change accent frequently and to appear in various satirical costumes, it is particularly important that they researched each role in depth so as to have at hand the important details that prevent the characters being merely larger than life. It is these details that are exaggerated and not the general, stereotyped aspects of the characters.

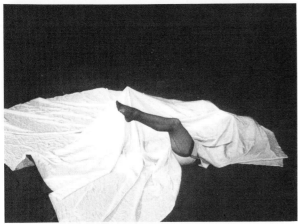

takes them beyond any personal ambition as an artist. This is what an actor should strive for in any rehearsal period. But even in the best possible situations, the rehearsal period will not be free from tension, anxiety, despair and elation. Actors are—after all—human.

THE PERFORMANCE

The pressure of an opening night is enormous. Most actors are probably relieved if they get through a first night without bumping into the furniture and forgetting their lines. Yet the actors must continue many of the processes used in rehearsal as they perform. Playing to the public does not mean you stop working at the part, and developing your character. You have to find how to reproduce your performance afresh each night, while maintaining a level of commitment and truth found in the rehearsal rooms. You must imagine every night before you go on that you are playing the part for the first time. Every night it will be different because you will be affected by the events of the day. If you find you are tired or frightened, try dedicating your performance to someone or something you admire, respect or love. It could be a great artist or the victims of an earthquake, it could be anyone alive or dead, but it must be someone who you feel a link with. It is this connection that you are exploring and using on stage. Imagine an electric current between you and that person and think to yourself that you are dedicating your performance to that person. Addressing someone particular and sharing the time on stage with that person, whether you are conscious of it constantly or not, will release you from self-consciousness and can reduce the fear or expectation you have of an audience.

Acting is an extremely lonely activity. The actor performs in front of an audience and, despite all the experiences of rehearsal and the help given by the director, during the performance the actor stands alone. Perhaps the most important attributes of an actor are concentration and imagination, and the performance depends on how much is put into it.

Acting styles A formal scene from Shakespeare's *Richard II* (**1**) demands a ceremonial style of acting. The atmosphere is enhanced by the grouping and the strong focus on the central figure of the King. His clasped hands and heavy, draped costume in matching tones, suggest a static tableau. His high throne gives him isolated dominance. A burlesque atmosphere can come from a throne scene as in this moment from Charles Dickens's *Nicholas Nickleby* (**2**). The central figure's open stance and the stylized hand gestures and costumes suggest a climactic tableau or act ending. In another scene from this production (**3**) Nicholas holds the dead weight of the unfortunate Smike. Their pathetic, inward stance closes them in while the other actors' positions and gestures indicate they are passive observers.

5

4

6

Variations on the chorus

Singing and dancing in exotic costumes to produce stunning musical and visual effects is the most common form of chorus (**4**). This line-up is from the musical *A Chorus Line* which looks at the making of such a group. Another scene (**5**) shows the same performers during auditions and holding photographs of their previous work. Individuality is stressed here in contrast to the uniform, disciplined chorus they become. Peter Hall's production of Aeschylus's *The Oresteia* (**6**) has a chorus of masked men functioning as a rhythmic group. This chorus from a classical Greek drama seems far removed from a modern musical, but it uses the same combination of unified body movements and music.

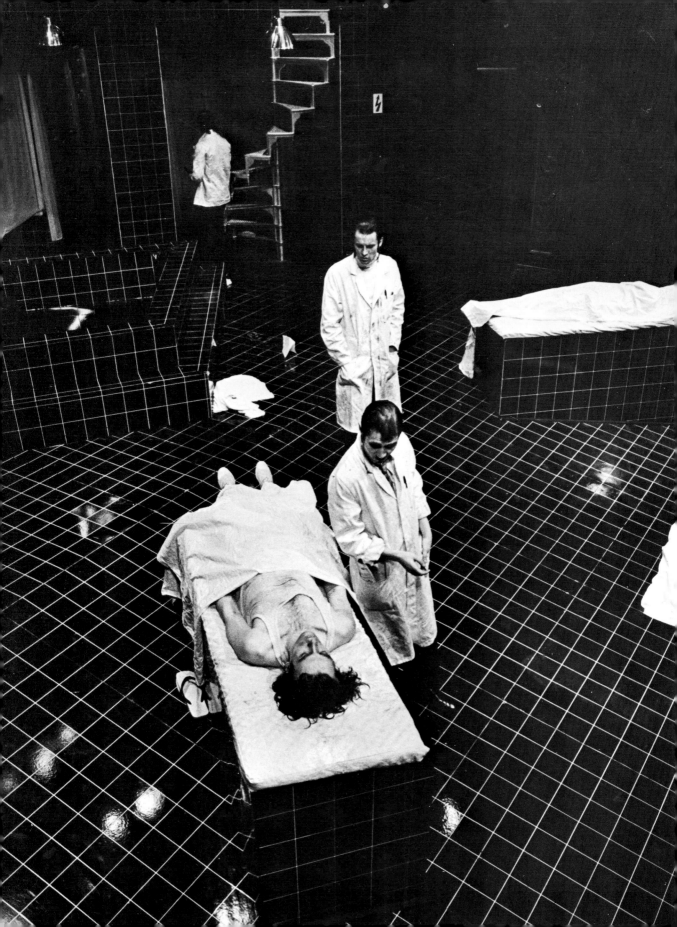

CHAPTER FOUR

SET DESIGN

STAGE DESIGN TODAY

SKETCHES · MODELS · PLANS

THE DESIGN PROCESS

TECHNICAL REHEARSALS · TOURING

Designing for the theater is a particularly abstract art. The theater is a live and unpredictable medium, and the designer's work is before each audience only for a few moments. Those few moments cannot be repeated and are not usually recorded, and so they can never be recaptured. The many elements of the performance must work in unison, and events on stage are beyond the designer's control. In the past, theater design was regarded as an adornment to the play. This century has seen it evolve into something entirely new. Revolutionary changes in the theater have reshaped stage design particularly in the past 30 years. The British director Peter Brook sums up, in his book *The Empty Space*, some of what is required of a set designer today: 'What is necessary ... is an incomplete design, a design that has clarity without rigidity, ... unlike the easel painter in two dimensions, or the sculptor in three dimensions, the theater designer thinks in terms of the fourth dimension, the passage of time—not the stage picture but the stage moving picture'.

STAGE DESIGN PAST AND PRESENT

Before the twentieth century, there was little cooperation between the various elements in the theater. The designer rarely discussed a production with the playwright, the director or the actors. The theater owner or manager may have given general directions but usually the designer was left alone. Scene design was an extra, an adornment to the performance. It was not a principal part of it. Being on their own, designers indulged in whims and fanciful ideas, deciding for themselves what was appropriate to the play. Sometimes their ideas had no connection with other elements on stage.

From the middle of the sixteenth century until the late nineteenth century theater designers were painters or architects, respectable artists using the stage to create their illusions. They painted magnificent scenes and incorporated ingenious tricks to amuse the audience, giving little thought to the purpose of the play. Their real concern was to demonstrate their skills. This did not matter since the task of the designer was to provide a backdrop for the performers, something for them to be seen in front of. The theaters were traditional proscenium arch theaters where the audience sat in front and viewed the set as if it was a framed picture at the back of the stage, usually painted in a naturalistic, two-dimensional style.

By the end of the nineteenth century, the theater began to change. New styles of acting were emerging and the traditional backdrop set was beginning to be questioned. Stage designers started to ignore the traditions by stripping out theaters and creating new types of settings for performances. Their new

Left Good set design is a vital ingredient of successful theater. This production of Büchner's *Woyzeck* at the Glasgow Citizen's Theatre was designed by Philip Prowse. He used a Turkish bath as the setting with a real bath up left. The glossy tiles reflecting cold, white light suggest an abbattoir or mortuary, as well as a hospital operating theater. The sinister atmosphere serves to underline the play's theme while providing a realistic setting for the doctor's experiments on Woyzeck. This kind of set makes no attempt to recreate the actual physical locations of the individual scenes.

1

2

4

3

Various approaches to one space This striking variation on a traditional perspective set (**1**) uses seven arches leading back to a cloud cloth. It provides an illusion of great depth and can be used to create a false proscenium. It will also concentrate attention on an upstage figure. A box set on two levels with a partial ceiling shows (**2**) how good use of props and furnishings can create an impression of period clutter while leaving the actors room to move. An exotic effect (**3**) is created with colored gel back lighting, unusual set colors and freestanding scenery units. The sturdy false proscenium creates a frame within the main acting area, emphasized by the white arch and the pillar which has opened into a fan on stage left. A different approach uses only light and a simple prop, this type of set (**4**) can eliminate the need for masking in a proscenium arch theater. It is also useful for situations where the audience surrounds the acting area since the entire stage is visible from all sides. Sally Jacobs designed this set (**7**) for Peter Brook's famous production of *A Midsummer Night's Dream* at Stratford. It showed that Shakespeare's verse did not require the help of a traditional setting of realistic woodland to create the magical atmosphere of the play. A non-professional company may find the flying apparatus and coiled wire trees too expensive, but this approach of taking a fresh look at a familiar text is important for any designer.

5

6

All these sets show how important a floor cloth can be in creating an overall effect. This box set (**5**) uses red to suggest a warm enclosed space in contrast to the blue window. The floor cloth picks up colors from the walls and the upholstery. The white tablecloth provides another strong color focus. This colorful set (**6**) achieves strong visual effects through four brightly colored book flats and a floorcloth. This type of set can be used to define an acting area within a large space such as a hall and is ideal for touring. The open air atmosphere of this set (**8**) is created through a variety of textures – wooden flooring, leaves and hung branches catching the light. The contrasting finished wood of one bench and natural wood of the other reflects the themes of *Love's Labours Lost*.

7

8

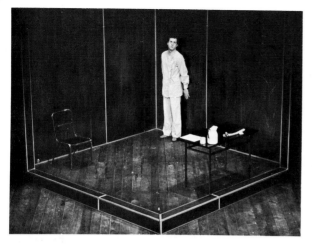

Solving problems of space
Both these productions faced problems of space. In an open area (**above**) the designer has created the illusion of limited space by erecting two solid walls to close off the upstage area. The strong panel lines suggest the missing two walls which imprison the actor. In the cramped space of the second set (**right**) the door and window are reduced to open frames. This gives a feeling of space and solves the problematic sight lines for the audience.

philosophy of set design was to take it beyond being just an extra to make it an art with a vital role in dramatic production.

With this change in attitude to the role of stage design came a change in working methods. Designers were often no longer working alone but as equal partners with the playwrights and directors in planning a production and deciding how it would be projected to an audience. Changes came fast as designers moved away from using traditional flats painted to represent a scene. But this method remains ideal for certain plays and may even come back into fashion. Meanwhile, set design has become more three-dimensional. The stage space has been completely reorganized, by thrusting it forward or using the entire space right to the back wall. Sets have been designed to relate directly to abstract qualities in a play rather than creating the physical setting for the play. Designs have been based on symbolic imagery rather than on landscape or historical details. Bare, simple structures are used alongside three-dimensional textures and dramatic costumes. Modern technology has been combined with traditional building methods to produce effects, and, even without using projectors and other multimedia devices, more than one focus of attention can be created on stage.

In the past, the theater audience would look into a frame and see moving pictures. Now the relationship of the audience to the acting area has completely changed and at times they are incorporated into a performance. Stage design has never looked back from that important move away from the traditional proscenium arch theater. It has never been less inhibited or more exciting than today.

THE
STAGE DESIGNER'S ROLE

A stage design must work in relation to the actors who will move around in it and in relation to the words and actions of the play. It is quite different to, say, an interior design of a room. In that case, the client will suggest domestic preferences and needs, but the designer will have no knowledge of, or interest in, what happens in that room after he or she has left. The conversations and actions which take place in the space on stage, however, are of great importance to the stage designer.

The stage designer's most significant function is to manipulate stage space in relation to human actors, their movements and how they create the visual experience of a play for an audience. There are no limits as to how this stage space can be used, but deciding what to do with it is the most crucial decision the designer takes. It is a decision that directly affects the actors and director and is certainly more important than which color the set is eventually painted. Do not be frightened by the space, however big or small. Think of it horizontally, diagonally, vertically and flat. Be prepared to

Creating acting areas In an open space a clearly defined acting area can be created by using floorcloths, rostrums and props. This seven sided floorcloth (**1**) gives a stylized, asymmetrical feel. Combined with the color matched furniture, it creates an impression of cool elegance. This very simple set (**2**) has been created using only a desk and a map fixed to a black backing flat to suggest a surveyor's office. Such a set is ideal for one act plays sharing a bill and for small scale touring because only the map and personal props need to be toured. In another approach (**3**) the deckchair, the upturned tub, the washing drier and the children define the acting area. Without stage lighting and with only simple props and costumes, the actors make a strong theatrical impression. In this set (**4**) three rooms have been suggested by different floor coverings, varying levels and furniture which clearly indicates a particular room.

1

2

3

4

redefine the space until you find the right framework for the play. The stage can be masked to leave only a small area, or the whole area behind the stage can be used showing the flies and bare lights. The aisles and orchestra pit or even the foyer or lobby could be part of the space, and seats can usually be taken out or moved around.

In recent years, directors and designers have forced actors to become more integrated with the set by creating scenery which they cannot avoid using as they move through, in and around it. The designer must take responsibility for expanding the actors' movements and for defining them. For example, an actor may have to relate to a room which, literally, has no walls.

Each production will present new problems for a designer. The play will not be the only influence; the company you are working with is also of great importance, as are the theater, the director and actors, the budget and helpers available. However, these influences should not compromise the designer since with spirit and enthusiasm, plenty of energy and faith in a good play, you can go far. If a budget for a play is very low and there are no workshops or helpers, you will need virtually to be a slave to the production. Be prepared in this situation to do all the work yourself and design accordingly. But if you are going to resent such conditions and feel the organizers of a project are foolish, then do not take it on.

Designing for the stage is both exhausting and complicated. The many different aspects of the production must be kept under control and there is an enormous amount to deal with. Anyone who thinks that a designer simply hands over basic, sketches or drawings to the producer and then returns all dressed up for the first night some time later has been cruelly misled.

THE DESIGN PROCESS

Unlike most creative artists, the stage designer does not work in isolation, but is a member of a team. Surprisingly, the closer the teamwork in theater, the greater the rewards for each individual and the better the results on stage. How a designer works with other members of a company, and how the work is organized varies considerably. No two companies are the same and no two designers will follow exactly the same work pattern. But there are certain common features in the planning and preparation for a production.

Interpreting the script The first step a designer must make is to read the play. The first reading is important and cannot be repeated. At this stage, the

---

SET DESIGNER'S TASK PLAN

Pre-rehearsal period: read the play thoroughly and work out basic ideas • discuss the production with the director • study the theater space to be used • obtain plans and elevations of theater • research the play in any way possible • find material to provide ideas and inspiration • make first sketches of your design • make simple model of proposed sets • discuss the model with the director and stage manager • make any changes required • finalize model • discuss the model with the costume and lighting designers • decide on prop and furniture requirements • draw up a prop list with the stage manager

During the rehearsal period: present the proposed set to the cast, explaining any level variations, openings, entrances, exits and other points • explain the set in detail to the set builders • do the technical drawings and elevations of the set • select the materials to be used to build the set • work out building schedule with the set builders, supervize the set construction closely • organize and select props with the stage manager • attend as many rehearsals as possible and liaise with the director on possible changes • ensure that the cast can move freely on the set • work out building problems and ensure that the set is progressing on schedule

Production week: ensure the set, props and furniture all ready • organize the load (get) in and fit up • attend the technical rehearsal • note all problems and try to solve them • make sure props, furniture and lighting work well with the set • attend dress rehearsal

First night and performance run: supervize any necessary repairs • ensure all borrowed and hired items returned

---

play should be approached with an open mind, and without considering physical or technical problems which may arise. After thinking about the play, the designer will probably discuss it with the director so that they can exchange ideas.

During the second reading of the play, notes should be taken of details which seem important so that the designer can discover the flavor of the characters and their environment. Most playwrights rely on the designer's contribution as an artist so it is not sufficient merely to decide, say, that the windows should be stage right and the door center back. The designer must discover what is vital to the play by questioning everything—for example, does the room have to contain all the things a room normally contains?; does the room have walls?; should the audience be able to see beyond the room?

Get to know the theater you are designing for. Walk around it and sit in the auditorium, absorbing the space fully. With the third reading of the play, perhaps using plans and elevations of the stage, you should be able to decide on the precise area you want the play to be created within. It may be important to talk again with the director before starting to put down your ideas. Surround yourself with visual references and research relevant to the play. Read background information and perhaps seek out photographs or pictures of the period and subject which the play deals with.

Sketches and models There are two main ways of putting down design ideas for others to see, and many designers use both. Sketches can be used, drawn in perspective and showing different scenes and colors for the set, with rough outlines of the stage floor plan. Alternatively, a model of the stage can be made in light wood, such as balsa, or in card, and this is usually the best method. It is often far easier for other members of the production team to understand a designer's ideas if they can consider a three-dimensional model rather than only two-dimensional sketches.

It often surprises a designer to realize just how much like the first model a finished stage set can be, so it is worth becoming a good model maker. It should be made to a scale of about ½ inch to 1 foot or 1 cm to 25 cm. Use children's modeling clay and anything else which will help to express your ideas exactly. Do not assume you can leave the interpretation of your ideas to others, everyone involved in the production must be able to see immediately from the model what you are planning to do. A valuable reference aid is a scale model of an actor which you can move around the stage space.

The director is the most important viewer of the model. The discussions about the first model and sketches depend entirely upon the personalities involved, but many ideas should come out of it. Some directors are technically minded, others not; some will have definite ideas on how the set should look, others will not. All of them will be thinking about the possibilities of movement on stage for the actors. You must think ahead in these discussions, working out whether the ideas suggested are practical and right for the play. It is now that the designer and director must solve any differences of opinion on the interpretation of the play. This can be difficult, but it must be done. If the two are working well together as the ideas emerge, the designer will not remember which were his or her ideas and which were the director's.

Following discussions with the director, adjustments will probably have to be made to the model, and the whole should be refined and made more accurate. Remember at this stage to keep in mind the limitations on your ideas imposed by the amount of money available, the working conditions

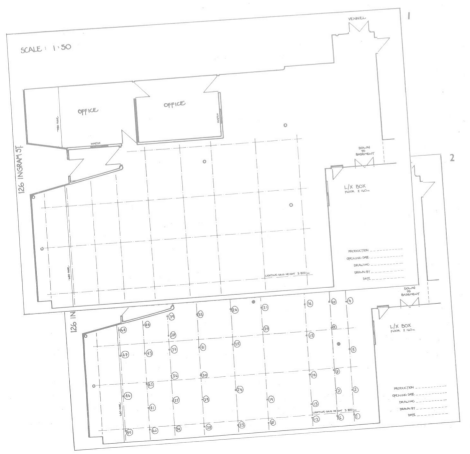

Theater plans If a company regularly uses a particular theater or hall, it is worthwhile drawing up and duplicating or photocopying basic plans of the building. These can be used by set designers, stage managers, set builders, lighting designers, and so on, for each production. This plan (**1**) shows a theater with no fixed acting or audience areas. The position of the lighting and scenery grid has been superimposed on it since this always has to be taken into account when designing sets and lighting. On a copy of the plan (**2**) the lighting socket positions have been shown on the grid to aid the lighting designer. There will be many similar uses for the plan. The three small circles on the main plan indicate permanent pillars in the building which will always have to be taken into account when arranging the acting and audience areas.

SCALE : 1·50

OFFICE

OFFICE

126 INGRAM ST

Research and inspiration
Designers should be enthusiastic collectors of magazine clippings, postcards and other visual references to aid them in creating the right feel for a set. Libraries are an important source for references, as are museums and historic buildings. Here is a typical selection of visual references – a picture of Arab Hall in Leighton House, a late Victorian building in London (**1**), J.M.W. Turner's painting *Petworth: The Library with a Spinet, c.*1828 (**2**); postcards, glossy magazines and interior design catalogs (**3**).

A production requiring a set of a 1930s interior could be inspired by these references. They show a private suite in the Radio City Music Hall, New York, designed by Donald Duskey in the 1930s (**4**) and the living room of a house at Roquebrune, designed by Eileen Gray in the late 1920s (**5**).

This initial sketch (**6**) by the designer shows the elements from both rooms which can be blended to create a set with an authentic 1930s feel.

for set building, and, most important, the abilities of the production team. Designers are only as good as the people they work with. You must know precisely what you are wanting to make and have a method in mind for a real piece of stage set as you build the model piece.

At the earliest possible stage in the design process, the set designer should have detailed discussions with the lighting designer, whose skills and knowledge will be essential to the design. Materials used in the design, such as gauze, shiny metal or velvet, can be affected by the lighting or only become effective when lit. Discuss the sort of lights to be used, and the lighting positions, so that any necessary adjustments can be made to the model. The set design and lighting should enhance one another.

The stage manager is another important person to discuss the model with, since he or she may notice difficulties you have overlooked. The stage masking—cutting off those areas you do not want the audience to see—should be worked out.

In a traditional theater, the whole of the backstage area was masked off by black fabric which soaked up any light falling on it, and this can still be a useful practice. Masking is not always required and there have been many successful productions, particularly in recent years, which expose all that masking

usually hides—stage lights, pulleys, grids, ropes and wires. If masking is to be used, it must be tidy and generous, since nothing is worse than gaps or patches which would distract the audience.

If the designer is not in charge of costumes, which would perhaps be ideal, then there must be a discussion of the model with the costume designer. Particular reference should be made to the overall feel of the stage design and the colors to be used.

On the first day of rehearsals, the stage plan will usually have been marked out on the rehearsal room floor. The model should also be present at this first meeting of the director and the whole cast. The stage can then be explained and actors can ask questions concerning distances and props. This is another important discussion, which should produce useful ideas and suggestions.

Technical drawings Detailed diagrams, known as technical drawings, are the next step in the process. Based on the model, they are used by those who build the set. Professionals normally use scene builders, however in the amateur theater this may be done by the designer with help from the stage crew. Technical drawings require skill and accuracy. Make sure that they are crystal clear and to an accepted and recognized scale. They should show proportions, measurements and specific details of

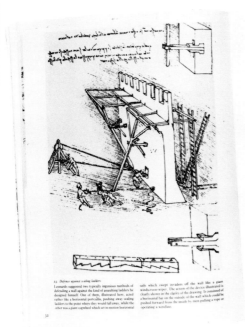

The design process Adrian Vaux was the designer for Bertolt Brecht's *Edward II* at the Round House in London. His research led him to study paintings of battles by the Italian artist Paolo Uccello and Leonardo da Vinci's war machine drawings (**1**). He sketched ideas based on these. An early idea was based on da Vinci's drawings (**3**) while a later development (**2**) used a complex seige machine and incorporated earth on the ground, lances and a billowing tent. This tent idea was eventually used in the form of a hanging draped over a solid wall (**4**), while the earth became pebbles and the lances were painted bright red for the actual production (**5,6**). The red lances moving across the muted colors of the set make a strong visual impact, helping to define, and focus attention on, the acting area.

all elements of the design. Front and side elevations and plans must be drawn not only for the set but also for all the props that are being made, such as pillars, statues or pieces of furniture. Mark the drawings carefully, add notes for anything complicated and always make a copy of the drawings. No matter how precise the drawings are, it is always important for the designer to visit the workshop where the scenery is built as often as possible to watch over progress and make sure the drawings are interpreted correctly.

From now on the professional designer will constantly be on the go, supervising the creation of the set, visiting carpenters, painters and prop people, and spending time in rehearsals and discussions with the stage manager and the director. In the amateur theater, the designer may actually participate in the set construction. Whatever the circumstances, it is important for the designer to keep a close eye on all aspects of the set construction. For professionals and amateurs alike, details such as fire regulations and safety have to be worked out. At this stage, there may have to be cut backs in the budget. Designers should always bear the production's budget in mind, but should also be prepared to justify expenses where they are vital.

Choosing and finding props All objects on stage, from a glass to drink from to a sofa to sit on, are called props and they should be selected as quickly as possible because the actors will want to work

3

6

MAKING A MODEL SET

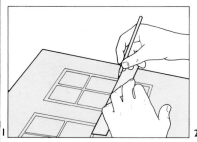

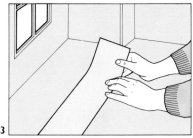

A simple and effective model of a proposed set design can be made by drawing up the basic elements of the set on card or balsa,

being careful to make them to scale (**1**). Cut out the shapes and affix them in their correct positions, adding colors, textures and

perhaps pieces of fabric and tiny props made from modeling clay to give as much detail as possible (**2,3**).

Time devoted to making a model is invariably well spent. With a three-dimensional reference, it is far easier to discuss the set and to spot any potential problems or weak aspects of the design. The director, costume and lighting designers, stage staff and set builders can express their opinions and become familiar with the proposed set. Actors also find it helpful to see a model so that they can rehearse keeping the set in mind and so that they will not find the transition from rehearsal room to stage as traumatic as it might be. If a company regularly uses a particular hall or theater, it is useful to have a model of it, complete with auditorium, so that it can be used for all productions and will indicate any possible problems with seating and visibility.

Building a model does not involve a major outlay on materials and equipment. The basic requirements are listed here. In addition to these materials, the designer should try and use anything to hand which will convey the details of the proposed set to give a clear indication of colors, fabrics and textures to be used.

Equipment
Craft knife
Scissors
Tracing paper
Pencils
Brushes
Glue
Ruler
Small nails
Hammer
Adhesive tape
Tweezers

Stapler
Felt tip pens
Thumb tacks
Sandpaper
Drawing pins

Materials
Cardboard
Balsa wood
Metal strips and rods
Foil
Plastic rod
Polystyrene sheeting
Modeling clay
Wire
Cotton thread
Fabric samples
Paints

Glitter spray
Cotton wool
Beads
Cocktail sticks
Colored paper
Match boxes
Egg boxes
Dolls' house furniture

Planning lighting effects
The model cannot show the full effect of the set since this will be greatly affected by the lighting. Sketches should be made, using the model set as reference, to show the various effects that can be achieved. This series (**right**) was prepared for a production of Mozart's opera *The Magic Flute*. Such sketches are of great importance to the designers and director in working out the precise effects required for the production.
The three designs (**below**) shown in the same model theater illustrate how effective models can be when shapes, colors and textures are carefully reproduced to scale.

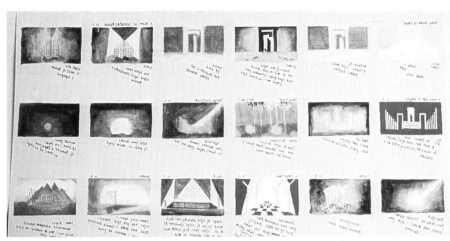

with them in rehearsal. They can involve finding anything from a stuffed crocodile to an electric wheel chair. A list of all props should be drawn up by the designer and stage manager and, if appropriate, the person responsible for obtaining props.

This list can then be broken down to those things which are to be made, those which can be found by others such as a props person or assistant stage manager, and those which the designer will want to find in person.

You can spend days hunting through second hand stores and other likely sources to find the right piece of furniture, or you may prefer to rent or hire furniture or other props. This is fine if the company has the money to spend on this, but often, if the budget is low, many of the props will have to be found for free. One approach worth considering in this situation is borrowing furniture and other props from private sources such as shops or even members of the theater group. Businesses are often generous in this way, but great care must be taken to ensure these props are not damaged and that they are returned promptly. The businesses will usually expect nothing more than a credit in the program.

With the stage manager, use your ingenuity to come up with other sources of free props. Hospitals

often give away old bedding, and city dumps can yield discarded furniture which can be painted and used. Railings could be found on demolition sites, and the banks of rivers or beaches can be treasure troves for old rope and broken timber. Often in circumstances where money is low and imagination high, wonderful effects can be achieved.

When selecting a particular prop, remember to choose it carefully in relation to the space on the set and its position on stage. It is crucial to allow enough space for movement on stage and to ensure that a piece of furniture fulfills its function. For example, if five actors need to sit down at a table to eat, the table must be large enough.

Fabrics are used in many ways on stage including for upholstery and drapes. Finding the right fabric at the right price can involve shopping around or finding free sources as you would for other props. If the right fabric cannot be found or afforded, it might even mean that it will have to be printed and dyed especially for the play. This can, however, be expensive, but may be worthwhile for a particular show.

Technical rehearsals When a set is first erected on stage, a process known in the United States as the 'load-in' and in Britain as the 'get-in', the designer should always be present in case of problems. A

1

4

2

5

3

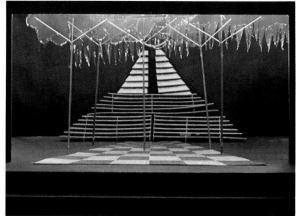

Models for all types of set

This wide range of models shows how effective they are no matter what the production or the design. This Restoration set (1) uses proscenium arch doors with paintings, furniture and architectural features depicted on the walls to suggest an artificial mood associated with Augustan theater productions. This box set (2) is in stark contrast to the Restoration set. Using practical furniture, doors, windows and other details it presents a room which is lived in rather than a set to be acted against. The atmosphere of fantasy created by this set (3) is achieved through one dominant color to set the mood and by using natural materials in unusual ways.

Oversize figures complete the effect. Another example of a detailed interior (4) shows a rustic peasant home, with stained walls, rough furniture, leaning pillars and balastrades. In another contrasting approach, this simple Renaissance set (5) has two formal downstage entrances and the possibility of upstage exits behind the classic arches. The oriental effect of this set (6) is achieved through using a checkered floor cloth, translucent borders and wood strips in a stylized design.

A rather fussy set (7) gains a strong sense of enclosure from the red wallpaper which is broken up by points of focus such as the large window and bulky stove. The hunting trophy requires

7

10

8

11

9

12

attention. Another example of an oriental setting (**8**) uses slatted hangings and a flown bamboo arch. By contrast, this more traditional set (**9**) divides the acting area with strong vertical pillars. The effect of these is softened by an irregular gauze netting downstage. In this design (**10**) both an exterior and an interior are created. A room is

suggested by a window, furniture and a difference in level from the exterior created by a skycloth and stylized palm trees. Another contrasting approach is seen in this set (**11**) where the juxtaposition of the festive bunting hung across a wide empty space creates an uneasy atmosphere. This final example (**12**) is the same basic set as (**9**) but

the spaces have been filled with furniture, a flown birdcage and a cloth hanging replaces the netting. With their tiny characters in costume and precise miniature props, these excellent models have been made with skill and imagination. They show clearly that the more care taken in building a model, the more useful it will be.

87

MASKING THE THEATER

Masking the offstage areas

Today's theater productions often use no masking to hide lights and other equipment offstage. But masking is still widely used, particularly in proscenium arch theaters, since an audience can be easily distracted by stage staff and actors in the wings. Masking is done in many ways. Traditional painted scenery (**1**) has masking flats at each side leading to a backcloth. For quick changes, rotating, three-faced flats can be made. Hanging cloths (**2**) can be used for both scenery and masking. It is important to ensure that the gaps between the hanging cloths are covered by supplementary masking. A deliberate decision not to use masking can produce an effect of starkness and isolation (**3**). The unlit areas beyond the actors extend into the distance with no pieces of vertical scenery to define the stage area.

1

2

3

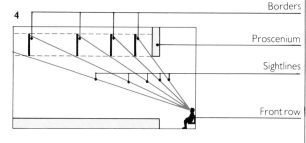

4

Borders

Proscenium

Sightlines

Front row

5

Sightlines extending above borders

6

Backcloth

Wings

Offstage area

Sightlines

Front row

In proscenium arch theaters borders should be placed so that the front row of the audience cannot see above them. Because of the angle of vision, there will be wider gaps between the borders toward the back of the stage (**4**). Incorrectly placed and spaced borders will allow the audience to see above them (**5**). The sightlines for side masking must be carefully worked out from a position at the far ends of the front row (**6**)

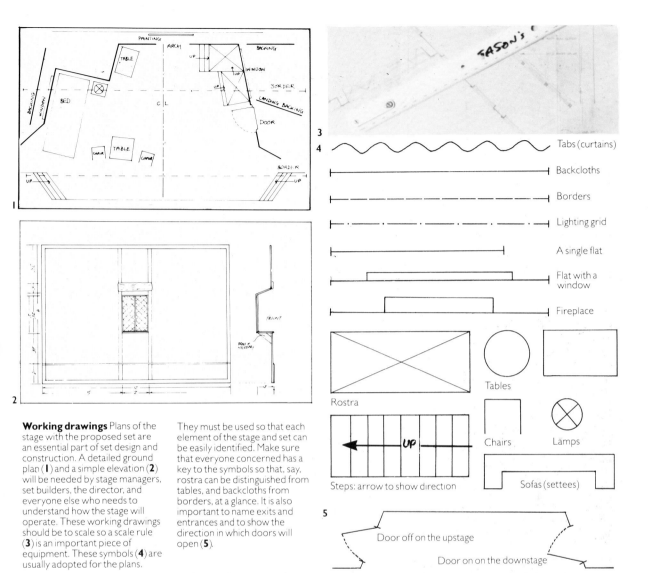

Working drawings Plans of the stage with the proposed set are an essential part of set design and construction. A detailed ground plan (**1**) and a simple elevation (**2**) will be needed by stage managers, set builders, the director, and everyone else who needs to understand how the stage will operate. These working drawings should be to scale so a scale rule (**3**) is an important piece of equipment. These symbols (**4**) are usually adopted for the plans.

They must be used so that each element of the stage and set can be easily identified. Make sure that everyone concerned has a key to the symbols so that, say, rostra can be distinguished from tables, and backcloths from borders, at a glance. It is also important to name exits and entrances and to show the direction in which doors will open (**5**).

small error on a technical drawing or plan can create difficulties, and the designer should be there to sort problems out and—if necessary—to take the blame. Hopefully this complicated process will go to plan and there will be a short period in which the designer can put the finishing touches to the set. This often involves a little painting, sorting out props and so on with the set in place.

Technical rehearsals will take place so that the actors can get to know the set, the lighting can be tested, cues worked out and all the other details looked at and rehearsed. The first time the actors get on the set, they will want to walk around to orientate themselves and to go through actions such as opening doors. The actors will often be nervous about their performances and may blame the set when things go wrong, or they may be surprised by the set. The designer should be there to sort such worries out. The technical rehearsal is always a long day with problems for everyone—doors may jam and props may not work. It is sensible to take detailed notes from the auditorium if you notice any points concerning the set or props. This will help you sort out difficulties quickly after the rehearsal. Always keep a cool head during the technical rehearsal and try to be positive and constructive.

TOURING

Many non-professional companies may have the opportunity to tour shows. Taking a play on tour creates special problems for a designer. The entire set will have to be transported, unloaded and erected perhaps daily. The designer must know several aspects of the tour before beginning work on the production. A ground plan of each of the spaces to be visited should be obtained. There may be extreme differences in the types of theater on the tour, varying from school halls to sophisticated college or university theaters. Another important consideration is the size of truck available to move the set, since the size of the scenery and props must be calculated to fit into it. Thirdly, the designer must know how many people will be unloading and erecting the set. For touring, a simple set is often the best idea.

Touring can produce other problems. For instance, the opening night may take place away from the company's base which involves special organization for the designer and stage manager. If a schools' tour is planned, there are other problems. Children tend to get right in amongst any scenery used. They will want to handle props and are generally inquisitive. The designer must take special precautions for the safety of the children and, particularly, once the set is standing, make sure that it will not fall over.

Designing for the theater can be a great challenge. Many professionals today have special training. However, in the amateur theater this is not so frequently the case. The main attributes needed for designing are senses of color and space and good visual ideas about transferring the typed or printed word into three dimensions. However, designers should also have a keen eye for the practicalities, and be prepared to temper their inventiveness in accordance with the requirements, both practical and financial, of a particular production.

Hamlet old and new
At first glance, these pictures appear to show a wide variety of plays from different periods. In fact they are all of *Hamlet*. Even the most well-known of classic plays should offer a challenge to directors and designers. Early this century Edward Gordon Craig designed this massive, sculptural set (**1**), while Johnston Forbes-Robertson chose instead to use detailed, Viking realism (**2**). Two *Hamlet* productions from 1980 could not be in sharper contrast. Both rely on costumes and positioning for visual impact against a bare stage. British actor-director Stephen Berkoff staged it in the round using modern dress (**3**), while the Royal Shakespeare Company chose simple, timeless clothes (**4**).

3

4

American director Charles Marowitz freely adapted *Hamlet* for his 1975 production at the Open Space Theatre in London. Many outstanding visual effects were achieved through the unusual set designs, costumes and action on stage. Hamlet swung on ropes during some of his most famous speeches (**6**), displaying his collegiate loyalties on his Wittenberg University sweatshirt. Claudius was in stylized military attire (**5**), and the postures and gestures of all on stage here reflect the bold approach of the director. It was not, however, a production of mere gimmicks, but one based on a new reading and understanding of Shakespeare. A rather more traditional, but still highly original, approach was seen at The Royal Court in London in 1980. This time the period suggested was the seventeenth century and for this scene in Gertrude's closet (**7**), a hanging cloth was used to suggest a tapestry. This cloth also cut down the stage space drastically to achieve a particular effect and atmosphere.

CHAPTER FIVE

LIGHTING

PRINCIPLES OF LIGHTING

BASIC ILLUMINATION

THE LIGHTING REHEARSAL

RIGGING · FOCUSING

Lighting is a crucial element in any stage performance. Without a creative and technically efficient approach to lighting, the audience cannot fully appreciate the sets and costumes or, most importantly, the actors on stage.

Lighting equipment is expensive and complex. Amateur theater groups who have a theater or hall which they always use for their productions will find that one of their most important investments will be in providing an adequate, flexible lighting system for that space. Those who do not have a regular base will have to provide lighting to suit various different spaces and, although purchasing the equipment will make a large hole in their budget, it should serve them for many years.

A good electrician is an essential member of any group, as is someone who understands the principles behind stage lighting and who has the creative ability to produce effects required and interpret the needs of directors and designers. Few groups will have a lighting designer as such, but, if a person with skills in using electrical equipment can be encouraged to learn about lighting and can work closely with a stage designer, then responsibility for lighting will be more than adequately covered.

Today stage lighting is generally seen as much more than just providing basic illumination for the stage. In general terms, the requirements of the lighting designer vary only slightly whether the design is for a large civic theater or a small informal space. The lighting designer has to work closely with the others involved in the production—the director, set and costume designers and, even, the make-up artist, as well as the actors and stage management staff. The lighting designer's job is to illuminate what the others decide on. In some smaller companies, one person may do several, or even all, of these jobs, but the functions themselves are separate.

GENERAL PRINCIPLES

The human eye cannot function without light. Too little light will have an audience peering to see a performance, but too much will actually hinder their ability to see by producing distracting glare. The eye is always attracted to the brightest object on stage. A spotlight moving across stage attracts the audience to anything it illuminates. If a stage is flooded evenly with light, the audience will first see the stage as a whole and then be attracted to those areas on stage where the light is most intense. For example, a bright follow spot moving across a dimly lit stage will determine what the audience sees because the eye naturally looks at the brightest area on the stage.

Intensity The intensity of light on stage is determined by the power of the lights used, the quantity and distribution of the lights, the angle at which the beams of light strike objects and actors, the color of

Lighting is now recognized as a major and vital part of the creative process of theater. Lighting is used to create a stage space, or to change an existing acting area. If the lighting designer works well with the set designer and the director, they can create visually exciting effects which enhance the production's meaning. This striking silhouette effect (**left**) was used in the Royal Shakespeare Company's *Iphigenia in Tauris*, part of *The Greeks*. It was achieved through back lighting. With skill, lighting can in some ways take the place of scenery in creating a visual style for a play.

LIGHTING DESIGNER'S TASK PLAN

Pre-rehearsal period: read the play · discuss the production with the director and stage manager · study the theater and obtain detailed plans · find out precisely what equipment is available · discuss the set model, masking, sight lines and other details with the set designer · discuss costumes · start to plan lighting using stage grid and studying the play

During rehearsals: go through the play scene by scene with the director to plan precise lighting details · work out presets and cues and help stage manager to mark the prompt book · buy or hire equipment as needed · work out a lighting synopsis with the stage manager

Production week: rig and focus lights · attend technical rehearsal to test lighting and solve problems · make final adjustments and prepare controls

the lights and the reflective quality of the objects being illuminated.

If a set is painted in pale colors, light will reflect off it and too many or too powerful lights will produce glare. This will result in details being lost so that the set and costumes and, most importantly, the actors' faces will not be seen clearly. Anything painted white will stand out when it is lit, and, conversely, the darker an area of the stage, the less it will attract attention. Consequently, flats or drapes used for masking are normally black. Similarly, if a set is painted in dark colors, it will merge into the background no matter how brightly it is lit.

It is important to realize that light spreads three-dimensionally. An actor dressed in a white costume who appears against a dark background will reflect a great deal of light. The actor will immediately stand out when the stage is lit because of the stark contrast between the object being lit—the actor—and the background—a dark set. An actor whose costume blends in with the set is in danger of being upstaged by that set because of a lack of contrast between the two elements. However, increasing the power of the lighting on the whole stage will not improve matters for the actor, because a pale set will reflect light and drown out the actor in glare, while a dark set will absorb the extra light so that the audience remains without a point of focus.

One answer to this problem is to light different areas of the stage carefully in different ways, so that the actor is more brightly lit than the set. Achieving a balance between the object being lit and the background is a fundamental task of the lighting designer and technician.

Angle Angle is thus the second vital factor in lighting. In general terms, 45 degrees is a good, basic angle which gives a reasonable effect. A light shining at 45 degrees is steep enough to avoid casting unnecessarily long shadows from the actor to the set and low enough to illuminate an actor's face satisfactorily. To light a face completely—that is to light the front and both sides of the face—basically two lights are required. If the lights are placed so that they both shine at 45 degrees and are positioned 90 degrees apart, this will illuminate the actor and allow some movement within the limits of the beam from the lights used.

Different types of lights can be used at varying angles. The actor can be lit by a bright light which does not fall on the set. With the correct equipment the possibilities are almost endless.

A traditional, proscenium stage will be lit from above, from the sides and from the audience area, allowing great flexibility. When lighting open or thrust stages, care must be taken not to have the lights shining on, or in the eyes of, the audience. Also lights must be carefully placed so that they do not obscure a view of the stage.

LIGHTING EQUIPMENT

Lighting equipment consists basically of the lights themselves and control system. The number of lights and the degree of sophistication in the control system will depend on the financial resources of the group and the requirements of its productions. Purchasing lights is, of course, expensive, but lights and other equipment can usually be hired or rented. This is particularly useful for special or unusual effects. There are four main types of light.

Beamlights These give a very narrow and intense beam of light. They are used to give a strong shaft of light, such as indicating sunlight.

Floods Floodlights are used to provide general lighting, such as giving soft light from above and lighting cycloramas or backdrops. The spread of light varies, but, in general, floodlights give a very wide beam which is difficult to control.

Fresnel spots These lights are relatively versatile, giving a softer light than a profile spot. The beam can be adjusted using shutters called barn doors and by moving the lamp relative to the lens. The most common sizes for amateur theaters are the 250 watt and 500 watt, which are suitable for general lighting in small theaters. The larger 1000 watt version can be used for lighting from out front, for backlight or for offstage effects. Fresnels also come in 2000 and 5000 watt sizes, but these will be used mainly in larger, professional theaters.

Profile spots These lights, usually called lekos in the United States, provide a sharp beam of light which can be shaped using shutters or special types of masking, called irises and gobos, in the light. The

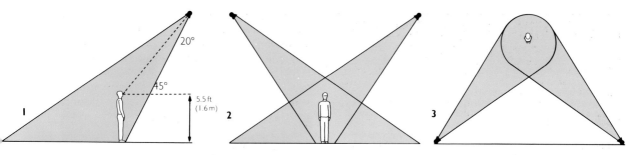

1 20° 45° 5.5 ft (1.6 m)

2

3

4

Lighting the actor on stage A figure on the stage is usually lit by a beam, or beams, at a 45° angle. This is steep enough to reduce shadows from the actor falling on the set, and low enough to illuminate the face (**1**). If the actor is to be lit completely, at least two lights are set to shine at 45° and positioned 90° apart (**2**). This allows for some movement within the illuminated area (**3**). This lighting bar rig (**4**) has been erected in a converted church. It will give saturation coverage for the stage area, as well as providing scope for lighting particular sections or figures within that area.

High density lighting Beam lights, floodlights and PAR lamps are some of the range of lanterns available for stage lighting. Beam lights provide a strong shaft of light which can be used for high intensity lighting such as sunlight. In groups they are used for back or side lighting. PAR lamps are powerful fixed-beam spotlights. There are various types of floodlights. They are often grouped together along battens. Floods are usually used to provide general lighting from above and for lighting cycloramas and cloths. Floods, as their name suggests, have a very wide beam and they can be difficult to control.

Parblazer 4 1000W Beamlight

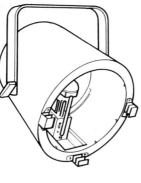
750 Beamlight 1000W

Floodlight 60 500W

Floodlight 137 150/200W

IRIS 1 Cyclorama Flood 1000W

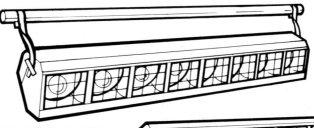
F/63, S/64 Batten 8×150W

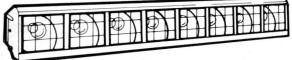
F/63F, S/64S Foot Lights 8×150W

Equipment for softer lighting
Profile spots (called lekos in the
United States) and Fresnel spots
are widely used. The beam is
adjustable, using shutters (known
as barn doors) and by moving the
lamp relative to the lens. The
lamps are available from 250 to
5000 watts but the range to 1000
watts is suitable for most
purposes in small theaters.
Fresnels are versatile and give a
softer light than profile spots.
They are useful for general
lighting, back lighting and for
effects. The 1000 watt version
gives greater power and spread
than smaller ones and can be used
for lighting the front of the house.
Profile spots, lekos, give a sharp
beam which can be shaped using
shutters or masking devices. The
narrower the beam and the
smaller its angle, the brighter the
light.

Model 743 1000W Fresnel spotlight

Harmony F Fresnel 1000W

Prelude F Fresnel 500/650W

Minim Fresnel 500W

23 Profile Spot 500W

828 Fresnel Spot 2000W

Model 814 1000W Prism Convex
spotlight

Prelude 500/650W Prism
Convex spotlight

Prelude 16/30 Profile 500/650W

T-spot 84 1000W
variable spread
profile spotlight

The use of color in lighting

Color is a vital part of lighting the stage. It can be used to produce strong responses from an audience. Color indicates particular atmospheres and moods, it can suggest a season or part of the day, it will show the state of the weather or merely lead the audience's attention to one area of the stage. These samples of cinemoid (**far right**), one of the most widely used color mediums, provide a handy reference for the lighting designer. A backcloth with a gobo and color medium (**1**) creates a striking effect. Blue light (**2**) gives an impression of coldness and separation, while red light (**3**) suggests warmth and intimacy.

2

3

Additive color mixing can produce a broad range of subtle effects. If lights with red, blue and green color mediums are directed at a central point, the result will appear as white light. If one color beam is removed, then color will appear in the beam. This diagram (**above**) shows the possible variations. A yellow medium transmits yellow, red and green light, while a blue medium transmits blue, blue-green and green. If a yellow and a blue medium are place together in a lantern, they will through only their common color: green.

Projected scenery and special effects are part of the lighting designer's responsibilities. An effects projector (**below left**) can be equipped with moving effects attachments to simulate such things as thunder clouds, fleecy clouds, storm clouds, rain, snow, running water, smoke or flames. Some of these effects can also be created mechanically. Projected scenery can be both useful and effective but care must be taken to ensure that the projected image is clear and undistorted. The projector can be used from behind or in front of the screen. Back projection offers a brighter picture because the light comes through the screen rather than being reflected off it. Also, the closer the projector is to the screen, the brighter the image.

Another useful device is a color wheel (**below right**) which allows for color changes on a particular light during the course of a scene.

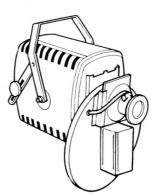

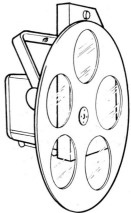

Lighting control systems As technology becomes increasingly sophisticated, lighting systems with memory controls and visual display units are now available at comparatively reasonable prices. The minimum requirements remain a dimmer pack and a dimmer board. Dimmer boards come in various specifications (**bottom left**) with 6, 12, 18, 24, 30 or 36 channels and extensions are also available. Such systems can be expanded to meet new demands as budgets allow. Even the simplest system allows for cues to be preset so that the next cue can be set up while the first cue is in operation. A patch board allows the designer to group a number of lights on one channel of the control system by replugging during the show, without having to touch the lights themselves. The tendency now is for the control systems to have more channels than formerly but the patch board is still a useful adjunct to the control system. Memory control systems (**below**) are increasingly common. Their great virtue is in the capacity to record and store the dimmer levels for each cue as it is finalized. This means that it is no longer necessary to write down each level and state. With all the best equipment, the ultimate desire of any lighting controller is to work with a clear view over the stage (**below right**).

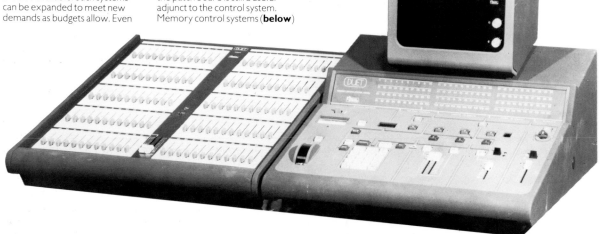

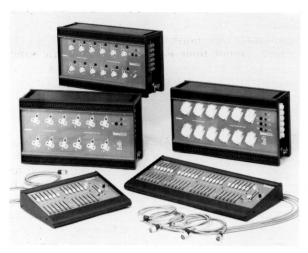

intensity of the light depends on the width of the beam. The narrower the beam—and the smaller its angle—the brighter the light. Profile spots are usually used for any long range coverage of the stage as well as for side or special lighting on stage. These lights can be controlled precisely thanks to the ways in which the beam can be shaped.

Control systems There is an enormous range of control systems for theaters today. The introduction of computer-based technology and miniaturization has led to constant advances in sophistication and technical capacity. However, the main basic requirements for stage lighting are dimmer packs and a preset desk. The level of the lighting seen on stage is controlled from the control system, and the degree of flexibility available to the lighting designer depends, naturally enough, on the equipment.

A basic control system consists of one or more dimmer packs which each contain a number of channels. Each channel is linked to the preset desk and can be operated independently. The channels each have a maximum load of, say, 2000 watts or

5000 watts. This means that the light or combination of lights fed into that channel must not exceed its total wattage. Within these limits, the channels of the dimmer pack can be used in a wide variety of ways, depending on the requirements of the production. The lighting designer decides which combination of lights to attach to which channel in the control system.

One vital factor in stage lighting is that, unlike most domestic lighting, it is not simply on or off. Stage lighting depends on being used at a variety of levels. These levels are determined in two ways. The basic lighting operator's desk consists of a number of fader levers each linked to a channel in the dimmer pack. The faders can be set to specific levels on a scale, usually from 1 to 10, marked on the desk. In addition, there is a master fader which operates all channels simultaneously.

Most plays involve a number of lighting cues, each of which may use a different combination of lights and therefore of channels in the control system. For this reason control systems include a system of 'presets'. A basic system will have two or three presets. This is why the dimmer desk consists not just of one row of controls but of several. Each row of controls relates to one preset. This means that the levels for the lights can be established one or two cues in advance, making the operation of the lighting much simpler. Normally, the levels of the lights for a particular cue are set on one of the presets, and the combination of channels is brought in on cue using the master fader. Even a very basic control system allows enough flexibility for, say, only one channel or, conversely, many of them to be used at one time.

Many companies find that their basic control system does not provide the variety required by their productions, especially if more lights need to be brought in than can be catered for on the channels of the dimmer packs. A patch board is a simple way of altering the lights on each channel of the control system during the performance. Today there is normally no separate patch board, but each dimmer channel usually has two or more output sockets at the dimmer pack. This method is simpler than using a traditional patch board, but is still called 'patching'.

Color Color is another basic element in lighting. It can be used to enhance the effects of the overall lighting or to achieve special effects. Color can be introduced into a light by means of filters, called gels, which are placed in front of the lens. Commercial manufacturers produce a wide range of different colored gels. The effects achieved with gels can vary tremendously, from a subtle warming of the light using a straw colored gel to an eerie red glow, or a cold effect using blue or steel gels.

Gobos and irises If a gobo or iris is inserted in the gate runners of a profile spot, the shape of the beam will be determined by the shape cut into the gobo or iris. For instance, an effect of softly dappled woodland light or a sharp jagged shape can be achieved with different shapes of gobo. An iris is used to cut down the area of the beam.

Other special effects Interesting special effects can be obtained using more specialized lighting. Projectors can produce static or moving effects, for example. However, for amateur companies, a little ingenuity can give good results. A home slide projector, for instance, can produce interesting effects when used in conjunction with stage lighting.

Safety Safety is a prime consideration with all lighting equipment. When using new or unfamiliar equipment, check the instructions and safety regulations carefully. All existing equipment should be regularly checked, especially before it is to be used. When using a new or unfamiliar theater, it is wise to check electric power and wiring before hanging any lights. Both lighting designer and operator should be mindful of the safety of not only themselves but all those involved in the production, as well as the audience. The manufacturers of stage lighting equipment are normally helpful in dealing with queries about their equipment concerning safety and other matters. Among the largest manufacturers are, in the United States, Strand Century, Berkey, and Kliegl, and, in Britain, Rank Strand.

BASIC ILLUMINATION

The simplest way to illuminate the acting area, which includes stage and set, evenly is to extend the principles established in lighting a single figure by dividing the acting area into a grid. The size of squares in the grid should be based on the optimum illumination which can be obtained from the lights used. On average, a spotlight will cast a beam about 10ft (3 meters) in diameter. However, as the intensity of the beam decreases near the edges, it is best to reckon on between 6ft (2 meters) and 8ft (2.5 meters) as the top limit of illumination from a spotlight.

Thus, an acting area measuring 24ft (7.5 meters) wide by 16ft (5 meters) deep can be divided into 8ft (2.5 meter) squares. There will be a total of six squares, three from stage left to stage right and two from downstage to upstage. For the purposes of writing down the lighting plot, label each of the squares with a letter, in this case from A to F.

To give a basic illumination to the stage, lights will

USING A LIGHTING GRID

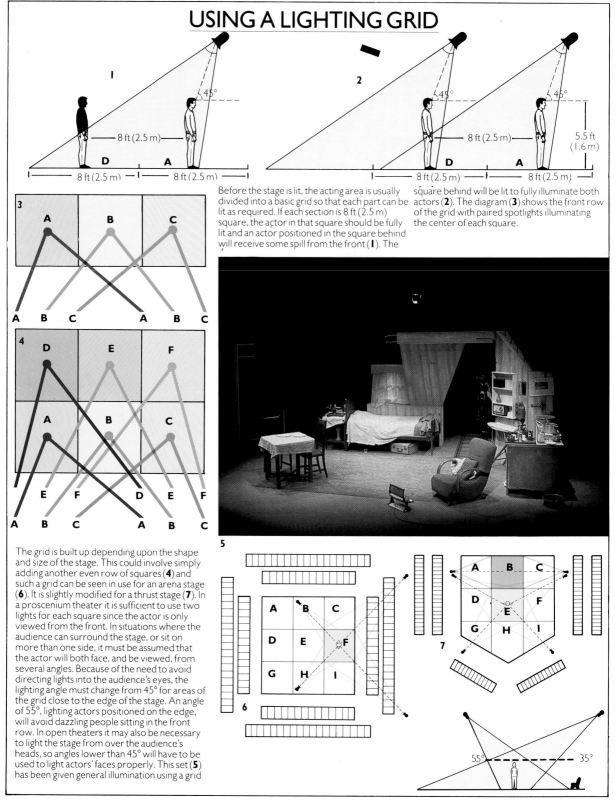

Before the stage is lit, the acting area is usually divided into a basic grid so that each part can be lit as required. If each section is 8 ft (2.5 m) square, the actor in that square should be fully lit and an actor positioned in the square behind will receive some spill from the front (**1**). The square behind will be lit to fully illuminate both actors (**2**). The diagram (**3**) shows the front row of the grid with paired spotlights illuminating the center of each square.

The grid is built up depending upon the shape and size of the stage. This could involve simply adding another even row of squares (**4**) and such a grid can be seen in use for an arena stage (**6**). It is slightly modified for a thrust stage (**7**). In a proscenium theater it is sufficient to use two lights for each square since the actor is only viewed from the front. In situations where the audience can surround the stage, or sit on more than one side, it must be assumed that the actor will both face, and be viewed, from several angles. Because of the need to avoid directing lights into the audience's eyes, the lighting angle must change from 45° for areas of the grid close to the edge of the stage. An angle of 55°, lighting actors positioned on the edge, will avoid dazzling people sitting in the front row. In open theaters it may also be necessary to light the stage from over the audience's heads, so angles lower than 45° will have to be used to light actors' faces properly. This set (**5**) has been given general illumination using a grid be hung on the lighting grid above the stage. They will be hung on bars, called 'battens' in the United States and 'pipes' in Britain. The angle at which the light should be hung from the batten (pipe) so that it hits the actor at 45 degrees depends on its position and height above the stage. It also depends on the angle of the beam emitted from the light. A common beam angle is 20 degrees, and, obviously, the area which the light will illuminate will vary considerably depending on the height of the light above the stage. So, if the batten (pipe) is about 18ft (5.5 meters) above the stage and a few feet in front of the stage, a light with a beam angle of 20 degrees will give a good area of illumination, and two lights positioned at 90 degrees to one another will illuminate one 8ft (2.5 meter) square of the grid. To light the other areas, repeat the process for each square.

Obviously, it may not always be possible to achieve an exact 45 degree angle, but aim for a close approximation. During focusing, which normally takes place prior to the technical rehearsals, the squares should be matched and joined up carefully so that there are no breaks in the coverage of light and so that the whole acting area is lit evenly.

Once the acting area has been basically lit, more specific requirements can be considered. Actors are three-dimensional, and lighting them from the front only ignores this. So, providing the production and budget permit, the actors, and indeed the set, should be lit from as many angles as possible. Having established an even illumination, remember that the light for each square in the grid can be controlled individually so that illumination in each area can be dimmed, intensified or eliminated independently.

LIGHTING A SHOW

The fact that an amateur group is unlikely to have a person whose sole interest and skills lie in lighting can be seen as a definite advantage. A production will always suffer if lighting is not regarded as an integral part of the design, so if one person designs both sets and lighting this problem should be avoided. What is essential is that at least one person can fully understand and maintain the lighting equipment. If a person can be found with both technical and creative skills, all the better.

The successful lighting of a production will affect every element of that production. It is essential to have constant discussion and exchange of ideas between the director, the designer, the costume designer and the technicians. The person who designs the lighting must know the text of the show as well as any other member of the company, so the

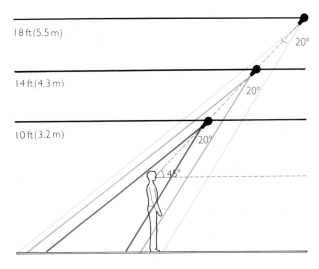

Positioning lights The angle of the beam emitted from a light remains constant. As a result of this, the area covered by that beam varies considerably depending on the height of the light. The lower the light, the smaller the area covered by its beam. This diagram (**above**) shows some possible variations for a light beamed at an angle of 20° from higher and lower levels.

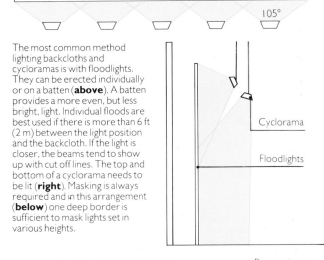

The most common method lighting backcloths and cycloramas is with floodlights. They can be erected individually or on a batten (**above**). A batten provides a more even, but less bright, light. Individual floods are best used if there is more than 6 ft (2 m) between the light position and the backcloth. If the light is closer, the beams tend to show up with cut off lines. The top and bottom of a cyclorama needs to be lit (**right**). Masking is always required and in this arrangement (**below**) one deep border is sufficient to mask lights set in various heights.

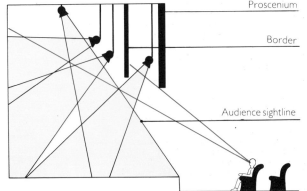

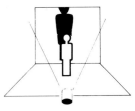

Lighting the face Lighting from directly above with a single light leaves shadows and obscures the eyes.

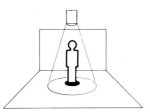

Lighting from below with a single light leaves shadows round the eyes and gives the nostrils undue prominence.

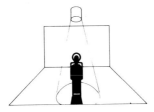

Backlighting by itself produces a silhouette. This can be used as an effective dramatic element if no facial expression need be seen.

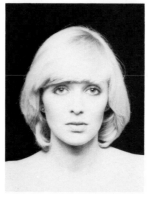

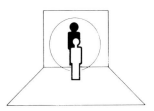

Lighting directly from the front at the same level as the subject tends to wash out the nose and is liable to hurt the actor's eyes over a long period.

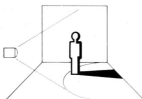

A single light from the side, at the same height as the subject, will light only one side of the face, leaving the other side in shadow.

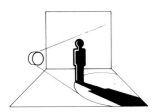

A backlight from the side gives a certain amount of facial contour and a halo effect in the hair.

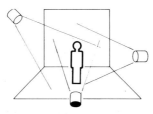

A high, side backlight, with a side backlight at the height of the subject, plus a direct front light, gives a normal appearance to the face.

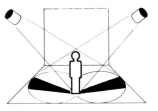

High front lights used with lights from both sides do cancel out shadows usually cast by side lighting but some fill is needed to fully register the eyes.

first step is always to read and understand the play thoroughly. It is vital to obtain a copy of the play as early as possible.

On a second or subsequent reading, take notes on any lighting requirements which relate to the action and setting of the play. Then discuss the text and how it is to be interpreted in detail with the director, designers and stage manager. The lighting designer must come to this meeting knowing precisely what lighting equipment will be available for the show and in what positions those lights can be mounted in the theater to be used. The electrical wiring of the theater is also important so that the lighting board can be considered, and, with this, the degree of flexibility and control which will be possible during performances. Lighting will be discussed with reference to the proposed set designs and as ideas are suggested, the lighting designer must know if they are possible in practical terms.

A basic lighting layout plan must be devised as early as possible in conjunction with the director and designers. In doing this, the requirements of the play must be matched with the equipment available and the exact layout of the theater and set. The sets and costumes should be carefully considered for lighting. Each production has its own lighting needs which must be answered. For instance, the setting may be a period interior which must appear to be lit by daylight, candles and oil lamps. It may have an outside setting which could vary from a pastoral woodland to an urban street. The set design may be futuristic or abstract. There could be several changes of environment or from daylight to darkness during the play and each one will require different effects.

Whatever a particular play demands, one thing always remains the same. The performers must be the central attraction for the audience and they must be seen clearly at all times. If an audience cannot see an actor's facial expressions, they cannot hope to understand the feelings and emotions that actor is communicating.

The lighting designer should attend as many rehearsals as possible so that he or she becomes familiar with the action on stage and the feel of the production so as to follow any changes to the play which will affect lighting. Close cooperation will also be needed with the stage manager, carpenters and set builders, costume designers and technicians, so that problems can be sorted out as they occur and so that everyone knows what the others require. It is also important to make sure there are sufficient helpers to tackle endless tasks from replacing fuses to rigging lights.

As rehearsals progress, the lighting designer should draw up the final lighting layout plan. It is easiest to base this on the designer's ground plan and it can be drawn in on tracing paper. The lighting plan should show the exact position of each light, its angle, circuit and any other relevant information such as gels, gobos or other accessories required. This plan should, ideally, enable all the lights to be rigged without the lighting designer being there.

The last main part of the lighting designer's job in rehearsal period is to draw up the cue synopsis. This needs to be done normally during run-throughs of the play near the end of rehearsals. It should list the number of the cue, its timing and place in the script, together with a short description of each lighting change. This synopsis should be drawn up by the lighting designer in cooperation with the director, designer, stage manager and the person who will operate the lighting board during the show. It should obviously be based on the technical capacity of the available equipment.

RIGGING

Rigging involves the construction of the set and the hanging of the lights and normally takes place before the technical rehearsal. Good planning and coordination with the others using the theater will help save time and energy in what can be a long and frustrating process. Check with the director and stage manager when you can have access to the stage and whether any lights can be rigged before the set is complete. The lights have to be hung in position and adjusted to the required angles. The lighting designer will probably need the help of several other people to rig the lights, as the designer must supervise and make sure that the overall design is adhered to.

Tall ladders or platforms will be needed for reaching the lighting grid above the stage, so safety is once more a prime consideration. Never put yourself or anyone else in a position of uncertainty or danger. If working above the stage, warn everyone else around *before* you go up. In general, be considerate about what the other people are trying to do, and they will, hopefully, reciprocate.

If you cannot gain access to the stage, time need not be wasted. All equipment should be checked before being rigged. This includes not just the lamp itself but also any shutters, barn doors or other accessories. Clamps and safety chains should also be in good order, as should the feed cable going to the light. This should also be marked with the circuit number. Rigging also involves putting up masking for the lights if the director wants them hidden from the audience. Sort this out in advance.

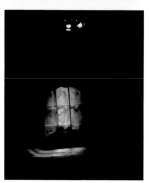

Creative and practical effects

A highly inventive set design, using a false proscenium arch and a massive fan, is brilliantly illuminated with the colors of the rainbow (**1**). Using such strong color gives a set the atmosphere of a fantasy. In contrast, the realistic, warm glow of an electric fire is created with a red filter (**2**). A similarly realistic effect produces daylight at a window (**3**). The lights can be seen above the window. Blue and yellow color mediums have been used to give a range of tones, and the lights are shuttered to avoid the beams spilling over the rest of the set. A split level set achieves three separate points of focus through lighting (**4**). The acting area of any set is often defined by lighting. Contrasting background flats (**5**) add to the atmosphere and such neutral flats can indicate different locations by merely changing the color in which they are lit.

FOCUSING

Before focusing can begin, the lighting designer must know the exact function and destination of each light. It is vital to be able to communicate clearly with the operator of the board and the people up the ladders focusing the lights. A combination of words and hand signals is often best. For basic focusing, each area on the original grid should be illuminated in turn and the light made to focus on the center of the square. The lighting designer should check and assess the effect of each lamp. Look out for any irregularities, unnecessary spill of light, the effect of color, the projection of shadows and so on. When moving from one area to the next, keep the first area lit so that you can check that the beams overlap sufficiently and provide unbroken coverage. Check how far upstage the lamps need to be directed and try to achieve a balance between too high and too low. If they are too low, a gap will appear in the coverage of the acting area, and if they are too high they may cause a flattening effect on the back wall and cast ugly shadows. This process can take a long time because each circuit and each individual cue must be focused and assessed.

At this stage a focus plot is useful. This lists the designation of each instrument beside its representation on the ground plan, together with details for lights from the side and so on. This enables lights to be refocused quickly if they are knocked or moved

LIGHTING REHEARSAL

The lighting session usually takes place soon after focusing is complete. The length of time taken normally by rigging and focusing mean that a short break will be needed before the lighting rehearsal can begin. First make sure that you can communicate clearly with the lighting board operator and that the theater is ready for performance. This means putting exit lights on and turning working lights off.

The purpose of the lighting rehearsal is to run through the lighting cues in conjunction with the director and designer so that they can comment on the lights. This is called working 'cue to cue'. The director will want to be able to see the actors, the designer wants the set to look good. The lighting designer should be positive and constructive and try to maintain a balance between demands which may conflict. However, the final appearance of the show is the responsibility of the director. The lighting rehearsal normally takes place without the actors, so the first time all the elements of the show come together is at the technical rehearsal.

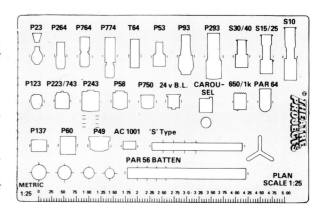

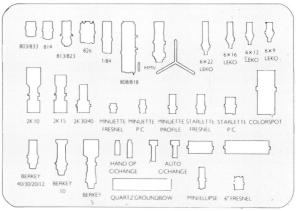

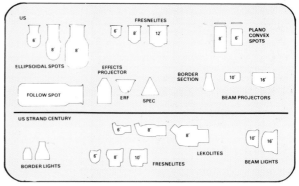

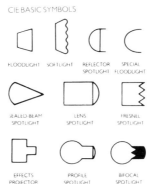

Lighting symbols and stencils
With an enormously wide range of lights in use today, it is important to draw up a lighting plan showing precisely which lights are hung where when a stage is rigged. This saves an enormous amount of time and helps with planning. International symbols have been created for each type of light in use and these are available on plastic stencils so that they can be easily reproduced to scale on a lighting plan.

The lighting plot Before the lighting plot is drawn up it must be carefully planned.

In the plan (**right**) the positions of each light are marked together with an indication of their function: shining upstage left, downstage right, and so on. The individual lights are indicated by the standard symbols. Specials are also categorized by their function in the play. For example, 'telegram', 'reader' and 'TV studio spots' refer to particular moments in the production. The whole show has been lit on the grid system which is indicated by the letter A-H, one letter for each square.

When all the elements of the lighting rig and plot have been finalized, it is best to then combine this information on to a cue graph sheet (**below**). This becomes a master sheet, showing all the various lighting plans and checklists. It also gives brief details of the whole show. The cue graph sheet enables the lighting staff to double check whether the effects being created are the ones intended. It also helps the crew to spot any problems or faults, such as lamp blowing or a light being moved, quickly. If the show is going on tour, this plot is essential since it gives an accurate account of what is required. The same applies if the show has to be dismantled and then relit.

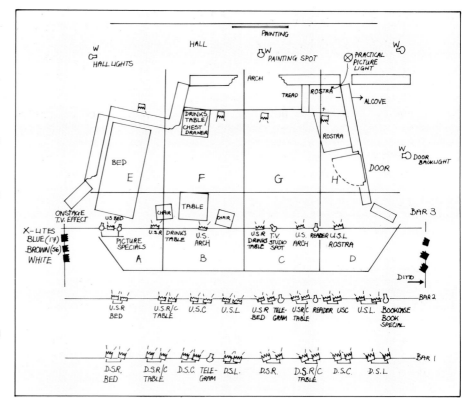

Type of light (Rank Strand numbers here)

Colors used, indicated by manufacturer's numbers

Direction of light and area to be lit

PRODUCTION:	POSITION	B	A	R	O	N	E	B	A	R	T	W	O	B	A	R	3	STANDS UL	UR
"MARK OR DAVID OR NINA"	LANTERN Nº	1	2	3	4	5	6	1	2	3	4	5	6	1	2	3	4	1	2
	TYPE	23	23	23N	264	264	123	123	123	743	743	743	123	60	60	60	60	23N	23N
	COLOR	50	50	50	67	67	67	50	50	50	67	67	50	6	6	32	32	67	67
KENWYN THEATRE	SETTING + FOCUS	UR	UL	TABLE U.C	UR	UL	TABLE U.C	DR	DL	UR	DL	DL	UR	CY	CLO	RA	MA	WIN	DOW
OPENING: JULY 5th	CIRCUIT	1	1	2	3	4	5	6	7	8	9	10	11	12	12	13	13	14	14

PAGE	WORD CUE	DESCRIPTION	TIME	Q																		
1		PRESET			6	6	7	6	6	7	6	6	6	6	6	6	2	2	2	2	—	—
8	Butler: "damn"	CLOSE TO TABLE	25 sec	1	0	0	9	0	0	8	3	3	3	3	3	3	0	0	0	0	—	—
15	Enter Birtles	BUILD TO GEN	45 sec	2	5	5	9	5	5	8	5	5	5	5	5	5	3	3	3	3	3	3
17	Music: "Gather at the river"	BURIAL SERVICE	5 sec	3	3	3	0	0	0	0	0	0	2	0	0	2	6	6	6	6	8	8
21	Enter Garrett	BUILD TO GEN	45 sec	4	6	6	7	6	6	7	6	6	6	6	6	6	6	6	6	6	0	0
25	Bonney "Got to do"	BLACKOUT	SWAP	5	0	0	0	0	0	0	0	0	0	0	0	0	0	0	0	0	0	0
26	Visual	(NIGHT) BUILD TO INT	60 sec	6	5	5	7	5	5	7	3	3	3	4	4	3	4	4	4	4	0	0

Page of script

Description of effect cue should achieve

Time taken for cue

Cue

Levels on each channel

FINAL REHEARSALS AND PERFORMANCE

Adjustments to the lighting may still be required in the technical rehearsal. However, for the lighting, the main purpose of the technical rehearsal is so that the cues and presets can be run through with the cast on stage. On occasion, the lighting and technical rehearsals may be combined. This is much less satisfactory as the whole process is slowed down while the lights are altered.

All changes to lights and cues at lighting, technical and dress rehearsals should be carefully noted down and incorporated on the cue synopsis. It is important that not just the lighting designer but also the board operator knows exactly what changes

have been made. The dress rehearsal may be the first time that the lighting board operator has to run all the cues in the time and sequence of the actual performance. Timing and accuracy are crucial, as is a cool head to arrange the presets correctly.

After the dress rehearsal, all that remains is the performance. The lighting equipment and board should be checked before the audience are allowed into the auditorium. The person who operates the faders and master faders of the lighting board carries the responsibility for weeks of planning and hard work and plays a vital role during the performance. Cues should be accurate and on time. The lighting will probably be taken for granted by the audience, but this should not worry the lighting designer or the board operator. If the lighting is noticed, it is usually because it has gone wrong.

Operating cues using presets
The dimmer board shown here (**1**) has two presets (**A** and **B**) ready for operation. Each preset has a master switch dimmer. When cue one is in operation (**2**) on preset **A**, its master dimmer is on full. The lower preset **B** is set for cue two with its master dimmer off. The cue sheet (**4**) shows the level on each circuit of the preset (circuit 13 is not in use

for this cue) and the arrow indicates that the cue is being brought up. When cue two has been operated (**3**) the master dimmers have changed position. Preset **A** can now be cleared and set up for cue three. The cue sheet (**5**) shows that cue two is a crossfade between presets which is simply done by operating the master simultaneously.

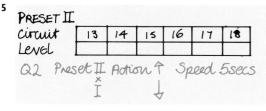

4
PRESET I
Circuit

	13	14	15	16	17	18
Level						

Q1   Preset 1 Action ↑   Speed 5secs

5
PRESET II
Circuit

	13	14	15	16	17	18
Level						

Q2   Preset II Action ↑   Speed 5secs
        ×
        I   ↓

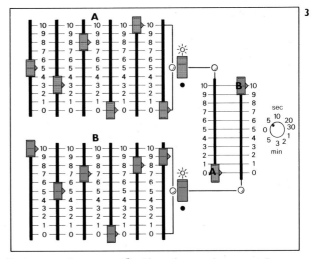

Cue one operating on preset **A**, with cue two ready on preset **B**.

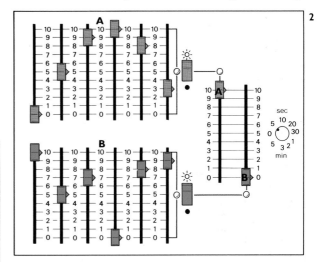

Cue two operating on preset **B**, with cue three ready on preset **A**.

CHAPTER SIX

COSTUME

THE DESIGN PROCESS

RESEARCH · HIRING · BUYING

PATTERNS . CUTTING · SEWING

TRIMMINGS · ACCESSORIES · HATS

Actors wear more than just clothes on stage. Their costumes have an important role in the production—they are like three-dimensional portrait paintings. Costumes express to the audience aspects of the character, highlights of the personality, and give a clear idea of the time, place and style of the period in which the play is set. The eminent American stage designer Robert Edmond Jones concisely outlined some of the main factors in costume design: 'A stage costume is a creation of the theater. Its quality is purely theatrical and, taken outside of the theater, it loses its magic at once … Each separate costume we create for a play must be exactly suited both to the character it helps to express and to the occasion it graces.'

GENERAL PRINCIPLES OF COSTUME DESIGN

There are numerous elements to consider in approaching costume design, but one basic fact is unavoidable—costumes are worn. Their purpose is to cover the human frame in its many shapes and sizes. Fashion historians have discovered three basic reasons for the way clothes have been worn over the centuries. The first is utility—dressing is a form of protection; the second is hierarchy—dressing is a way of indicating social rank; the third is seduction—dressing is a method of attracting atten-

tion. It is always worth considering these three influences when approaching a new production, since they are fundamental to all costume, all over the world, throughout history.

There are two main types of approach to a play's costumes. They can be either realistic or they can be abstract. Realistic costumes will aim to be accurate to the historical period of the play and to reflect the true characterizations of the cast. This may mean, for example, using drab and unfashionable outfits for a shabby character, or flamboyant accessories for a dapper rogue. The abstract approach involves exaggerating elements of the character by stylizing the clothes and human form to suit the atmosphere of the play. A gangster's suit may be given vastly padded shoulders or a jolly, fat innkeeper could have an enormous round seat to his pants.

Both approaches have their place in theater, dance and opera. The choice for any particular show is not up to the costume designer alone, but should be worked out in discussions with the director to achieve a common perspective on the presentation of the play.

CREATING COSTUMES

Ideally both the stage design and the costume design for a particular production will be done by one designer who has control of all visual elements. However, this is not always possible for various

Left Stage costumes are one of the most important visual elements of a production. In line with the atmosphere and style of the show, they may be simple everyday clothes or abstract creations. Their function is not merely visual, since costumes inform an audience of sex, status, period, personality and occasion. This extravagant, glittering gown of rich colors gives a clear indication of monarchy, especially when worn with a crown, orb and scepter. Using fabric squares with a painted design, the costume was made from a patchwork. This is a simple but highly effective design.

	① NIGHT FOREST	② MARIE'S AREA	③ FAIR GROUND	④ MARIE IN BED	⑤ SHAVING CAPTAIN
WOYZECK (R. HOOPER)	FULL GREY FATIGUE MASK	BELT REMOVED →	FATIGUE STRAPS REMOVED →	POCKET GOING →	→
ANDRES (MAT)	FULL FATIGUE MASK				
MARIE (MAGGIE STEED)		DRESS SHOES	DRESS SHOES	BRA, KNICKERS PETTICOAT EARRINGS	
MARGARET (JUDY LLOYD)		BLOUSE - CHIFFON TIGHT SKIRT BELT, SLIPPERS			
DRUM MAJOR (SAM)		HIGH BOOTS DRESS UNIFORM HELMET MOUSTACHE	WITHOUT HELMET →		
BARKER (MAT)			BRA · CHECK SHIRT STAND COLLAR BOW TIE, SHOES WHIP, HAT LUREX SOCKS?		
SGT JUDY ?			DRESS UNIFORM		
CAPTAIN (ROBIN SOANS)					
DOCTOR SAM ?					
1st DRUNK (MAT)		LONG COAT ~			
2nd DRUNK ?					
KATHY (JUDY LLOYD)					

MALE CHARACTERS		
CHARACTER	ACTOR	COSTUME
MINISTER	TONY	SUIT, BOWLER
PORKER	TONY	BALD WIG, SUIT WITH SEE-THROUGH RAINCOAT
RICH PIGGE	LEWIS	SUIT, WAISTCOAT
TOAD CROAK	KEN	SUIT, BOWLER
RATMAN	ROBIN	HUNCHBACK COAT GLASSES, MITTENS, HAT
BERNIE FLAME	ROBIN	WELDING VISOR, GOGGLES BLACK ANORAK
MARLOWE (HUMP BOGART)	TONY	COAT, HAT,
Q. MASTER	KEN	CHECKED JACKET
CONTESTANT	ROBIN	BERNIE FLAME
2 40's FELLAS	KEN/LEWIS	OVERCOATS, WHITE SCARVES, ARMBANDS
		HAT OLOE SHIRT

Planning for a production
A simple chart showing the scenes of a show and all the characters (**left**) will enable the designer to see what costumes are required for each actor and where there are potential problems such as costume changes or actors playing two roles. A list of actors, characters and the details of each costume (**below**) provides another important planning guide.

reasons. If there are two designers, one for stage sets and one for costumes, they must work closely together, keeping in touch constantly and discussing ideas, colors and objectives.

Interpreting the play No two productions are the same so each play has to be carefully studied. Certain decisions have to be made, and this will involve detailed discussions with the director and stage manager as well as the set designer. These decisions will involve the budget available for costumes, the number of people available to make them and their equipment.

During these discussions as the play is read and thought about, ideas will be suggested, characters will be analyzed and the text interpreted as the production is shaped. The costume designer must explore all avenues and make sure he or she has all questions answered. Will the play be set in the time it was written? In which country will it be set? Will it be set in modern dress?

Having established the basic requirements of the play, the costume designer must then do some research. Using anything relevant for reference,

such as books, illustrations and magazine articles, the designer should search for inspiration and information which fits with his or her ideas about the play. Wonderful costumes have been inspired by a chance photograph discovered in an old magazine, for example.

If the play is set in a particular historical period, it is important to research the visual artists of that period. This will help in discovering the feel and style of dress of the period, particularly with reference to different social types. This is not often found by merely using text books on period costumes. However, it is important not to become a slave to historical detail, since this is both restricting and unnecessary. Reproducing costumes that are historically correct in every line and stitch will probably involve missing what could be said through the costumes about the life and personality of the characters and other significant aspects of the play and the production.

Planning with a chart Having steeped yourself in research and inspirational images of style and color, it is time to consider the practical details of the

Research and inspiration

Visual references provide not only information but are often a good source of inspiration. Books, paintings, postcards, magazines and museums will all assist the costume designer. Early photographs (**1**) and old fashion catalogs (**2**) are extremely useful. This fashion magazine (**3**) is from the 1950s. A late sixteenth century portrait (**4**) shows fashionable female costume and a painting of James I as a boy (**5**) depicts other clothes of the period. French formal dress worn in 1779 is shown in this fashion engraving (**6**), while a portrait of Lord Nelson (**7**) shows British naval uniforms of that period. Eighteenth century style, particularly in hats, is featured in this portrait of the novelist Fanny Burney (**8**).

4

5

6

7

8

1

2

3

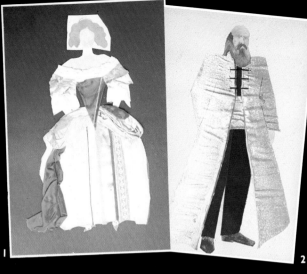

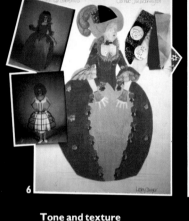

Presenting design ideas

The costume designer must put his or her ideas down on paper as soon as possible so that they can be discussed. Fine illustrations are not necessary but it is essential to convey ideas accurately to the set designer, director and actors. A face can be left blank (**1**), but if possible add some of the material to be used (**2**) to indicate texture. Simple color sketches (**3**, **4**) can be very effective, and combining two characters (**5**) shows how color tones will be matched. A full record of a costume may be useful for reference after the production. This will involve a detailed sketch of the design, material samples and a photograph of the actor wearing the costume (**6**).

Tone and texture

combinations Fabrics must be chosen carefully to ensure that there is harmony of tone and color on stage. They will also affect whether or not a particular character merges with other actors on stage or stands out. Choose fabrics together so that effects can be planned. The muted pastel shades of these samples (**right**) suggests a domestic interior, but the dark colors and woven textures (**far right**) indicate an outside scene. The women's dresses blend, but the bright red fabric contrasts with the dark blues, greens and blacks so the character wearing the red will stand out. The range of possible atmospheres, color contrasts, harmonies and blends is enormous and should be planned carefully in the early stages of costume design.

RICHARD CHISWICK (Home 603 8509)

Roles: Kantsky
Policeman
Wounded man
Group Leader
Kier Hardie

Needs 3 Costumes

Measurements:
Chest 41"
W 35"
IL 32"
Height 5'10"
Collar 16
Shoe 9½

① Policeman, 1887, Winter
Helmet
D.B. coat
Belt/truncheon
Boots

② Dark Gray Lounge suit with waistcoat
Shirt, stand collar + bow tie
Tweed type, covert coat
Black shoes
Square crown felt hat
Watch chain

③ Kier Hardie - As pictured
Reefer jacket D.B
Check trousers
Soft tweed peaked hat with ear flaps
Waistcoat
Grey shirt with collar, thick knotted tie
Watch chain
Black boots

Bloody Sunday - November 13th, 1887

Costume checklist For each actor, the costume designer should prepare a checklist showing the role or roles the actor is playing, the garments he or she will be wearing, the actor's measurements and number so that fittings can be arranged. In a London production of David Zane Mairowitz's *Landscape of Exile*, one actor had three costumes for his roles as a London policeman of 1887, as Kier Hardy the Labour politician and miners' leader, and various minor male roles. The costumes were realistic period dress. A photograph of Hardy was the basis for one outfit – a copy of his actual clothes (**left**). For the policeman's uniform, a newspaper cutting of 'Bloody Sunday' 1877 was referred to and, as an event related to the play, it was useful to the entire cast.

production. Drawing up a chart at this stage will make sure that all details are taken into account, and it is particularly important in a play involving many characters and scene changes. The chart should include all costume changes, time and place changes, the doubling of characters by one actor and so on. For instance, an interior scene may be followed by a scene outdoors in winter, so the characters may need coats. Some costume changes may be complicated. and have to be done very quickly. All such points should be charted, so that the designer can check the needs of each character and the progress of the play at a glance. Details are always important and never more so than in a small theater where the audience is close to the stage.

Design sketches Once all necessary information has been amassed, the ideas have been discussed and the details put on to a chart, it is time for the designs to be put on paper. Designers will all work differently in producing sketches of the costumes they propose. Some use a full painting with water-colors or acrylics, others merely produce pen drawings, and yet others may create complex collages incorporating the textiles and fabrics they intend to use. No method is better than any other and the designer does not have to draw perfect figures. The most important consideration is the use to which the sketches will be put. They must provide information for other people and accurately communicate the designer's ideas.

You must know exactly what your design entails as you work it out. Do you want a leather belt or a cloth sash? Are there buttons on the back of the costume? Where is the opening? Are the shoulders really to be that shape? These are not only the sort of questions you should ask yourself, but they are also the questions you must be able to answer for people looking at and working from the sketches.

The people who actually make the costume will use these sketches as a basis for their work so they must be right. The sketches are also important for the actors. The instinctive feel of a character that the

Interpreting the design

This dazzling chorus girl costume was created for the musical *Pal Joey*. The designer's sketch (**1**) was a pencil drawing with a watercolor wash. To this glitter and sequins were added. These, together with samples of fabrics to be used, gave a clear idea of how the final costume should look. The costume maker was given a similar sketch (**2**) annotated with detailed notes explaining the elements of the costume. Rough patterns were then drawn (**3**) as a guide to constructing the skirt. The outfit was in fact a simple one consisting of a body stocking decorated with sequins and glitter. A wide skirt of organdie and net, supported by buckram, was attached to a hip band decorated with fabric poppies. More poppies were attached on wires to the fabric turban. The final effect on stage (**5**) shows how closely the actual costume was to the initial sketch of the design. Designer's instructions for even the most complex looking headdresses are also quite simple. Again, a sketch of the design is done (**4**) with detailed notes of fabrics, trimmings and other materials to be used.

1

2

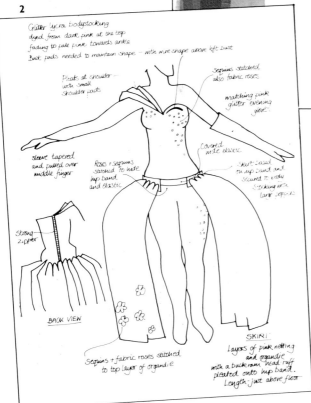

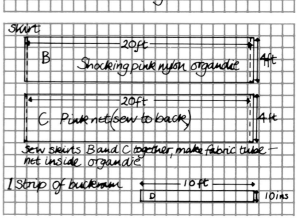

Glitter lycra bodystocking
dyed from dark pink at the top
fading to pale pink towards ankle
Bust pads needed to maintain shape – with wire shape above left bust

Pleats at shoulder with small shoulder pads

sequins stitched also fabric roses

matching pink glitter evening gloves

sleeve tapered and pulled over middle finger

Roses + sequins stitched to hide hip band and elastic

Covered wide elastic

Skirt cased on hip band and secured to body stocking with large poppies

Strong zipper

BACK VIEW

Sequins + fabric roses stitched to top layer of organdie

SKIRT

Layers of pink netting and organdie with a buckram head ruff pleated onto hip band. Length – just above floor

3

Hip Band

20
A
30
4ins

For dancer W 24ins
H 35ins

Cut in brocade, pink lining and interlining.

Skirt

20ft
B Shocking pink nylon organdie — 4ft

20ft
C Pink net (sew to back) — 4ft

Sew skirts Band C together, make fabric tube – net inside organdie

1 strip of buckram — 10ft —
D — 10ins

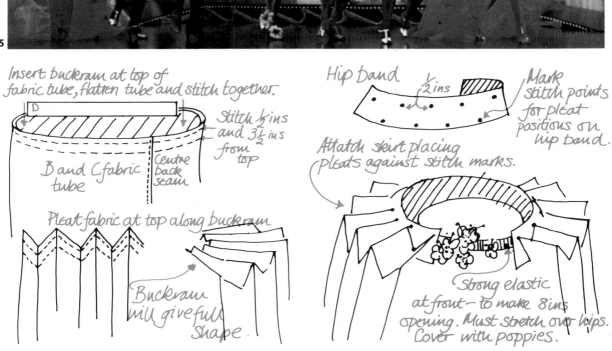

Insert buckram at top of fabric tube, flatten tube and stitch together.

B and C fabric tube

Centre back seam

Stitch 5ins and 3½ ins from top

Pleat fabric at top along buckram

Buckram will give full shape.

Hip band — ½ ins

Mark stitch points for pleat positions on hip band.

Attach skirt placing pleats against stitch marks.

Strong elastic at front — to make 8ins opening. Must stretch over hips. Cover with poppies.

115

COSTUME DESIGNER'S TASK PLAN

First stage: read the play • discuss the production with the director, stage manager and set designer • research the play

Second stage: draw up a planning chart for the whole play • draw up a character and costume chart for each actor • note all details which affect costumes • sketch designs • obtain fabric samples

Third stage: annotate sketches for construction and discuss costumes to be made with costume makers • supervize making of garments • search out free sources for accessories, trimmings and other costumes • hire any costumes as necessary • attend fitting sessions with actors • complete all costumes • attend dress rehearsal and organize any last minute alterations

costume designer portrays in a sketch is often a real help to the performer. The total effect, the line and flow of a costume are often difficult to put down in sketches, but they should not be overlooked. Back views and side views are valuable, as are fabric samples and notes. In fact, include anything that will provide information for the other members of the company when you are showing the designs.

During discussions about the sketches be prepared to make changes and remember that changes may be necessary at any stage of the production, right through rehearsals to the first night. Sometimes a play has to be designed before casting is completed, and concepts may change because of the actors who eventually get important parts. Occasionally a good costume idea will have to be thrown out because a certain performer cannot, or will not, wear it. Changes can include details that arise from the plot, such as a character requiring a cloak rather than a coat or needing extra large pockets in a jacket. Usually such changes can be easily coped with, but occasionally the basic concept of a design will require alterations and this can cause extreme aggravation for the designer. It is always worthwhile discussing and investigating the reasons for changes in case you do not agree with them or you find that a simple change can cause complex problems in other areas.

Always recognize the limitations imposed on designs by factors such as budget, helpers and skills available, as well as suitable space for building costumes and the level of enthusiasm of those you are working with. Spectacular images can be created on small budgets but this depends upon the skill and dedication of the designer and the makers. Not every play can or should be treated extravagantly or flamboyantly. The play's requirements are all important, and designers must use their judgement in not forcing a style of costume which does not suit the production and performance.

Cutting and sewing costumes
A skilled costume maker will measure out (**1**) and cut patterns from the designer's sketches. Alternatively, commercial paper patterns can be adapted for costumes. Linen roughs of garments are often useful and so are old costumes when unstitched and used as a guide. As with all tasks involved in costume making, the more skilled helpers available the better. The patterns are outlined in chalk on the fabric (**2**) and then cut out (**3**). These apparently simple tasks require great care.

3

4

Care and skill are also needed in sewing the costume. Hand sewing is often involved (**4**) whether for elaborate decorations or merely basting sections before machine sewing. An industrial sewing machine (**5**) is usually essential since domestic models are not always designed with the stitch strength required for making many costumes. A dressmaker's dummy (**6**) is useful for constructing and fitting garments, but the important fittings must be done with the actors who will wear the costumes on stage.

5

6

MAKING COSTUMES

Clearly a costume designer's skills and knowledge must go further than those of a dressmaker, yet it is essential that the designer understands the basic techniques of pattern cutting, sewing, using fabrics and other aspects of costume construction. Professional designers rely on the cutters and makers they are working with. Their particular skills and experience will often produce solutions to problems, so it is always worthwhile discussing methods with them. In the amateur theater, the costumes may be designed and made by one person. So bear in mind what you can achieve yourself!

A wide range of fabrics are available today including shiny plastics, clever imitations of fur or leather and sparkling cloth. The costume designer must understand fabrics and develop a sixth sense to appreciate what fabrics look like when made up, how they hang and whether they will crease and appear crumpled during performance. Consider too whether the costume will need to be particularly sturdy—does the actor have to move energetically or fight, for example. The costume should be designed to stand up to necessary wear and tear.

It is essential to show fabrics to the lighting designer. A fabric which appears dull could look radiant under certain theater lights, or the opposite may be true. Colors can also be affected by lights, for instance a lovely emerald green may look like a dirty olive on stage under certain colored lights.

If the right fabric cannot be found, the designer may decide to solve this, and achieve the right effect, by printing, painting and dyeing cloth. Appliqué can also be used to create certain effects, but all these methods involve extra work and expense. It is essential to take into consideration what can realistically be achieved.

In recent years, particularly in straight plays, there has been a tendency to assemble costumes from a wide range of sources. Markets, rummage sales and second hand stores can be searched to find just the right article of clothing or to find some element of a costume. Altering old clothes, adding to them, recutting and perhaps dyeing or painting them can result in impressive designs. Pieces of fabric can be patched together and unusual contrasts can be achieved if things such as old bedding or furnishing fabrics are used alongside metallic or plastic fabrics. Even historical periods can be effectively interpreted using this method. However, since it requires a great deal of work and enthusiasm, the same considerations apply as for creating complete costumes from original fabrics.

Renting or hiring costumes Many theaters have

Costume details

Painting fabric is often the most effective way of creating a pattern. The paint can be combined with glue and applied with a glue gun. This method was used to achieve the criss cross pattern on a garment (**1**). A striped bodice in green and yellow was given matching stockings by coloring a pair of white socks with felt tip pens (**2**). Clip-on studs provide a bold metal trimming for these black shoulder epaulettes (**3**). Many female period costumes require padding on the hips and a roll of fabric (**4**) is usually worn under the skirt for this.

Trimmings and decorations

Costume designers and makers should collect in one place anything which could be used to trim and decorate the outfits they create. Dressmaking departments in stores carry a wide range of ribbons, beading, feathers, lace, sequins and so on, and they can also be found as furnishing accessories. But such trimmings can be picked up less expensively in secondhand clothes stores, flea markets and rummage sales. Many of the trimmings shown here (**right**) are not standard costumiers' accessories but all of them can be highly effective on stage. Curtain rings and ring-pull can tops could be used for chain mail. Shells can be attached to garments if a small hole is drilled in them. Bamboo makes an interesting noise when hung on costumes and even dried pasta can be used. Many odds and ends such as net packaging for fruit, should be saved for trimming hats or adding a final touch to exotic creations.

good costume stores, and it is useful to contact their wardrobe departments in order to arrange a visit. Just the right costume or the perfect ostrich feather could be found there. If your company has a good reputation for looking after and returning borrowed costumes, the fee can be reasonable. Always check the fee in advance to make sure you do not exceed the budget.

There are, of course, large costume companies which provide for television and film productions as well as for the theater. They often have a sliding scale of charges and, the theater being the poorest and most akward customer, they may consider your requests too much trouble if your company is not well known. Obtaining costumes in this way can be more expensive than making them, but, if it is decided to use a costume company, make your arrangements as soon as possible since they usually require plenty of notice.

Renting or hiring costumes must be carefully supervised. It is not sufficient merely to provide measurements, period and color preferences. Time must be spent searching through the racks to find several possibilities for each actor and more than one company may have to be used. It is important to arrange for fittings to take place early on in the rehearsal schedule and at the premises of the

Fabrics that shine
Lighting can have a drastic effect on color and texture, particularly on satins, lurex, brocades, taffeta, shot silk and other reflective fabrics. If they are used, there must be close consultation with the lighting designer to ensure the right effect is achieved. The same fabric samples look quite different under different colored light. These samples were tested under white light (**right**), then under blue (**below**) and yellow (**below right**).

costume company. Try and make sure that the look you want can be achieved during the fitting. Take note of any alterations required or details which are not quite right.

Using your chart, make sure that each actor has everything needed for a performance, including accessories and costume details. A deep pocket may be required here, a large cloak there and bright yellow stockings for that last scene. After the fitting, discuss if anything is missing and any necessary alterations with the costume assistant so that any work can be finished for the collection date.

Rented costumes are particularly useful for certain period plays where the clothes required are difficult to find and expensive to tailor. However, try to avoid the final effect on stage appearing as if you have merely obtained a range of costumes of approximately the right period. Keep hold of a design style. This can be achieved by, say, choosing plain colors for all the basic costumes, but enhancing them with bright accessories, such as handkerchiefs, hats and shawls.

Accessories No costume is complete without the right accessories. Whatever they are, in whatever play, they are all important and should never be left until last or chosen by an inexperienced helper. Hats, shoes, gloves, sunglasses, jewels and much more can be used to suggest important aspects of a character and help to create an effective overall design.

It must be decided whether accessories are to be rented, found in shops or made by the company. Often, using imagination and skilled helpers, good and effective accessories can be made. For example, unusual and dramatic hats can be created but they will take time. Shoes are perhaps the most difficult of all accessories. Not only is it difficult to find the correct period shoe, but it is almost impossible to find it in the right size. Modern shoes can often look right or be adapted. It is very expensive to have footwear made to order.

COSTUME FITTINGS AND REHEARSALS

When the busy rehearsal schedule is arranged by the stage manager, make sure that time is put aside for fittings. Each actor should have two fittings of at least 20 minutes for each costume. These fittings are of great importance and are not, as many actors believe, merely to see how fetching a costume looks. They are to make sure, to the designer's satisfaction, that the line, shape, fit, coloring, details, hem lengths and so on are all correct. Discuss the

costume with the actors, answering any questions, such as details about quick changes or when they should wear, for instance, a hat or gloves. The designer must enable the actors to feel confident in their costumes, remembering that costumes are often blamed when things go wrong. Make the actors move in their costumes and perform any actions, such as stooping and stretching, that they are required to make. Dress rehearsals can be brought to a halt by actors shouting 'I cannot move in this costume'.

Also take the opportunity to discuss make-up and hairstyles during the fittings. If there is a make-up artist or wig maker in the company, make sure he or she is present. Any pictures which the designer has used for reference are invaluable to show performers how to do their hair and make-up. Wigs, false beards and sideburns have to be treated carefully by the designer, since actors have strong opinions about their appearance. When having wigs made, the designer should provide sketches showing front, side and back of the head and perhaps a photograph or picture reference as well.

Company practice with costumes may vary. For instance, especially in the United States, in some companies there may be a 'dress parade' some days before the dress rehearsal itself. For this all the actors parade in their costumes—but without make-up or wigs—in front of the director, so that any comments or criticisms from the director can be acted upon well in advance. The dress parade is often the time for a picture or photo call as well, to avoid interruptions at the dress rehearsals.

As the crucial dress rehearsal approaches, there will be inevitable late nights to finish costumes. Do not panic and do not give up. The first technical and dress rehearsal is usually long and chaotic so be prepared for problems and take detailed notes

Making hats and headdresses Designers and costume makers can create amusing and imaginative head gear using an abundant trimmings box and plenty of creative flair. This wonderfully colorful concoction (**1**) is a simple combination of satin, dyed feathers, ribbons, plastic bananas, a large fabric poppy and shiny fake fruit. A magnificent mask is easily achieved by painting a basic papier-mâché eye mask in white. The eye holes are then decorated with paint, sequins and exaggerated false eyelashes. An enormous glass jewel builds up the effect which finishes with a flourish of peacock feathers (**2**). A delightful dove motif (**3**) is made with a papier-mâché bird body. The wings and tail are fine white feathers and it is completed with a bright red painted beak and a sequin eye. It is all fixed to a white hat base. An old fashioned maroon hat (**4**) has been transformed by the addition of a carefully tied shot silk bow and beautiful pink feathers.

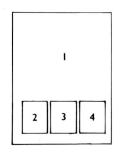

2

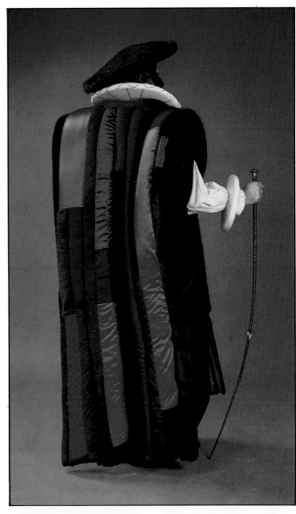

3

The style of the show

Designers face a new challenge with each production. Every show will have its own style demanding perhaps weird and wonderful costumes or everyday modern clothes. Basic principles will be decided with the director and set designer, with careful consideration to budget, equipment, time and skills available. Fantastic effects need not be difficult to create. The costume store could probably provide plain black trousers and full-sleeved white shirts. Two fantasy figures (**1**) have been created using them in conjunction with exotic animal masks, simple material ties and feather trimmed anklets. Another striking fantasy costume (**2**) is based on a painted red body stocking. A hand-held mask is topped with luxuriant feathers, and there are more feathers on the detachable collar. The bright skirt is

a wire frame covered in paper and decorated with paper shapes, paint, beads, feathers and tassels. This magnificent cloak (**3**) is a revamped standard cloak. Padded satin and fur applique strips have been sewn on and the wrist and collar ruffs are polystyrene cut-outs. When a formal male period outfit is required, the tailoring would exclude making it, so the costume would be hired (**4**). But a female period dress is easily sewn using a simple dirndl skirt, a lace trimmed blouse and wrap-over fabric shawl (**5**).

4

5

about your costumes from the audience seats. It is best to ignore remarks against the designs and do not allow yourself to be pressurized into making unnecessary changes at this time merely because someone does not like a particular costume or detail. Final rehearsals are a nerve-racking experience for everyone. It is vital to remain calm and constructive when dealing with problems.

At the end of a long day in rehearsal, there will be a list of things to be done which inevitably means more long hours in the work room. Make sure that the next day's schedule gives the costume department sufficient time to work on the costumes before they are required again. At the next rehearsal, more notes must be made from the auditorium but, hopefully, this list will be shorter. It is good to remember that many a costume to be worn in Act 2 has only been completed during Act 1 of the opening night. The designer will be working constantly until that first night is over.

If the show is a success, the critics will praise the leading actors and the director. Designers are rarely mentioned, and costumes are likely to be taken for granted by critics and audience alike. The majority of the public does not appreciate the skill and hard work that has gone into creating them. A designer must gain satisfaction from having a rewarding working relationship within a company, from being one of many who has contributed to an end result— a fine performance of the play.

Period costumes Recreating the dress of a particular historical period is perhaps the most usual challenge for a designer. However, the period used may not be that in which the play is set. In a recent production of *The Merchant of Venice*, modern dress was used (**1**) but it was carefully chosen. Portia's legal costume and the officer's uniform suggested the Venetian setting. The general atmosphere of the Renaissance was created in a production of *Hamlet* (**2**), but the costumes are not detailed replicas from the period. The mad and mourning Ophelia is in striking contrast to the couriers who surround her. Contrast is also important in this scene (**4**) from *All's Well That Ends Well*. The Edwardian setting is unusual as is the woman's dark formal dress while the men are in light summer suits. Two characters from Alexander Ostrovsky's *The Forest* (**3**) are both down on their luck yet show very different faces to the world through their costumes.

6

The use of masks Two traditional theater forms, ancient Greek tragedy and the *commedia dell'arte* of sixteenth century Italy, used masks as a dramatic device. Aeschylus' *The Oresteia* was first performed in 458 BC. A production appeared in London in 1981 at the National Theatre, with men playing female roles, as in the classical Greek theater. A unified and highly stylized effect was achieved through simple costumes, wigs and traditional full-face masks (**5**). The pale masks of the chorus in the foreground are very similar, highlighting their function as a group rather than individuals. Clytemnestra, in the orange dress, wears a red glove to indicate the blood she has shed in killing her husband. The influence of *commedia dell'arte* is clear in this production of Shakespeare's *Comedy of Errors* (**6**). The plot involves two sets of twins so the masks are a useful traditional device for adding confusion and creating doubles.

CHAPTER SEVEN

MAKE-UP

BASICS · EQUIPMENT · WHAT TO BUY

CHANGING THE FACE

STYLIZED AND FANTASTIC EFFECTS

STEP-BY-STEP APPLICATION

M ake-up is usually an essential aspect of most stage performances. Merely standing on a stage under bright lights has a drastic effect on a human face, and if that face is to express something to an audience it will require highlights and definition. The main purpose of make-up on stage is to make the actors look right to the public in the context of a particular production. Make-up is not a last minute consideration to be slapped on just before the curtain goes up. Each production will require a particular type of make-up, and it must be related to the various aspects of that production—the overall style of the show, the design of the sets and costumes, the characters being portrayed, the lighting and the size of the theater or space. Nowadays, actors may wear virtually no make-up in small studio theaters as the audience sits so close.

Most amateur groups will not have a make-up artist and often make-up will be applied by the actors themselves. It is a great help to performers if one person is able to take overall responsibility for the make-up on a production. That person can discuss the make-up with the director and designers and then explain to the actors how to achieve the right style and effect by simple means. The same person could help out before performances and check the finished faces. If a company takes the trouble to make sure that one person, it may be the director, set designer or even a stage hand, knows the fundamental skills of applying make-up, it will be very worthwhile and avoid the problems which arise from individual actors having complete control over their own make-up.

THE RIGHT MAKE-UP FOR THE SHOW

Make-up can range from the grotesquely heavy to none at all and still be right for a particular production. There are four basic types of make-up: straight, character, stylized and fantastic. Which of these is used depends completely on the show and the type of make-up will be decided upon as part of the show's overall style. A naturalistic interpretation of Chekhov's *Three Sisters*, set in nineteenth century Russia, will require straight make-up. A powerfully dramatic interpretation of Shakespeare's *Richard III* may require character make-up. If Gilbert and Sullivan's comic operetta *The Mikado* is being produced with traditional Japanese sets and costumes, a stylized make-up will be used in Japanese style. While, if a children's show features actors as animals, then a fantastic make-up would be appropriate.

The type of lighting and the size of the theater are important considerations once the general type of make-up has been decided. The basic effect of strong lighting and of looking onto a stage from a

Each production will require a certain style of make-up. The musical *Evita* (**1**) required quite heavy make-up to emphasize the characters' features. A simple, natural make-up was worn by English actress Helen Mirren (**2**) in a production of *Faith Healer.* The haggard face of *The Witch of Edmonton* (**3**) was created with heavy make-up, but the contorted and disfigured character of *The Elephant Man* (**4**) was depicted through the actor's expression and posture, without the help of make-up. In a famous scene from *King Lear* (**5**), the King's face has been aged and Gloucester's eyes are made-up to appear as if gouged out.

distance is to eliminate detail and fade colors on the face. In large theaters and opera houses, this effect is at its greatest so faces need to be made up in strong colors, and features should be strongly accentuated. The smaller and more intimate a theatrical space, the lighter and more natural the make-up should be.

STRAIGHT AND CHARACTER MAKE-UP

Straight make-up does not necessarily mean natural make-up. It should appear natural on stage, but achieving this can be more difficult than painting the face of a clown. A basic make-up will be applied to the whole face and throat. The actor's features must be defined so that they are clearly visible and can be expressive even to the back row of the audience.

Shading and highlighting are particularly important in character make-up, but they are often used in straight make-up. The actors may have to appear exhausted or unwell, or they may wish to improve a structural detail of their face by shortening a nose or strengthening a chin. Highlighting and shading will achieve this. Generally, in straight make-up, the actor's face is improved and heightened but not distorted or changed.

Character make-up may change the appearance of an actor considerably. It is used to show a particular type of person, so an evil character may have his or her eyes made to look close set, or a sad and humble character may be given a drooping expression with sad eyes and a forlorn mouth.

Character make-up is often used when a younger actor is playing an old person. Sagging skin, wrinkles, hollows and color changes must be applied through make-up using shading, highlights and lines. Another common use for this type of make-up is when a performer's features need to be changed to those of another nationality or race. The most common problem when doing this or ageing an actor is that a mere stereotype is produced. It is essential for the make-up to maintain an individual character and not produce a wooden appearance. People vary enormously no matter where they come from. Europeans from southern Italy look subtly different from Milanese. Chinese people have similar features to Eskimos, but they look nothing alike. If you are trying to make an Asian actor look French, merely applying light make-up and a jaunty beret will not be sufficient. While, if a young, red-haired Irish beauty is called upon to take the lead in *Hedda Gabler*, an ash blonde wig and heavy worry lines will

Basic make-up requirements The range of make-up shown here includes all the essential elements for creating a natural face on stage. These products will also be used for changing the features using shading and lines in order to age an actor or alter the face in other ways. It is not necessary to acquire everything shown, and once the basics are bought, add to them only as necessary.

not turn her into an overwrought Scandinavian woman. It would probably be better to leave her in a straight make-up.

When appying character make-up, it is always easier and more effective to adapt the features of a face, rather than set out to change them dramatically. A make-up that is painted against the natural structure of a face may look convincing if the face never moves, but as soon as the actor speaks or even smiles it will distort horribly. If you are ageing a face or altering it for a particular character type, consider carefully how the natural features would change if that person were older or infinitely evil. Where will wrinkles appear and sagging occur? Could the mouth successfully be adapted to an unpleasant

Three types of foundation or base are shown here – cream, cake and greasepaint. They can be combined, but it is usual to choose one of them. The number of tones required will depend on the production and this also applies to color sticks, eye pencils and so on. These products are from various manufacturers.

1 Remover oil
2 Cream make-up in foundation and other tones
3 Blending powder
4 Cleansing cream
5 Cake make-up in various tones
6 Greasepaint color sticks
7 Wand mascara
8 Cake mascara
9 Cream and cake liners
10 Greasepaint foundation sticks
11 Eye pencils
12 Rouge
13 Black greasepaint

MAKE-UP CHECKLIST

One person should always take responsibility for the make-up during a production and should do the following: discuss make-up requirements with the director and the designers • if a fantastic or stylized make-up is required, obtain sketches from the designer of the exact effects • make sure you have an adequate supply of make-up to cover both practice sessions and the performance run • buy any new products required • discuss make-up with each actor, working out precisely what is needed for his or her character • if any wigs, beards or hairpieces are to be hired, send the actors' measurements to the wig maker • organize practice sessions with the actors • pay particular attention to those who have to alter their features, particularly those involving false hair or nose putty • make sure that make-up areas are adequate and properly equipped • work out the time taken to apply make-up with each actor • help actors prepare for the dress rehearsal • note all necessary changes and explain them to the actors

sneer? The same applies to changing basic features. Most races have various types, so choose the one closest to the face being made-up. There are, for example, Japanese with high noses and long faces, as well as those with round faces and snub noses.

Research is important as well. If you are doing your own character make-up, look around you and constantly observe people. Watch how expressions change with emotion and see how a face ages or changes from one type of person to another. Use pictorial aids such as photographs of different races or portraits from the historical period in which your play is set. Always try and use faces that are basically like your own for research as this can aid you in adapting rather than changing your face. For

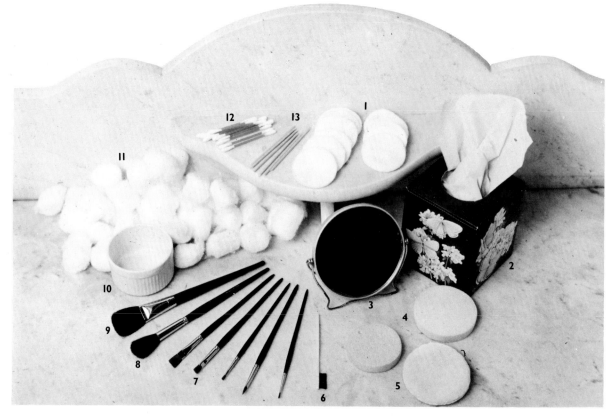

straight or character make-up, the audience should think how right the performers look in the roles, not what a wonderful make-up they are wearing.

STYLIZED AND FANTASTIC MAKE-UP

Clown make-up is perhaps the most well known form of stylized make-up used in the Western world. It is traditional and carries a message to the audience about the performers which goes beyond their particular role. Many traditional theater styles use stylized or fantastic type of make-up.

Stylized make-up is also used if a play's design, sets and costumes are intended to override individual characterization. In these cases, the actors' faces will be part of the design. The person who controls this type of design should also design the stylized make-up, as an integral part of his or her work. Actors will be given a very detailed brief on how their faces must look and the make-up process should be carefully controlled. Extra colors and types of make-up will be required from those needed to achieve straight or character faces.

Fantastic make-up goes even further than this and should also be controlled by a designer. It is used to create weird and wonderful faces, and it may have no relationship to the actual structure of a face. It is

Above Make-up equipment
1 Eye make-up remover pads
2 Paper tissues
3 Hand mirror
4 Cosmetic sponges
5 Velour powder puff
6 Mascara brush
7 Sable brushes: 1/8in (3mm) square ended and 2 Filbert for eye lining and fine detail; 6 Filbert for lips and eye shadow; 1/4in (6mm) and 3/8in (10mm) square endeds for blending
8 Rouge mop brush
9 Powder brush
10 Small bowl
11 Cotton wool balls
12 Cotton buds
13 Manicure sticks

A fully equipped dressing room may not be available but an adequate make-up area (**below**) is easily constructed. A large mirror with a work surface in front of it is essential. The face must be lit from the front so lights round the mirror arel needed.

difficult to apply, will require specialized products and, again, should be overseen by someone who knows what they want and how to achieve it.

In stylized and fantastic make-up, the design on a face must be bold enough to be seen clearly by an audience and should not come across as a meaningless mess of different colors and shapes. It must also be in complete harmony with the costumes and sets used in the production and should be approached as if applying a mask, so the actors should be prepared to lose their own identity behind it.

BASIC MAKE-UP AND EQUIPMENT

There is a great range of make-up products available, but, particularly for amateurs, it is definitely not necessary to buy more than the basic requirements and add to these for particular productions. Amateur companies should buy the absolute minimum to begin with, since make-up is expensive and easily wasted. Take advice from the professionals, if possible, and consider what the various trade name ranges have to offer. In the United States, Bob Kelly, Max Factor and Stein are the most popular makes. In Britain, Leichner and Max Factor are widely used and fairly easily available, but Bob Kelly and Kryolan are also well known. You may find it necessary to have products from different companies and to mix and match these.

Foundation In simple terms, there are two main types of base, a greasepaint or cream foundation, and a matt or cake type. Decide on one or the other since what you use as a base affects the rest of your requirements. Traditional greasepaint comes in sticks. More than one stick color is often required, since they may have to be blended together on the face. If you decide to use greasepaint, first select basic colors for foundations. When buying for a company, make sure you obtain colors suitable for fair, female complexions, for brunettes, and for men with florid and with fair complexions. Cream foundations come in basic shades and so do not require blending.

The most well known matt or cake make-up is Max Factor Pancake. It is probably the most simple base to use, but it cannot have other tones blended into it and the matt finish it gives can tend to obliterate details on a face. Again choose a basic color, or colors, to begin with.

Powder Powder will also be needed, and it is best to get a beige or honey beige tin of powder produced by the leading brands. This should suit both male and female make-up.

Eye make-up A selection of black and brown liners are always needed, greasepaint or standard eye-liners can be used. A basic shading for the eyes is achieved by mixing dark blue and dark carmine, and again these can be bought in greasepaint or liner colors. The eyes will also need black or brown mascara, and a white liner may be needed for productions in large theaters.

Mouth and cheeks If you are using a greasepaint or cream base, a carmine color in the same range will be needed for lips and cheeks. A moist rouge, available in several ranges, is a good product for lips and cheeks.

Shading and highlighting For a greasepaint or cream base, the best shaders are darker colors, even sometimes a greenish shade. Highlights are best done with light colors. Cake make-up in dark colors should be used for shading under a pancake base, choose one suitable for men, and another for

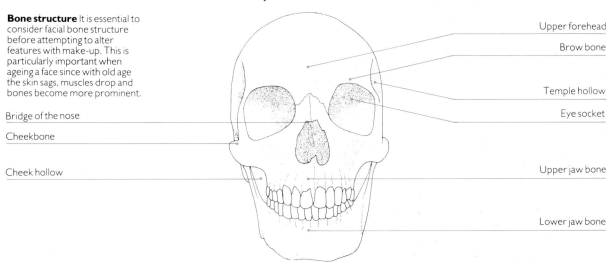

Bone structure It is essential to consider facial bone structure before attempting to alter features with make-up. This is particularly important when ageing a face since with old age the skin sags, muscles drop and bones become more prominent.

Bridge of the nose

Cheekbone

Cheek hollow

Upper forehead

Brow bone

Temple hollow

Eye socket

Upper jaw bone

Lower jaw bone

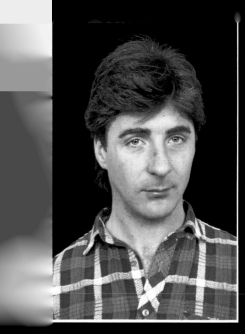

Straight make-up 1. To make the face appear natural as it will be seen by the audience in a large theater, the features should be given more emphasis with carefully judged make-up. It may also be appropriate to alter a particular feature. Study the face before starting to make up. Here, for example, the eyebrows are heavy and curve downward so these can be reshaped.

2. Dab the whole face with a flesh-tone stick of foundation and smooth it evenly right up to the hairline and down the neck. Apply light flesh tone to the outer side of each eyebrow to disguise the shape. Go over this with a red-brown make-up stick and stroke the same color under the eye and onto the cheekbones. Blend it in with the fingers and powder the face lightly.

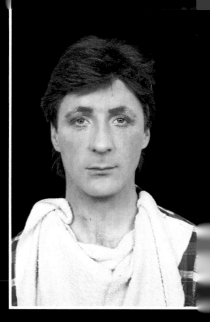

3. Apply deep pink and dark blue to the palm of one hand and mix the colours with the fingertips. Smooth the mixture over the eyelids, but not above the crease lines of the eye socket. With a fine brush, draw lines of black cream around the eyes, just outside the lashes. Draw the lines out toward the eyebrows. Correct the lines if necessary by dabbing with a cotton bud.

4. Draw in the new shape of the eyebrows with black greasepaint, applied with the end of an orange stick. Use red-brown again to cover the disguised area. With the blunt end of the orange stick touch in the inner corners of the eyes with carmine and the outer corners with white. Apply a heavy layer of brownish-black mascara to the upper lashes of each eye.

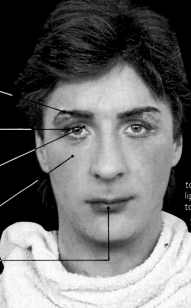

Eyebrow reshaped and browbone highlighted

Black grease eyeliner and mascara on upper lashes

Mauve-pink shading on eyelid

Brown-red cheek color

Lips shaped and reddened

5. For the final touches, redden the lips and outline the top lip finely in black. Apply pale highlight above the brows.

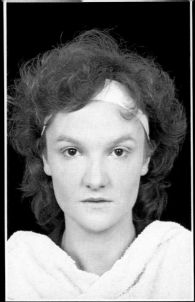

Straight make-up 1. Start by making sure the face is completely cleansed of ordinary make-up. Look carefully to see whether any correction should be made to the features. In this case, a little corrective shaping can be applied to emphasize the bone structure and narrow the face. Again, the following make-up technique gives a natural appearance in a fairly large theater.

2. Apply stick make-up in a light flesh tone, smoothing it over the whole face and neck with the fingertips. Put brownish-red under the eyebrows and on the cheeks below the outer corners of the eyes. For corrective shading, mix deep red and dark green in the palm of one hand and blend the mixture down each side of the face and inward under the cheekbones. Dust lightly with powder.

3. Use a dark mixture of red and blue across the eyelids, blended softly with the fingertip up to the socket creases and out toward the brows at the outer corners. With a fine brush draw lines of black cream liner below the lower lashes and over the upper lashes, taking both lines just past the outer corners of the eyes.

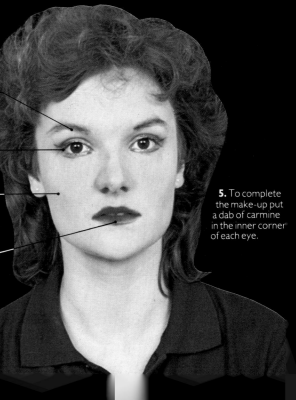

Eyebrows emphasized with black

Red on upper lids, eyes lined with black and upper lashes blackened

Corrective shaping with mixture of red and green make-up sticks

Carmine applied to the lips

5. To complete the make-up put a dab of carmine in the inner corner of each eye.

4. Emphasize the eyebrows with lines of black greasepaint. Pick up the grease on the tip of an orange stick and apply it with light, feathery strokes, not as a harsh line. Thicken the eyelashes with brownish-black mascara, applying two or three coats to the top lashes. Color the lips with carmine and blot them on a

FALSE HAIR AND NOSE PUTTY

Equipment There are various makes of nose putty which come in either lumps (**I**) or sticks (**2**). Some are softer than others, but all require softening between the fingers before using. Putty can be used for building up other parts of the face such as the chin or ears, but should, if possible, not be used for areas which move with speech or expression. For areas other than the nose, spirit gum should be applied to hold the putty in place.

False beards (**3**) are fragile and expensive so the less expensive and more flexible alternative of crepe hair is often used. Crepe hair is supplied in braids (**6**) which must be soaked and teased out before use. Spirit gum (**4**) fixes the beard to the face and a mild spirit gum remover (**5**) is also needed. In addition, a pair of sharp hair-cutting scissors are used for trimming false beards and cutting the crepe hair into sections. A linen towel is required.

Applying nose putty Using these sketches for reference (**below**), draw the profile of the nose and shade in the shape you require. Minor changes to the nose can make a significant difference to a face, and it is rarely necessary to use a lot of putty. It is important to be able to see the profile of the nose clearly so either use a triple dressing mirror or large hand mirrors with a wall mirror. Ensure the face is clean and completely free of grease before starting.

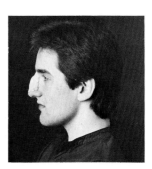

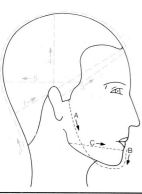

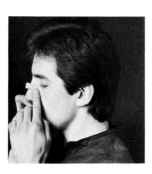

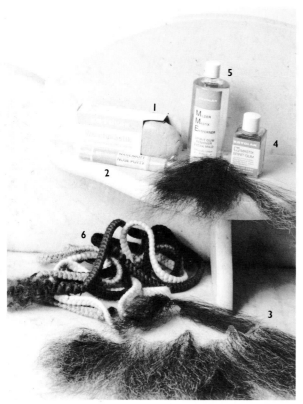

I. Cream your hands lightly before kneading the putty required between your fingers. It should be supple but not too soft. Put the putty on the part of the nose to be shaped and press it down firmly.

2. Referring to the sketch of the required shape, start to mold the putty. Use both hands to make sure the shaping is even and symmetrical. Build up the putty until the nose is roughly as required.

Accurate and detailed head measurements must be supplied to wigmakers when ordering wigs, hairpieces or false beards.

Wig measurements
I Circumference of head
2 Hairline to nape of neck
3 Ear to ear across forehead
4 Ear to ear across top of head
5 Temple to temple across back of head

Beard measurements
a Sideburn to sideburn under chin
b Lower lip to end of beard under chin
c Width of beard across jaw bone

3. Continuing to use both hands, squeeze and press the putty to the final shape. It is important to blend the edges smoothly against the skin so that the putty does not stand out.

4. Finally, apply a grease-based foundation. Lightly spread it over the putty with the fingertips, smoothing the surface and giving the nose a natural color.

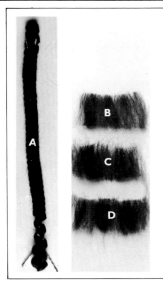
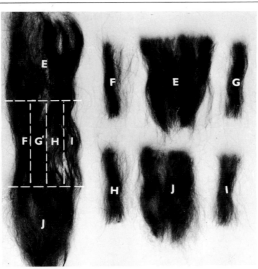

Using crepe hair This method of creating mustaches and beards is less expensive than using hair pieces, but it does require care and skill. The crepe hair braids (**A**) must first be soaked in water and teased out. This is done by combining the hair on the surface of the water. Blot the long piece of hair between two pieces of linen towel. When it is completely dry, divide it into sections (**left**) using sharp haircutting scissors. For a mustache only, three wide strips of hair (**B,C,D,**) are used. For a full beard, two large wads (**E,J**) and four strips (**F,G,H,I,**) are used with the mustache pieces. This step-by-step guide shows how to create a false mustache and a full false beard using crepe hair (**below**).

Mustache 1. Apply gum to the mustache area. Allow to dry. Paint a second light coat of gum just above the lip. Hold section (**B**) as shown, pulling down with the thumbs and pushing up with the fingers.

2. Gently press this section against the line of gum. Spread the hair with the fingers so that it twists out slightly. Press hair with a damp towel.

3. Paint a thin line of gum above the first section of hair and covering the ends of that section. Position section (**C**) in the same way as before. Then paint a final line of gum above this section.

4. Divide section (**D**) in two, holding one piece between each thumb and finger. Position the pieces just beneath each nostril and spread them out. Press with a damp towel. Allow to dry. Remove loose hairs and trim.

Full beard 5. Apply gum to the area to be bearded and allow to dry completely. Put a second light coat under the chin and position section (**E**) with the hair coming forward from the throat to the chin.

6. Lightly paint gum along the jaw line and position pieces (**F**) and (**G**). They should be in line with the first section and just touching it. Press with a damp towel.

7. Apply a light coating of gum along the jaw line and position pieces (**H**) and (**I**). They should in line with and just touching section (**F**) and (**G**). Press with a damp towel. Paint gum on the remaining area.

8 Position piece (**J**) below the mouth. Press with a damp cloth. Allow the whole beard to dry completely. Stroke the beard to combine the sections and remove any loose hair. Trim it with sharp hair-cutting scissors.

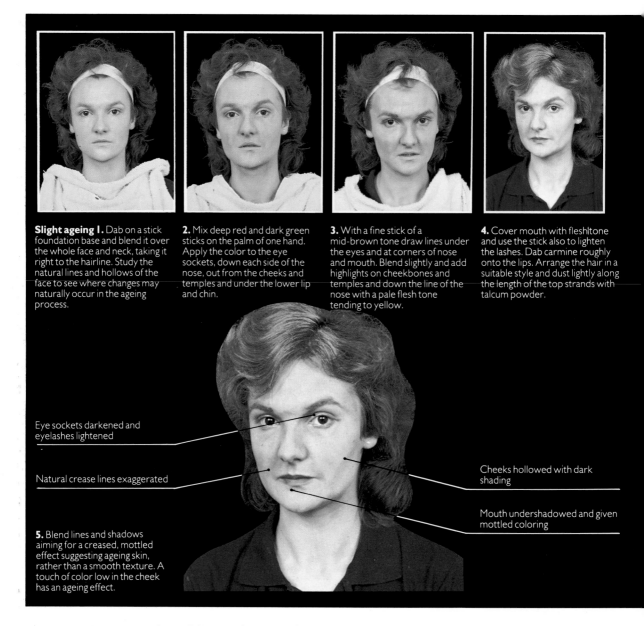

Slight ageing I. Dab on a stick foundation base and blend it over the whole face and neck, taking it right to the hairline. Study the natural lines and hollows of the face to see where changes may naturally occur in the ageing process.

2. Mix deep red and dark green sticks on the palm of one hand. Apply the color to the eye sockets, down each side of the nose, out from the cheeks and temples and under the lower lip and chin.

3. With a fine stick of a mid-brown tone draw lines under the eyes and at corners of nose and mouth. Blend slightly and add highlights on cheekbones and temples and down the line of the nose with a pale flesh tone tending to yellow.

4. Cover mouth with fleshltone and use the stick also to lighten the lashes. Dab carmine roughly onto the lips. Arrange the hair in a suitable style and dust lightly along the length of the top strands with talcum powder.

Eye sockets darkened and eyelashes lightened

Natural crease lines exaggerated

Cheeks hollowed with dark shading

Mouth undershadowed and given mottled coloring

5. Blend lines and shadows aiming for a creased, mottled effect suggesting ageing skin, rather than a smooth texture. A touch of color low in the cheek has an ageing effect.

women. Eyebrow pencils and liner colors are also used in shading.

Other requirements Make-up tables should conform to a traditional style but this need not be elaborate. A shelf about 18in (45cm) wide can be attached to a wall with a mirror behind it. One light should be placed at the top of the mirror or it can be lit all around. Very little equipment is needed but make sure that you have a selection of: 3 watercolor paintbrushes; large velour powder puffs (swansdown or lambswool puffs are unsuitable); orange sticks; cotton wool balls and tissues; small mirrors on stands; and cream or oil for removing make-up.

APPLYING MAKE-UP

Sitting in front of the make-up table, it is best to wear a robe or dressing gown and to have a towel over your lap to catch any powder which falls and to wipe your hands on. Keep tissues close by to clean hands and wipe away smudges. The face should be clean and the hair fixed back from the face.

Foundation If you are using greasepaint base, you may be blending two colors. Take the lighter stick and draw four good stripes across the forehead and down both cheeks, and two stripes down the sides of the nose. Then, if necessary, draw two stripes of

Heavy ageing I. Dab on flesh toned stick foundation make-up and smooth it over the face and neck with fingertips. Note the natural hollows of the face in temples, cheeks and chin and the lines of the neck.

2. With a stick of brownish-red, draw in bags under the eyes and hollows in the cheeks. Use deep red to emphasize creases in eye sockets, between nose and mouth and under the lower lip. Reinforce the shading with touches of dark blue.

3. Use a soft brownish-black pencil to make lines under the eyes and at the corners of the mouth. Highlight temples, nose, cheeks and chin with a pale flesh tone and lighten the eyebrows slightly. Make hollows and highlights in the neck also.

4. Touch in the lips with dark red, and with a brown make-up pencil reinforce the lines around mouth and nose. Hold up strands of hair and coat them down the length with a light gray powder.

Temples and bridge of nose hollowed with dark shading

Lines around nose exaggerated and flesh of cheeks highlighted

Creases around eyes drawn heavily in brown

Cheeks hollowed and given mottled colouring

Mouth barely emphasized but chin modelled with shadows and highlights

5. A heavily ageing make-up depends upon identifying every slight crease or dent in the flesh and emphasizing them with shadows and highlights.

the darker color between the lighter stripes. Spread the greasepaint over the face using both hands and blending the shades until an even texture and color is achieved. Avoid the hairline, but take the make-up down the neck where it fades into the natural skin color. How far down you take it depends upon the costume being worn. Adjust the color as necessary, using more of the light or dark sticks.

Wipe the hands clean and, using a darker color, rub a little on one of your fingers. Spread it along under each eyebrow and slightly over the end of the eyebrow, fading it down to the eye socket. With more of this make-up, shade in a shield shape on

the cheek, the center being below the outside of the eye and in a straight line horizontally with the top of the nostrils. Fade the edge of the color into the foundation with a clean finger.

Cake make-up is applied with a wet sponge which has most of the moisture squeezed from it. Wipe the sponge over the make-up and spread the color evenly over the face and neck to achieve a matt finish. Now apply rouge to the center of each cheek, about ¾in (2cm) on each side. Blend these with the foundation sponge, forming a shield or triangle shape. Dab the same colored rouge in a line under the eyebrows and smooth it with a light layer of

Creating Captain Shotover
Colin Blakely (**1**) played this role in London for the National Theatre's production of G.B. Shaw's *Heartbreak House*. A bald cap was applied and his nose was slightly altered (**2**). The actor painted wrinkles and age spots directly on to his skin (**3**). The full beard and back wig were positioned in layers (**4,5,6**). With very simple make-up, a small amount of putty and meticulous false hair, the actor has been transformed (**7**).

Hands Except for the most natural of make-ups, the hands must not be forgotten. An actor made-up as a farm worker cannot have smooth, manicured hands, while a wealthy aristocrat should not reveal tough, reddened hands. Hand make-up is also important when an actor has been made to look older. To age the hands, apply shadows and veins (**below**) using the same methods as for the face. Use cake foundation and pencils rather than greasepaint which rubs off.

foundation. The color should lie along the underside of the eyebrow and fade down the eye.

Shading and highlighting The basic uses of shading and highlighting are for improving on nature, changing the structure of the face to suit a special character or race, or changing the age group of the face. Basically, shading serves to recess the area over which it is applied while a highlight makes an area more prominent.

If you are using a greasepaint or cream base, then you will have greasepaint shaders. A muddy color which blends well with all flesh tones is achieved with a blend of two tones such as dark green and terracotta. Mix the two colors on the palm of the hand before applying and vary the intensity of the shading depending on how hollow you want the area to appear. Apply powder after shading.

If you are using a cake make-up base, shading

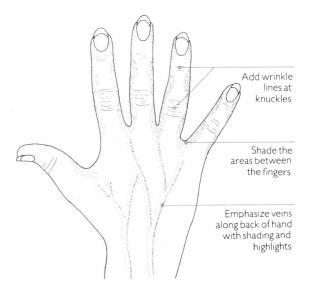

Add wrinkle lines at knuckles

Shade the areas between the fingers

Emphasize veins along back of hand with shading and highlights must be applied before the base. Dark colored shading colors are used and they should be applied with a brush and do not require shading in. Powder is applied over this before the base is put on. It is important to work in this order.

To slim or lengthen the face, shade lightly down both sides with heavier shading under the cheek bones. To shorten or widen the face, the hairline should be lowered either with the aid of a wig or by painting on a hairline below the natural one and filling it in with a color as close to the natural hair color as possible.

Noses can be altered with shading and highlighting. Shading along either side and highlighting along the center and down to the tip will lengthen the nose and make it narrower. To shorten a nose, shade the tip of the nose and apply highlight above this. To widen nostrils, highlight the widest portion of them, and, to make a large nose less prominent, paint it all in a slightly darker shade than the rest of the face.

Chins often require work. To emphasize a chin, quite heavy shading is used under the jawline, forming a diamond shape from the jawbone halfway down the neck. Do not make the shading too heavy, or it may look like a beard. A slightly receding chin can be strengthened by using highlight on the point of the chin. A strong jawline can be subdued by shading from under the cheek bones, down over the entire jaw and fading out on the line of the jawbone.

There are endless possibilities for shading and highlighting. In ageing a face, hollows are applied under the eyes and the skin should appear to sag below the cheek bones and into the neck. Bags under the eyes are best achieved by shading under the eye, drawing a line in a darker color around the actual shape of the bag, and then accentuating this with a corresponding highlight inside it.

Highlights should always complement shading, since on any face a hollow area is complemented by a protruding area. Highlights are usually applied last of all.

Eyes and eyebrows Begin with shading the eyelids, the basic color for this is a blend of blue and dark carmine. Rub the colors on the palm of your hand and blend them until a soft mauve results. With the same finger, spread it on the eyelids and slightly up and out from the end of the eye, shading the color as it goes. Men can wear gray, brown or carmine as an alternative, but they must be used with discretion. Women can use practically any color, but pale blue tends to look hard and green spiteful.

The next stage is drawing in the eye, which is done with a brush loaded with black or brown greasepaint, lining color or cake. Draw the brush across the make-up, making sure the brush comes to a fine point. Try it on your hand to make sure it is not too heavily loaded. Holding the brush at a right-angle, draw a fine line under the eye, starting below the inner corner of the eye and about ⅛in (3mm) below the roots of the eyelashes. Draw the line parallel until it reaches the lowest point of the eye, and then sweep slightly away and out, ending ¼in (6mm) from the corner of the eye and slightly below it. Repeat for the other eye. Load the brush again and draw a heavier line on the top of the eyelid, along the lashes and then curving up and out for about ⅓in (8mm) at the end of the eye.

To make eyes seem sunken from age, shade around the eye socket. Brown or gray are the best colors to use. To flatten recessed eyes, perhaps to make a face appear Oriental, use highlights in much the same way as you would shade to achieve sunken eyes. The shape of the eyes can be altered by varying the lines drawn around the eyes. To enlarge eyes, draw the lines further out from the end of the eye and draw the lower line further down. Narrow eyes by carrying lines well past the natural eye with the lower line painted close against the lower lashes. When lines have been extended out from the eyes, use a white dot in the outer corner of the eye.

Apply mascara thickly to the top lashes only, since there is no need for mascara on lower lashes when there is a line painted under the eye. To complete a basic eye make-up, place a tiny dot of carmine below the naturally pink inside corner of the eye with an orange stick. When the eyes are to be particularly bright, place a small white dot or triangle under the outer corner of the natural eye with an orange stick.

Basic eyebrow make-up involves applying black or brown greasepaint with an orange stick. Eyebrow pencil does not give the brows enough weight in a large theater. Draw the loaded stick along the top of the eyebrows with the point facing the tip of the nose. Bring the line slightly past the highest point, continuing out and down to just beyond the natural eyebrow. With light strokes of the stick, fill in this line to the thickness required. It is important that the eyebrow is painted along the line of the natural eyebrow and not separately above it, unless an exaggerated or unnatural effect is required. Eyebrows can be raised by blotting out all or part of the natural brow, and painting only the upper part of the natural eyebrow. Eyebrows can be emphasized by using heavier colors or by drawing them in a thicker shape.

Mouths To achieve a natural looking mouth, spread greasepaint darker than the foundation over the lips with a finger. Then apply a small dot of carmine to the lower lips and two dots of carmine to the upper

lips, and smooth them in. In a large theater, the lips can be emphasized with a lip or eyebrow pencil.

To diminish the size of a mouth, cover the lips with foundation and then paint in the mouth to the size required. Enlarge the mouth by painting it to the size required and outlining it strongly in carmine or black. A pouting effect can be achieved by putting a highlight in the center of the lower lip. A weak mouth is best achieved by painting a fairly large mouth without outlining it. Illness and age are best represented by pale mouths.

Stage make-up takes time to learn and understand so plenty of practice is essential so that you come to the point where you can achieve the various effects. Time spent experimenting will not be wasted, but do not choose to do it just before a performance. When you reach the dressing room, you should know precisely what make-up you are going to apply. But if you perfect a face for one production, do not make the mistake of automatically trying to use it again in the next. Each character has different traits which should be reflected in the make-up.

Any area of the body which is exposed on stage

Make-up for special effects
Stylized and fantastic make-up must be designed with careful consideration to the overall visual presentation of a production. When bright colors, glittering sparkles and other outstanding effects are used they should work in harmony with the colors and textures of the sets and costumes. There are many products available to create these effects.

1 Body make-up
2 Cake make-up
3 Black tooth enamel
4 False eyelashes
5 Glitter in various colors
6 Ugly false warts
7 Wet face make-up in bright colors
8 Fake blood
9 Color spray for hair

must be made up. Hands should be painted one or two shades lighter than the face. Remember that cake make-up is less likely to rub off on costumes than one of the more liquid varieties. Make-up may have to be used on other parts of the body and, in addition to cake, liquid body make-up is available in a variety of colors.

Practice as much as possible when creating a new character and always adjust make-up to the size of the theater. If you also make sure it serves to complement every other element of a production, your make-up will never look out of place.

Special effects make-up The styles of make-up demonstrated here are designed for use in a fairly large theater and may be modified and lightened for a smaller auditorium. This example shows a deliberately fanciful make-up for a sea-nymph, so the color and shaping are strong and unusual. First apply a smooth layer of foundation flesh tone. Add bold strokes of dark green sloping inwards under the cheek bones, down each side of the nose and up from the eyebrows.

Blend them lightly with finger tips and dust the face lightly with foundation powder. Make a strong dark blue line in the crease of each eye and blend the color over the lids (**left**). With a fine brush, outline the eyes with black cream liner, extending the lines from the outer corners. Highlight the inner corners with red and the outer with white, applied

carefully with an orange stick. Brush a heavy coating of brownish-black mascara onto the upper lashes. Apply black to the eyebrows with the stick, drawing them up into the forehead (**below left**). Finally, shape the lips with dark green, but not too heavily as opaque color deadens under strong stage lights (**below**).

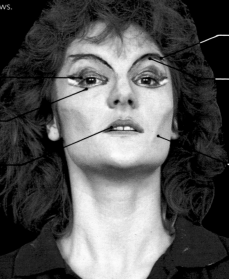

Blue shading on lid

Black liner and highlights round eyes

Mouth colored green

Eyebrows reshaped

Green under brow

Green shaping on cheek

Character make-up A character make-up, such as for an Arab man, may require a change of skin tone. The foundation color must be applied quite evenly before the individual features are created. Liberally dab on dark brown stick make-up and smooth it over the face right up to the hairline and down the neck (**right**). With the same stick darken the tone down each side of the nose, in the eye sockets and

under the eyes and cheek bones. Powder the face lightly. The powder will sink into the color though it may appear chalky at first. Paint lines around the eyes

with black cream, extending them slightly at the outer corners. Use a fine brush for the cream and then dab a red dot into the inner corner of each eye with the wooden end of the brush. Put in short white lines at the outer corners. Apply black mascara to the upper lashes (**below right**). Emphasize the eyebrows with black grease and highlight forehead, cheeks, chin and bridge of nose with flesh tone.

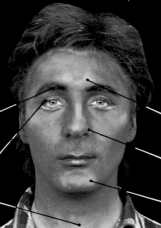

Eyebrows blackened

Eyes lined in black and eye sockets darkened

Skin tone extended down neck

Pale highlights on forehead

Sides of nose shaped

Highlights on chin

CHAPTER EIGHT

THE WORKSHOP

TOOLS AND MATERIALS

MAKING AND PAINTING FLATS

ROSTRA · SCENERY CONSTRUCTION

PLANNING THE WORKSHOP

There is no one ideal scenic workshop. The best workshop is the one most suited to the theater and the requirements of a particular group. The facilities needed will depend on the type and scale of the productions and, most importantly, the budget available for the workshop and scene construction.

BASIC REQUIREMENTS

Many amateur theater groups may not be able to have a permanent workshop area. However, if the group has a permanent base, it is a good idea to have an area which can be used regularly for scene construction. Obviously, a group which does several major productions in a year will have more need of a workshop area than one which only does one production a year. This section outlines some of the basic requirements for a permanent workshop area. Other requirements can be adjusted for the needs of a specific group.

The main requirement for a workshop is that it should allow smooth, efficient working. It should have a good firm workbench. The size of the workbench will be determined by the needs and resources of the group and the amount of space available. The bench should be firm enough to work at safely without being so heavy that it cannot be moved. It should also be possible to clear an area of floor space so that a large piece of scenery can be constructed flat. If possible, the workshop should have easy access to the stage with high, wide doors so that scenery can be moved without difficulty. The ceiling of the workshop area should be high enough to allow scenery to be stood upright for checking, painting and final touching up. If any large power tools are used, there should be a separate area for them, marked clearly on the floor. This is both for safety reasons and so that different types of work can proceed side by side. However, it is unusual for small amateur groups to have many large power tools.

When considering the exact layout of the workshop area, bear in mind the needs of your group and the type of production and scenery used. The workshop layout should allow for smooth efficient working, so think about the order in which work will be done. When constructing a flat, for example, the best order of work is usually to begin by cutting the timber to length from a list taken from the designer's working drawings. The timber should then be marked out for machining on a bench. Other pieces of wood, such as the supports and joints, should be machined. Finally fit the frame together on the workbench or floor. The flat should then be covered with canvas and painted. If the workshop is also being used for making props, consider the type of working area most suitable for the processes which are likely to be used and try to make allowances for them in the layout.

The set builder is the person who turns a designer's ideas into actual scenery. The sketches and models prepared for the proposed set must be carefully discussed so that the set builder can interpret them accurately and achieve the required effects on stage. Brilliant visual creations may look good on paper but they must be workable given the time, skills, personnel and resources available. If the scenery workshop (**left**) is to run efficiently it must be spacious, well-equipped and have good storage so that tools are not left to cause clutter and, perhaps, accidents.

TOOLS

A scenic workshop requires a selection of basic tools, most of which are also used for home repairs and do-it-yourself. Indeed, surprisingly little specialist equipment is required for scene construction. A basic selection of tools should include at least the following—hammers, mallets, screwdrivers, ratchet screw driver, cross-cut saw, rip saw, keyhole saw, plane, wood rasp and chisels. A brace and bit with a number of drills, as well as a hand drill, will also be useful. For measuring and squaring up, a square, ruler and measuring tapes are needed. Use a vise (vice) for holding materials firm: different models are best for wood and metal. Another useful tool is a craft knife for cutting and trimming.

Power tools make work much quicker, but some companies may not be able to afford them. A drill with a variety of bits and attachments, a sander, jigsaw and small circular saw make useful additions to the workshop's equipment. Other necessities include a selection of nails and screws, in a variety of sizes, and corrugated fasteners. Tapes, especially thick 'gaffer' tape and thinner insulating tape, are also invaluable.

MATERIALS

Scene construction requires only a few basic materials, most of which are readily available.

Timber Softwood is quite satisfactory for scene building. The most popular types are pine or deal. Hardwood is seldom used, especially by amateurs, except where there is a need for extra durability or strength in the scenery. When working with wood, remember that it tends to split along the grain, and so do not put in nails or screws in a straight line. This will help prevent the wood from splitting.

Plywood Plywood can be obtained in many sizes and forms varying from extremely thin to about 1in (25mm) in thickness. Plywood has none of the weaknesses associated with the grain of wood, and so it can be nailed or screwed close to the edge without fear of it splitting.

Blockboard Blockboard can be used instead of plywood where less strength is required. It can be obtained in the same sizes as plywood, but in fewer thicknesses, normally ½in (12mm), ¾in (18mm) and 1in (25mm).

Chipboard or masonite These types of board are not of much use to the scenic carpenter because they are brittle and cannot take heavy loads. They are best avoided by scene constructors.

Hardboard Hardboard is generally used for covering large areas, but it needs more support than the equivalent size of plywood. It tends to warp and is usually heavier than plywood.

Adhesives Adhesives can be very useful. They tend not to be used if the scenery is constructed with mortice and tenon joints, but can be useful for adding strength to the simpler types of joint preferred by most amateur companies. One type of adhesive used in the theatrical workshop is animal glue, which can be used for applying covering materials to frames and joints. Contact glues make a strong bond as soon as the two glue-covered surfaces are placed together and can be very useful for repairs. However, PVA—polyvinyl acetate—is the most widely used adhesive in scenery construction today. It can be used for many purposes including strengthening joints and attaching canvas to flats. It is extremely versatile. Epoxy glue is useful for quick, small-scale repairs, but is too expensive for other applications.

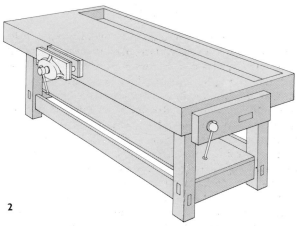

2

Workshop equipment Perhaps the most important piece of equipment in any workshop is a solid, large work bench (**2**) of comfortable height. The bench should be fitted with a vise and a bench screw, so wood can be held firmly as it is sawn, drilled or carved. A low platform underneath the bench provides a useful area of storage space. Nails, screws and tacks often spill and spread over a work surface. A simple magnet on a string (**3**) will collect them efficiently.

3

The tools required in a workshop will, of course, depend on the scale of the productions staged by the company. It is obviously best to have as many sophisticated power tools as can be afforded. But most amateur groups will find they can build the sets their company requires with basic workshop equipment (**1**):

Electric saw
Crosscut saw
Electric drill
G-clamp
Tenon saw
Square
Ratchet screwdriver
Standard screwdriver
Hammer
Crosshead screwdriver
Wood chisels – used with mallets
Folding rule
Hinge bar clamp
Pincers

JOINTS

The type of joint used when constructing scenery is extremely important. The strongest joint is the mortice and tenon. However, this requires fairly complex machining, so a simpler type will be perfectly adequate for most amateur purposes. One popular method uses corrugated fasteners strengthened by thin plywood plates. This provides an adequate joint and is simple to construct.

SCENERY CONSTRUCTION

Scene carpentry is not simply the application of ordinary carpentry to scene construction, it is a craft in itself. Among the special considerations for the scene builder are that the scenery must be capable of being assembled and struck—removed from the stage—very quickly. Remember the scenery is never seen at close quarters and usually only one face is seen by the audience. A final important consideration is that most scenery is only used for a comparatively short period.

Before embarking on scene construction, consider the order in which different pieces of scenery will be needed by the director, crew and cast. For instance, practical pieces, such as doors or windows which have to open, should be made as early as possible so that they can be used by actors during rehearsals. Pieces of scenery which require elaborate painting should also be constructed early. Flats which are to be flown—lowered into position from above—should be hung when the stage is clear of any other scenery, so try to hang them before the main fit-up. Keep the easily built pieces for last. Remember also that scenery used in rehearsal may need to be

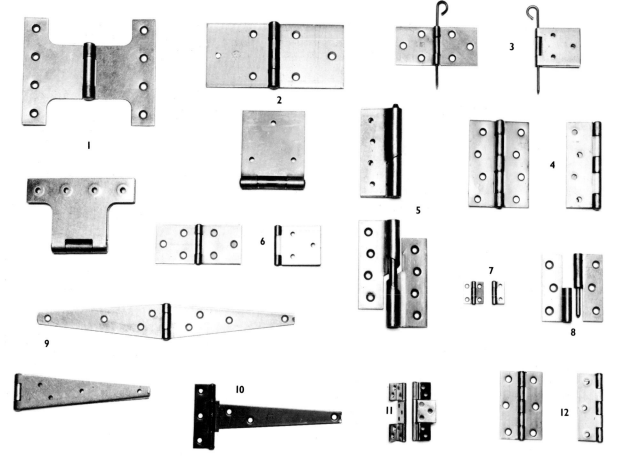

Hinges and hardware I h
hinges (**above**) are those m
often used in set building:

 1 Parliament hinge
 2 3 in (77 mm) back flap hinge
 3 1 ¾ in (44 mm) back flap hinge
    with loose pin
 4 4 in (102 mm) butt hinge
 5 Rising butt
 6 1 ¾ in (44 mm) back flap hinge
 7 1 in (26 mm) butt hinge
 8 Loose or lift-off hinge
 9 Strap hinge
10 T-hinge
11 Cabinet hinge
12 3 in (77 mm) butt hinge

Other hardware for making and
joining scenery includes:

13 Barrel bolt
14 Grommet
15 Pelmet clip and sleeve
16 Corner bracket
17 Corner plate
18 Cleat
19 Bolt with wing nut and plate
20 Flushing plate for flats
21 Screw eye
22 Screws
23 Hasp
24 Heavy duty castor
25 Nails
26 Corrugated fasteners
27 Tacks

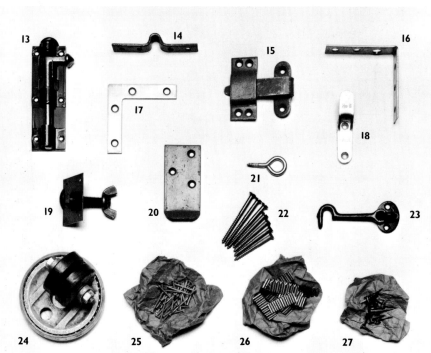

repaired or repainted before the first night. Careful planning is an important factor in scene construction, as it is in all other aspects of theatrical production, both professional and amateur.

FLATS

Flats are the most fundamental unit of scenery. About three-quarters of constructed scenery consists of flats in varying combinations. The frames for flats must be constructed to hold their shape, and to be reasonably strong, as they may need to be used several times. Flats can easily be repainted to suit different types of show.

Flats should also be portable and as light as possible. As flats are normally held firmly in position, usually by braces, they can be made from the cheaper varieties of softwood. Estimate carefully from accurate drawings the amount of wood which will be required in order to minimize waste. Work out how many long pieces of wood are needed and see whether all the shorter lengths can be cut from one piece. When the wood is cut, mark the faces and lay the pieces on the floor so that the measurements can be checked. Then join the frame together, working around the outside first. When the frame is complete, cover it with canvas. Finally the flat should be checked for accuracy once more, as it is much more difficult to rectify errors once the whole set is in position.

The size of flat required for a production depends

SET BUILDER'S TASK PLAN

First stage: meet with the set designer at the earliest possible stage • discuss the proposed set in detail • concentrate on any difficult construction requirements and work out immediately if they can be done given the skills, workforce, tools and finance available • check that proposed scenery can be built in workshop space • check that all tools and equipment required are available and buy any that are not • discuss the materials to be used, not only woods but also paints, trimmings and decorations • ensure that the effects required by the designer can be achieved • buy any materials needed with the designer • work out the schedule for the construction

Second stage: when construction starts, build the most complicated pieces first since they are most likely to take time and cause problems • next build any pieces which are practical on stage, such as opening doors • try and see if existing scenery, such as flats, can be revamped in order to save time and money • regularly check that work is progressing on schedule • demand extra help if necessary • ensure that the set designer checks scenery to see if end results are as required

Third stage: as scenery completed, check all flats, rostra, scenery and props built in the workshop will fit on the stage • ensure all angles are correct from the auditorium • check that any moving parts or moving scenery works correctly • make sure actors can move round the set • make sure it is steady • attend technical rehearsal and prepare for alterations and repairs • retouch scenery and make final adjustments

Woodwork joints The joint used when building scenery depends on how strong it has to be. Half lap and butt joints are the most commonly used but others may be required (**below**).

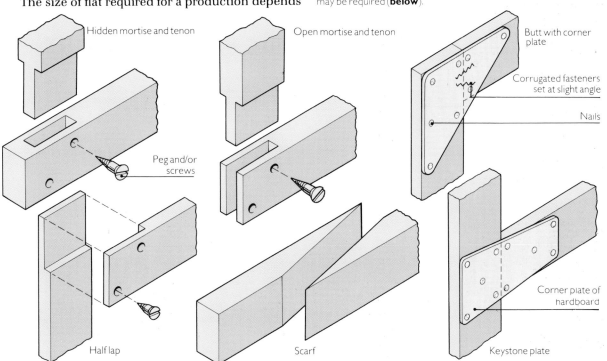

Hidden mortise and tenon

Open mortise and tenon

Butt with corner plate

Corrugated fasteners set at slight angle

Nails

Peg and/or screws

Corner plate of hardboard

Half lap

Scarf

Keystone plate

Scenery flats Traditional scenery flats remain the most versatile unit in constructing a set. Flats are wooden frames covered with canvas and are relatively easy to build. Flats can be built in a wide variety of sizes and with open areas, as these drawings show (**right**). This enables doors, windows, fireplaces, and other openings to be built into the set. The window flat (**far right**) shows the standard terms used to describe the basic components of a flat.

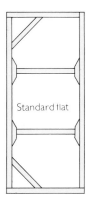
Standard flat

Door

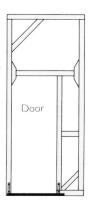
Door

Fireplace

Window

Making a flat 1. From the set sketch or technical drawing, work out the amount of wood required.

2. Mark out the lengths of wood carefully. Try to be economical, cutting short pieces from one length, for instance.

3. Cut the wood to length and square up the ends. Keep the wood steady in a bench hook and use a square to check the 90° angle.

4. Mark the positions of the pieces – head (top), sill (bottom) and style (side). Mark the face (or front) of each piece too.

6. Beginning with one corner, check that it is square and then join with corrugated fasteners. Nail in the fasteners at a slight angle. Repeat for each corner,

working your way round the outside of the flat. This creates the basic framework of the flat.

7. Repeat the process for the middle pieces, working round the outside first. Check the squareness of the corners carefully.

8. Make corner plates from thin plywood measuring about 8-9in (20-22cm). Position at the first corner and draw round the edge.

12. Work round the outside corners and then the inside corners. Position the window plates so that they do not obscure the opening.

13. When all the plates are in position, the basic frame is ready. When nailing the plates, take care not to put the nails in straight lines as this will simply

split the wood along the grain. The nails should be slightly longer than the width of the wood.

14. Turn the frame over and support on trestles. Place a piece of steel behind the wood and hammer the ends of the nails back.

Window

Door

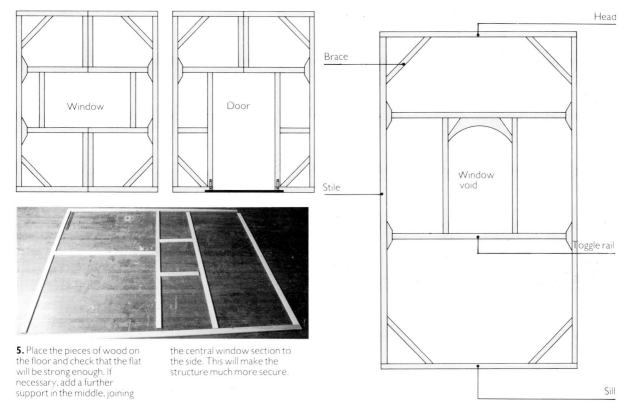

Head

Brace

Stile

Window void

Toggle rail

Sill

5. Place the pieces of wood on the floor and check that the flat will be strong enough. If necessary, add a further support in the middle, joining the central window section to the side. This will make the structure much more secure.

9. Spread PVA glue liberally inside the marked area. Take care not to put any outside the pencil lines.

10. Put the corner plate in position, rubbing it slightly in the glue to make sure the glue adheres well to both faces. Before the glue has dried, check once more that the corner angle is square. Use a combination square for this.

11. Using cement coated nails for added grip, nail the plate in position. Put the first nails at the corners. Use about 15 nails per plate.

15. This strengthens the joint considerably. Repeat for all external and then internal corners. The joint, often humorously called a 'dog and biscuit' joint, is now complete. Note the dovetailed angle of the fasteners and the pattern of the flattened nails.

16. Plane any rough edges and the outer corner of the wood so that the canvas does not catch in any splinters.

17. Cut four supporting corner braces to size, check the corners are square. Nail and then screw the brace in position.

Canvassing a flat 1. Measure the canvas, cut to size. Lay one piece on the frame. Tack each end and then tack from the middle.

2. Place the second piece over lapping the first by about 1-1½in (2.5-3cm). Tack as before, but do not tack the two pieces together.

3. The canvas should be pulled fairly taut, but not too tight. The overlap, two rows of tacks and gap between can be seen.

4. Lift the two canvas edges and paint PVA glue liberally to the wood. Smooth one edge of canvas down onto the wood.

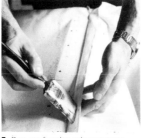

5. Repeat for the other canvas edge. Do not make the canvas too wet with glue. Press the canvas firmly down on top of the first layer.

6. With a craft knife, slit the layers of canvas in a straight line between the two rows of tacks.

7. Remove first the top strip of canvas and then the bottom strip. Apply more glue to the join.

8. Once more smooth down the edges. The two pieces of canvas should now meet. This is a knife joint.

9. Tack around the outer edge of the window frame, working from the middle as before. Ensure there is a tack at each corner.

10. Carefully cut the canvas at the corners. Use a craft knife which will produce a smooth, sharp cut.

11. Cut around the window opening so that the canvas overlaps the wooden frame by about ½-¾in (1.5cm).

12. Fold the canvas back and apply glue to the frame as before. Only put a little at the bottom edge.

13. Smooth the canvas down as before with a piece of canvas. Make sure there are no wrinkles in the canvas.

14. Pay attention to the corners. Put a tack on each side of the corner. Repeat for all the others to strengthen the join.

15. Trim the canvas along the edge of the window opening about ⅛in (3mm) from the edge. Use your thumb as a guide.

16. Now tackle the edges. Pull the canvas taut. Work from the inside out, smoothing at the same time. Tack near the inside of the frame.

17. Repeat for each side, working from the middle of each side to the edge to avoid wrinkles. Fold canvas neatly back around the edge.

18. Paint glue quickly around the edge so that it does not dry. Smooth the canvas down working toward the edge to avoid wrinkles.

19. Put in corner nails to strengthen the corners. The canvas should not be too tight, as painting will tend to make it shrink slightly.

20. With a craft knife, clip across the corner of the canvas leaving the wood exposed. This helps prevent damage to the canvas.

21. Using your thumb as a guide, trim the canvas about ⅛in (3mm) from the edge with a craft knife. A wooden edge is stronger than canvas.

22. This shows the gap between the canvas and edge of the wood, and the corner nails. Flats can be reused, so make them fairly durable.

The finished flat now awaits painting or other finishing (**24**). When viewed from the back (**23**) the details of construction can be seen. Here, an off-center window has been built into the flat. In order for the flat to stand upright it requires a brace. Two main types are used. The adjustable length brace (**25**) is hooked into a screw eye on the flat and either weighted with a special stage weight (as here) or screwed into the floor with stage screws. A French brace (**26**) is hinged to the flat and then weighted. The adjustable hinge which attaches it

must be positioned correctly to avoid movement and noise. The hinge is shown here (**27**) in the wrong position and also in the correct position (**28**). Flats can also be cleated together to ensure a close fit and greater stability.

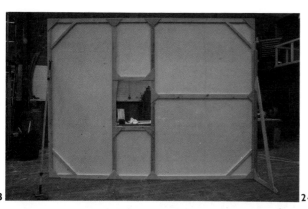

23

24

25

26

27

28

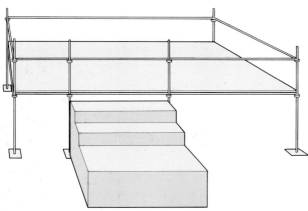

on the size and height of the stage area. For most stages, flats measuring approximately 6 feet (2 meters) by 12 feet (4 meters) will be sufficient, although it is possible to use flats measuring up to 8 feet (2.5 meters) by 24 feet (7.4 meters). When a long run of flats is required, multiples of single flats may be joined together. In addition to single flats, book flats are often used. As its name suggests, a book flat can be folded. The two pieces are hinged, so it will stand independently and is easy to store. This type of flat is also called a double or a two-fold flat. If a further element is added to the flat, it can be called a three-fold.

Flats can also be constructed with windows, doors and other openings in them. In such cases, the frame should extend around the opening for strength. Wings are flats traditionally positioned to mask the offstage areas. Set pieces are isolated pieces of scenery such as trees, towers or fences which stand free of the rest of the scenery. Profile flats have irregular edges illustrating, for example, foliage or rock formations. On a profile flat, it is best to have no more than 6–8in (15–20cm) projecting beyond the frame, otherwise the piece is easily damaged accidentally.

Where flats are fitted with doors, they normally are hinged on the upstage side and open offstage. However, particular shows may have their own requirements. This means that only one side of the door needs to be painted. If the budget allows, cheap paneled doors or sash windows may provide a quicker solution than trying to make such complex constructions. Books on bookshelves can be imitated by sticking the spines of books onto plywood cut to fit the shelf. Painting the background in a dark color helps create an illusion of three-dimensionality. Fireplaces are mounted into an opening in a flat with a space allowed for a simulated fire or basket of logs. The mantelpiece or other features should be mounted on the front.

The three-dimensional effects of ceiling or other moldings are now less common in the theater than they once were. However, the basic principle is to select and emphasize a few salient architectural details which will carry to the audience in order to create an overall impression of detail. Shadows and highlights can greatly increase the effectiveness of such devices.

Repairs Tears in flats can be repaired with patches. Make sure that the materials used for patching are the same as those already on the flat. For instance, patch new canvas with new canvas and painted canvas with painted canvas. Patching with different materials causes puckering and sagging. Cut a patch larger than the tear and trim the corners. Apply

Raising the acting area Set designs will often incorporate varying levels within the acting area. These are usually created with either wooden rostra or with scaffolding. The use of scaffolding (**above**) has become more usual in recent years and many varieties can be bought or hired. Scaffolding provides a strong foundation on which to place boards and is highly flexible. It was used here (**right**) for a balcony set. In a production of Christopher Marlowe's *Doctor Faustus*, a two level entrance was created (**below**) and used to great effect.

Wooden rostra constructions

Rostra are used for low level platforms and for audience seating. Even a slight change of level can affect the dramatic impact of both the set and the actors' positions on stage. This can be seen on this simple set (**1**). Very low units can be built from inexpensive board. If a company regularly uses one theater or space, it is worth creating a modular system of rostra which will provide both multi-level seating and scenery.

1

2

This basic rostrum (**2**) was built with a solid top and strengthened corner pieces to ensure stability. A view of the underside (**3**) also shows how it has been hinged so that it folds for easy handling and storage. Building stepped rostra requires great attention to perspective to ensure that the correct angles are achieved. This set of steps (**4**) appear uneven and lopsided but on a flat stage they will look correct from the audience's viewpoint. An underside view (**5**) shows the simple but sturdy construction of the steps. It is not usually possible to make steps fold since they need to be comp etely rigid.

3

4

5

A folding platform (**6**) is a particularly versatile piece of scenery, and can form part of a modular system. The hinges must be fitted with care (**7**) to ensure not only that it folds correctly but also that it stands firmly. This frame has a flat top, shown here from the underside (**8**). Locating blocks have been fixed to each corner and in line with the central gate of the platform to aid stability. Triangular rostra and ramps can be constructed in the same way.

6

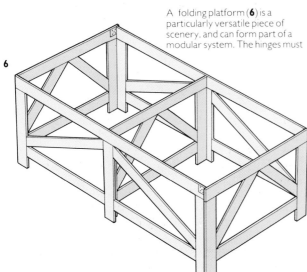

7

8

Building props and set pieces

Two dimensional cut-outs can be used very effectively in certain productions. This low budget show (**right**) used cut-out sheep and soldiers which worked well on stage and helped get over the problem of having only a small cast.

With skill and imagination, low budget productions can be given spectacular sets. For this production of Jean Moliere's *Scapin* (**left**) an ornamental pond was created on stage. The surround was cast in plaster by a member of the group, the bust was borrowed and the pillars were faced with corrugated cardboard. Hired plants completed the effect. Water can be used on stage provided it is placed in a secure container and does not come into contact with any electrical equipment or wiring. Remember also that it will have to be changed if the run is a long one. Fountains can be used on stage and are made from pumps and hoses found in any garden suppliers.

Masks can be used for both props and as costume accessories. They are not difficult to make but the painting and decorating should be done with care. Papier mâché masks (**left**) are styled over a clay model head. The result is a rigid mask which can hold decorations such as feathers, beads and false hair. A lighter mask, which is soft and stretching, and fits close to the face, can be made from rubber latex (**right**). A plaster mold is required and the liquid latex is poured into this. The more latex used, and the longer it is left in the mold, the thicker the mask will be.

1

2

3

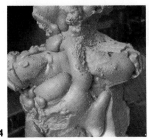

4

5

6

7

8

9

Making props Polyurethane foam is becoming a popular medium for prop making in amateur companies. It is suitable for large props, being both versatile to work and very light when set. The prop maker works from a sketch and a crude wooden core of the prop (**1**). There are two different component fluids from which the foam is formed (**2**). They must be kept in separate tins, and do not muddle the lids. Measure out an equal quantity of each liquid, and mix them together in an old tin. Stir thoroughly, and a malleable brown foam will start to form. This can be applied directly to the wooden core of the prop or spooned into a mold (**3**). Once mixed up, it will harden in approximately five minutes. It is better to apply more foam than appears necessary for the end result, as it is easier to rasp away any excess than it is to fill in gaps (**4**). Do not try to shape the foam before it sets, as it will become stringy. Rasp the prop into shape being careful not to remove too much foam (**5**). A surprising amount of detail can be achieved at this stage. Sand the prop down evenly and remove any loose crumbs of foam (**6**). Bind muslin onto the finished object with PVA for a smooth hard finish (**7**). Paint and varnish the foam prop as required (**8**). To make props such as this candlestick look old, the crevices can be painted black. The finished candlestick (**9**) looks both impressive and authentic, but is light to lift and could be made in a single day. Some of the carving has been emphasized with gold paint. Detail, made with other materials such as tubing or ping pong balls, could also be glued on.

Cutting and joining expanded polystyrene
1. Mark the block with a felt tip pen. Cut the sections needed along the mark with a hot-wire cutter.

2. To shape a curve, cut off surplus with a saw or hot wire and use a surform to round off the edges and corners.

3. Apply a latex-based adhesive to the faces which are to be joined.. Press the glued surfaces together.

4. Many types of finish are possible. Here a wood glue mixed with acrylic pigment and sawdust is used. Two coats are needed. Sand when dry.

155

PAINTING SCENERY

Flats are painted with a mixture of paint and glue, called size. This ensures that paint pigment does not rub off and also provides a good base for subsequent painting or texturing of the flats. The basic size mixture consists of two cups of glue added to ten quarts of water. Paint color pigment is then added to this as required. The mixture is made on a double boiler (**1**) with a container of water between the size and the heat source. This is to prevent burning. When adding the paint color pigment, remember that it will dry to a lighter color than appears when it is wet. The color of the dried paint is best gauged from the color of the pigment powder.

The size is applied while still hot. Always paint a small test area first to make sure the color is correct. Apply the first coat with a thick brush using criss-cross strokes (**2**). If the flat is to remain a single color without further decoration, a second coat should be applied (**3**).

Acrylic emulsion paint is a modern alternative to size. Painted directly onto the canvas, it gives a good finish and will not rub off.

Flats can be used for almost any effect. They can be painted as backdrop scenery or with abstract patterns and designs to achieve various textures. Different brush strokes produce a wide range of effects, but paint can also be applied with foam rubber or a feather duster for interesting textures. In addition, plaster, sawdust, polystyrene, newspaper and many other things can be incorporated into designs.

6

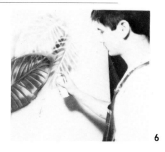

7

10

11

1

14

15

2

3

18

19

4

5

If a pictorial design is to be painted onto a flat, first sketch the design accurately and draw a grid over the sketch (**4**). Using a large grid on the flat, the design can then be transferred square by square (**5**).

Patterns can be made using stencils and spray paint (**6**). A dense effect is achieved by overlapping the stencils (**7**). A simple printing block made from foam rubber (**8**) gives an interesting random pattern. A large and detailed backdrop design may require final touches (**9**) to highlight colors. For a rusty metal effect: first paint the flat black, then sprinkle rust-colored paint onto it (**10**). Paint a second layer of black and rub this down with sandpaper until sufficient 'rusting' shows through (**11**).

Marbling can be done by applying two or three different colored paints to a roller being careful not to mix them. Tear off a piece of newspaper to get a jagged edge and hold this against the flat. Roll the paints over the newspaper (**12**) and repeat this at random to cover the flat. Apply the finishing touches with a paint brush (**13**). Pieces of newspaper glued to a flat (**14**) look quite rough, but from a distance they provide an effective mottled gray wall (**15**). The flat can be made to look like peeling plaster. A piece of

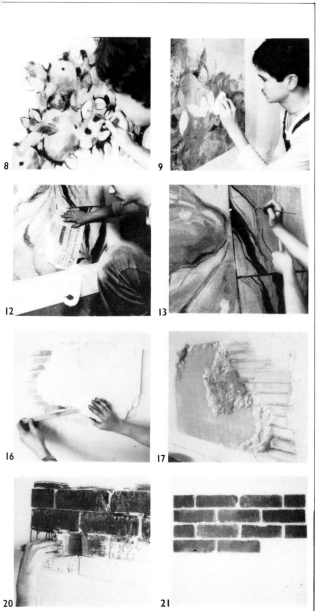

adhesive liberally to the face of the patch and place firmly against a board held in front of the flat.

ROSTRA

A second important component of stages and sets is the rostrum. These can be used to construct the stage area and to add different levels within the stage. Like flats, rostra are extremely versatile in terms of size, shape and usage. They can usually be folded away for easy storage and are quite easy to set and strike. For the non-professional company, rostra can provide cheap and versatile staging possibilities.

A rostrum usually consists of a framework for the sides and a solid top. The best materials for the rostra tops are blockboard or flooring timber. On no account use chipboard or masonite as it is not resilient enough to withstand the wear and tear of a show.

Stairs, or 'treads' as they are often called in the theater, can be specially constructed or made by putting rostra together. They can also be made from blockboard or flooring timber. Construction is made easier if the wood is the correct width to form the tread. The treads can be made in different units and joined by hinges or special hooks fitted into the rostrum top. To help avoid unwanted noise or creaking, it is a good idea to cover the treads in material such as canvas or felt. The set may, of course, require stairs to be carpeted which will also help with noise problems.

When the scenery is complete, check the following elements. Make sure that all verticals and horizontals are correct. Check the fit of doors and jambs, and of windows. The movement of practical doors and windows should also be checked carefully. Joints and hinges require separate checking and make sure that there are no spaces for light to leak through between joints. The positions of any special features such as bars for hanging pictures from should also be checked.

expanded polystyrene is cut into a rough shape and glued to the flat. Wooden laths are then placed to extend from under this (**16**). Gauze fabric is glued to the flat surface of the polystyrene and the whole area is painted white to create the final effect (**17**). Brickwork is done by first applying a layer of glue to the flat (**18**). Cut-out rectangles of either carpet felt or split wood are then arranged in a brickwork pattern (**19**). The entire area is painted with a pigmented paint (**20**) to give further texture. The 'bricks are then painted red/brown and the pointing is added using thickly pigmented white paint. The final effect (**21**) is a neat brick wall.

WORKSHOP SAFETY

Accidents can easily occur in a workshop so make safety a priority. It is important to have adequate shelving and storage so that tools are not left lying around.

Wear sensible, robust clothing and use eye goggles when splinters are likely to fly.

When cutting wood, ensure it is supported and always saw away from you. Also, always sharpen tools away from the body.

Remeber that blunt tools are as dangerous as sharp ones.

Always switch off the power after using electrical equipment and remove the plug. Take care to follow manufacturers' instructions.

Have a fire extinguisher to hand and take great care with heaters. Fumes can be a hazard, such as when cutting polystyrene, so maintain good ventilation. Glue can also produce fumes.

INDEPENDENT
THEATRE
PRESENTS

BUCHNER'S WOYZECK

FOLLOWED BY A "B" FEATURE

4th -15th OCTOBER

AT THE

THEATRE CENTRE
ISLINGTON ROW OFF FIVE WAYS

PROGRAMME BEGINS 7·30 p.m.
THEATRE OPENS 6·00 p.m. FOR

INEXPENSIVE MEALS IN THE OMELETTE BAR
MAXIMUM 30
FIRST COME, FIRST SERVED

COFFEE
IN THE FOYER

TICKETS
AVAILABLE FROM

TOWN HALL
PARADISE STRE
BIRMINGHAM 1
TEL. CEN 2392

OR AT THE D

STRATHCLYDE THEATRE GROUP
Presen

The Hypocrite

by ROBERT McLELLA

Directed by ALASTAIR CORDIN
in the Drama Cent
126 Ingram S
Tel. 041 552 582

Jan. 28th–Feb. 2r
at 7·30p

Financially assisted by SI

STRATHCLYDE THEATRE GROUP
LOTHIAN ROAD CHURCH EVERY EVENING 7.20pm 60p

WHAUR'S YER WILLIE WALLACE NOO?

BY JOHN FOWLER
DIRECTED BY HUGO GIFFORD

WORLD PREMIERE
OF A NEW SCOTTISH PLAY

RED RIVER BLUES
by JOHN FOWLER

Directed by
HUGO GIFFORD

7.20pm Tickets £1·00

ST. BERNARD'S
CHURCH HALL
DEAN STREET
EDINBURGH
MON. 20 AUG
to
SAT. 1 S
STRATH
THEATRE

MELMOTH

by
STEPHEN WYATT
directed by
ALASTAIR CORDIN

10.15 pm   tickets 70

GENESIUS PRODUCTIONS
JULIE C. DAUGHERTY PRODUCTIONS LTD
PRESENT

OWARD & DANIELLE KEEL & DARRIEUX

AMBASSADOR
A New Musical

Based on the Henry James novel "The Ambassadors"

MUSIC BY
Don Gohman
Hal Hackady
LYRICS BY
Don Ettlinger

A
DOUBLE
BILL

Thursday 11th - Saturday 13th Ma
8
The Drama
126 Inge
G

The Enlightenment of the Strawberry Gardener.
by Don Howarth

The Education of Skinny Spew.
by Howard Brenton

CHAPTER ELEVEN

ADMINISTRATION

FINANCIAL MANAGEMENT

PUBLICITY · POSTERS · PROGRAMS

HOUSE MANAGEMENT

BOX OFFICE · SAFETY

A dministration may seem one of the less glamorous of the many activities in the theater. However, the smooth running of a theater group and of a production can owe much to sensible, efficient administration. Nonetheless, good administration should be as unobtrusive as possible, oiling the wheels of the organization so that the group and its productions can proceed with as few hitches and problems as possible.

SETTING UP

The forming of a new amateur theater company is the result of a number of circumstances. Companies rarely emerge from a simple decision to create a theater group.

A common beginning is when people, with a strong interest and practical experience in drama, come together to mount one production. They may be disgruntled or adventurous members of an existing group who wish to break away to do a particular production. Alternatively a group may be united by a common interest in theater and the area in which they live. If there is a vacuum in local theater, they may make a bid to fill it with a popular production.

There may be no need to form a group immediately, but if this first production demonstrates that there is a demand for more theatrical activity in the area then other people can be drawn in to contribute. It will be necessary to have an organization which can take advantage of their talents and enthusiasm. If the prime movers in the original group wish to formalize their existence, they can call a public meeting at which an informal constitution is proposed and discussed. This should set out the basic aims and organization of the company and provide for the election or selection of a committee and officials. Details of membership should also be worked out. It will usually be necessary to have a chairperson, a treasurer and a secretary to the company. Other posts should be appointed as necessary, including such positions as stage manager, house manager, wardrobe manager, membership secretary and so on. If necessary other members could be brought onto the committee.

The constitution will provide opportunities for the group's members to demonstrate their opinion of the work of the committee through, perhaps, regular elections and through open meetings where policy and other matters can be discussed.

There are many ways in which theater groups can organize themselves. They will all have to decide which people are going to make decisions and which people will be taking action to carry out those decisions. They will differ in the extent to which those two groups of people overlap. The more democratic the organization, the greater the number of people involved in making decisions.

In the commercial theater the people working on a production are usually answerable to those who

Eye-catching publicity is vital for attracting an audience. The traditional publicity of the theater is the poster (**left**). Excellent results can be obtained from simple designs using few colors. Complicated posters are often confusing and definitely expensive. What must be clear is the name, time, location and, if possible, an indication of the type of play to be performed. The poster should be easy to read and attractive. Badges (**bottom center**) are inexpensive and effective for publicity. They are too small to convey much information but those wearing them can spread the word for a long time and over a large area.

are financing it. Profit may not be the major aim of the production team but their investors have to be convinced that they are likely to reap some financial dividend. It is true though that many 'angels', as investors are often known, are motivated by the opportunity to enter the world of show business and the chance to dine with leading actors. Others invest because of a love of the theater.

Some companies are financed by a funding body, usually through national, state or local government. An arts' council or organization will subsidize a company it considers worthwhile by giving grants to a governing body which must carry out agreed aims

As a result of these methods of funding, in much of professional theater, the ultimate decision makers are not the workers. An amateur company will usually be more democratic and will exist because its members wish to present plays, and the only external influences on it will be exerted by its audience.

FINANCIAL MANAGEMENT

The finances of a theater group can be divided into two parts. The first element is the constant expenditures and the income to pay for them. These expenditures are not related to any particular production. Usually they will include the upkeep and perhaps rent of premises, the purchase, maintenance and replacement of equipment and props and the cost of informing members of the company's activities. The income to finance these will probably come from membership fees. As the number of members of an established group will remain fairly constant, it will be possible in time to calculate a membership charge which will cover these costs and allow for inflation. In a large company it may be possible to expect a surplus from membership charges, but this should not be carried to excess as it will penalize those members who are less actively involved and whose support might be easily lost.

The second part of financing the group will be related to putting on productions. An amateur company is not created as a money making venture. That would be a contradiction in terms, unless the profits were to be distributed to charity. Nevertheless, it makes good sense for a group to make some profit on its productions in order to help fund future activities.

Once it has been decided to present a particular play, the treasurer should consult with all the departments involved—stage management, costuming, carpentry and publicity—and agree estimates

ADMINISTRATOR'S TASK PLAN

First stage: work out the budget for the production with the director and stage manager • check that proposed sets and costumes can be afforded • sort out any problems concerning the theater space to be used • check carefully all fire, health and safety regulations • discuss publicity, posters and programs

Second stage: organize the design of posters and programs • work out the best methods of publicity and get volunteers to distribute posters • organize advance box office • print tickets and set aside complementary tickets • contact newspapers, radio etc. with a press release for possible free publicity • contact local organizations for party bookings • get posters distributed • organize catering for the performances

Third stage: make certain every aspect of the auditorium and front of house is organized and functioning for the first night and all performances • ensure that box office and program sellers have small change

of their costs. The treasurer then has to add to this the cost of a hall and rehearsal rooms, insurance, scripts, royalties and any other expenses before he or she can determine the overall income required for the production. A sum, say between 10 and 15 per cent, should then be added to allow for price rises and unexpected disasters such as the cost of removing paint from hired or rented costumes. A further sum, say between 10 and 15 per cent, is then required in order to allow a reserve of money to build up in the bank. This will help prevent cash flow difficulties and provide a hedge against inflation and unpopular productions.

At this stage the treasurer has to estimate the size of the audience and hence calculate a ticket price which will provide an income to cover all the costs. This is the point at which the financial viability of the production has to be faced. If production costs, such as publicity and wardrobe, are very high, the treasurer may find that the ticket price to cover such costs is too high and will have to be trimmed. When a reasonable ticket price has been decided and the income assessed, it may well be necessary to cut some of those original estimates worked out with the various departments. This can lead to disagreements between the director and the treasurer, but it must be done, and it must be done accurately.

Worse problems will arise if the director is told arbitrarily what can be afforded. Too often, in both professional and amateur theater, cutbacks are demanded when it is too late for the director to spread the load over the whole production and one department, perhaps costumes, suffers disproportionately.

Detailed records should be kept of each production. They will provide invaluable help in estimating the costs of future productions, and if a disaster does occur they will help apportion the blame. These records should be clearly set out so they can be easily understood by future treasurers.

Most groups will find that they have other sources of income besides ticket sales. If the production has a program, it could provide a profit. Selling refreshments is another effective way of making money, but this should only be decided upon after careful consideration. Refreshments can provide particularly good returns when labor is free, and providing drinks and snacks will be much appreciated by the audience. Selling alcohol can also be an added draw for the audience, but can provide complications for the group. Some theater or hall owners will run their own bar and the group will not see any part of the profits. Alternatively, if a bar exists in a theater, the licensee may be prepared to run the bar during a production and give the group a share of the profits. If the company has the opportunity to run a bar using the free services of its members as bar staff, this will allow the maximum profit but there will be a large burden of responsibility attached. However, different countries and states have their own legal provisions for selling food and drink. Check carefully on local requirements.

PUBLICITY

The largest single cost of putting on a production is likely to be publicity. It allows endless possibilities for wasting money, and, although it is never possible to assess if money has been spent wisely, those in charge of publicity must make sure that it is spent effectively. Since the problem of publicizing one production is much the same as for any other, it is important that the company builds up a publicity machine which can come into operation each time. It will help if one person is permanently responsible for publicity, avoiding the need for someone to start from scratch without the advantages of learning from past mistakes and building on past experience.

Some aspects of publicity will always have to be treated subjectively, but much of the task can be approached systematically. An imaginative publicity person will not only use the usual outlets, such as posters and advertising, mailings and leaflets, but will look at ways of obtaining free publicity through mentions in local newspapers, on local radio stations and in other ways. Enterprising publicity people should have plenty of ideas such as using stunts or displays in store windows. Perhaps the most cost-effective publicity of all is word of mouth. Once the show has opened, the audience will be telling their friends about it, but before it opens members of the group and friends of the cast should

BUDGETING CHECKLIST

When budgeting for a production, take all the following items into account:

Publicity: printing posters, leaflets, programs; photographs for publicity and records; newspaper advertizements

Set: materials; equipment; hardware; paint; trimmings; hiring or buying furniture and props; rehearsal props

Costumes: fabrics and trimmings; accessories; hiring costumes

Technical equipment: lighting lamps; tapes; hiring sound or lighting equipment; buying equipment

Theater space: cost of rent; transport costs; ticket printing; catering; also estimate profits for catering, tickets, programs

Performing rights: cost of getting rights, copies of script

be encouraged to spread the word. They could be invited to an open rehearsal so that they know more about the play and feel involved in a production in which they have not participated.

Posters and leaflets Though printing costs have escalated rapidly, it would be difficult to imagine publicizing a play without the use of some printed matter. Posters should be distributed in large numbers and, ideally, printed in two sizes. Large posters can be displayed on billboards, which, however, can be expensive. But large posters can also be posted on public notice boards, such as those in libraries, schools and community centers, or in the windows of more generous local shops and stores. Generally, a smaller poster will find room on a shop window and in many other places. It is not enough to give a handful of posters to every member of the group and hope that they are displayed. The publicity manager should allocate sections of the local area to volunteers who should ask permission to display material in every store and on every notice board. If they take their own adhesive tape or putty, they will be able to put the poster up on the spot.

Leaflets can be left in the same places as posters, but they are most effectively used when more volunteers may be available to hand them out to individuals. A standard way to do this is to deliver them door-to-door in residential areas. It may be more effective to place leaflets securely on parked cars or to distribute them in shopping centers and other public areas at busy times. It may also be possible to place them in bags with purchases, rather than let them lie on the counter.

Before printed publicity reaches the public eye, it has to be designed and printed and this can be a complicated process. Graphic design is a skill which

Programs Creating a strong visual image for a production will attract attention. That same image can be used for posters and programs (**above**) and will save printing costs.
Programs come in a wide variety of shapes, sizes and styles (**right**).

They are an important memento for audiences and should convey as much information about the production as possible.

requires specialized training. It is wrong to assume that a competent artist or set designer will be able to design a good poster or leaflet. Commercial designers are expensive and beyond the financial reach of most groups. Small printers often have basic ideas for design which can be very helpful, and it is always worthwhile asking at general meetings if anyone knows a graphic designer who would enjoy doing a poster. It is better to aim for an informative poster which can be easily read at a distance.

Various printing processes are available and factors such as the quantity to be printed, the paper size, the design and the publicity budget will decide which is appropriate. Ask for price quotations from several printers and get them to explain fully the various processes they can use and the advantages of each. In time you should build up a relationship with one printer who can meet your requirements and can assist you with practical help. With modern printing processes, such as photocopying, the costs of printed publicity can be kept down considerably. It is still important, however, to avoid complicated designs using several colors, since the cost of printing is always related to the work involved.

If a group is willing to bind itself to a long-term publicity policy, it is sensible to commission a basic poster. This would display the name of the group and any other details which did not change with each production. As the cost could be spread over a number of productions, the poster could be well designed by a professional studio. If the reputation of the work of the group is good, then publicity which is immediately identifiable with it will be useful. The details of a particular production can be printed onto the basic poster and the printer will probably agree to store blank posters as they are a guarantee of future work.

Some display publicity can be hand painted, particularly large outdoor sites such as the front of the theater or billboards. Again, it is best to get professional help. If the group gradually establishes a design style for posters and leaflets, this can be repeated for other publicity material or letterheads.
Newspapers and radio Generally, if volunteers are available to hand out posters and leaflets, newspaper advertising will prove unnecessarily expensive. But in certain circumstances it can prove invaluable. In country areas where door-to-door distribution of leaflets is out of the question and the show has sufficient drawing power to attract people from a wide area, the local newspaper may be the only effective medium for publicity.

It is often possible to get publicity through newspapers without paying for advertising. Many local

STRATHCLYDE THEATRE GROUP
with the assistance of the Scottish International Education Trust
PRESENTS
OBSTACLES

TUE. 20 FEB. - SAT. 24 FEB. '79
7·30 P.M.
IN THE DRAMA CENTRE
126 INGRAM ST., GLASGOW
BOX OFFICE: 041 552 5827

Kathy Callagher

HCLYDE THEATRE GROUP

presents

OBSTACLES

tirely new show

researched, improvised and written by
athclyde Theatre Group members who have
project together over the last nine months.

ice things about art is that history
itself to you as a simultaneous volume
ch all events are happening at the same
ly accessible, all mutually referable
ual item enriched and complicated by
somehow implies every other event to
lar in that volume of history in which

Jonathan Miller

Alison Adams	Liz Gardner
Nancy Bannerman	Trevor Griffiths
Katie Birrell	Billy Johnson
Pamela Blackwood	Robert Johnstone
Kaye Coleman	Ace McCarron
Sheena Craig	Andrew McKechnie
Ian Crofton	Peter McCormack
Linda Dickson	Kevin McMonagle
Elizabeth Donald	Margaret Riddell
Donald Fraser	Kathy Rooney

The simplest and least expensive program is probably the typed sheet variety. One side of a photocopied leaflet can show an advertisement for the play and the program can be typed on the back of this (**left**). It can then be handed out as advance publicity for the play and at performances. Use an attractive but simple design for the front, conveying the name of the play and company, plus the time, date, location and box office number for the performances. The back should carry as much basic information as possible. A cast and crew list is essential and to this can be added notes about the play and dramatist, information about the director and leading actors, and anything else which is both relevant and interesting. But a long and boring program will not be read and, if it is given out as a handbill, could put people off the show.

newspapers have a section listing local activities, particularly those organized by charitable and amateur groups. Information should be sent to them well in advance of their publication date. Quite possibly they will review the show and carry a photograph automatically, but this may not appear until after the last performance so other, earlier mentions in the newspapers are important. They are keen to hear of interesting stories and appreciate suggestions, as long as they are not being asked to simply plug the production. Readers may be interested to read a profile of the director or to hear of the search for an obscure prop. Try to build your idea around a photograph which will be more eye-catching than just a short article.

PROGRAMS

The program is an important part of the ritual of theatergoing. After the performance the program becomes a keepsake of value to both the audience and the theater group. As with publicity, the production of programs will become much easier if a long-term policy is established. A small company which plays to only a limited audience will generally find a cast list is sufficient but most groups will find they can produce programs of several pages. This is

feasible if equal prominence is given to advertising as to information about the particular production.

When pricing the advertising space, it should be remembered that few advertisers will be buying space because they consider that it will help their businesses. It is more likely to be a goodwill gesture on their parts. The local businesses are trying to help the group by advertising and will only do so if the price is low and they are put to no inconvenience. It will prove easier to sell several small spaces than a few whole pages. But prices should be structured to offer a healthy discount to those who want full pages. Once prices have been agreed, someone should visit local businesses to sell the advertising space. This person should be able to answer technical questions concerning the printing of the program and to give an estimate of total sales and advise on artwork. As with posters and leaflets, you will find that getting estimates from several printers will give a clear idea of what is feasible for the size, number of pages, design and printing process. If the program is to be sold, not handed out free, the selling price should cover the cost of printing and advertising revenue would be profit.

If later programs are printed in the same format and the quality is maintained, it will be easy to persuade advertisers to repeat their purchases. A discount for advertising several times can be offered. More pages can be added to the program as time passes, though the overall design can remain the same and artwork can be used several times.

PLACES TO PERFORM AND REHEARSE

Often a group is not in a position to choose where it performs. It may be that there is only one possible space in the area or that there is a traditional link with one hall or theater.

For a new group, deciding for the first time where to perform is important because it will be easier if the same location can be used for future productions. Both backstage and house management (front-of-house) staff will find it easier if they only have to learn the idiosyncracies of one particular space. Scenery flats which are the right size for one stage may not fit elsewhere. If there are storage facilities, this will be of considerable benefit.

Purpose-built theaters have obvious advantages over community halls or other spaces. Lighting and sound will normally be available in a theater, seating should be fairly comfortable and all seats should command a good view of the stage. The theater will usually be cleaned by the owners and there may be good facilities including an advance box office and licenced bars. All these services will cost money but many such theaters are owned by local or municipal authorities and they may charge a theatrical group, particularly an amateur one, at cost or less.

A hall will have to be specially equipped by the group and will rarely be as comfortable. However, greater access may be allowed and it may be possible to rehearse there at little or no extra cost. It may also be possible to build scenery there, although this will depend on other uses of the hall.

Operatic companies will usually have to play in fully equipped theaters because of the nature of the productions. These groups have the drawing power to sell all their seats and so cover their higher costs, such as expensive sets, professional musicians and perhaps a director too.

The rehearsal space is as important as the performing space and to maintain a pleasant atmosphere attention must be paid to those who are present but not required throughout the rehearsal period. Ideally, they will have a separate room where refreshments are available and where they can talk without disturbing the rehearsal. A private house may be adequate, but this depends entirely on the production. Few houses have a room as large as the stage and wing space of a theater, but a smaller space may be useful for early rehearsals.

If it is necessary to hire a rehearsal room, it should be warm and well lit, so that the best work can be obtained from the cast in the limited time available. However, hiring can be a great expense.

HOUSE MANAGEMENT AND BOX OFFICE

The audience is attending more than a performance and much of their pleasure comes from details, such as efficient refreshments, an interesting and easily obtainable program, and a well run theater. Good organization of the theater is essential to any group, and it must be the responsibility of one person who cannot double as stage manager or director.

Ticket sales The box office is not only important on the night but how tickets are sold can have a major effect upon audience numbers. People are often impressed by publicity but forget about it by the time the show is actually in production, so advance ticket sales should be made as easy as possible. Once they have paid, people will not forget to attend and even if they receive bad reports of the show the group will still have their money. A telephone number should be displayed for advance sales which must be paid for within a fixed period. Often a travel agency or a record store will act as a ticket agent. It is reasonable to offer a commission of at least seven per cent for this service and this expense will certainly be justified in all cases other than those lucky theater groups who know they can sell out their seats without effort.

Selling tickets at discount, or season tickets, are two of the ways professional theaters have improved audiences in recent years. Season tickets have proved particularly successful by giving large discount to those who are prepared to book in advance for several productions. It helps the theater to make more accurate plans for the future, as it will have a better idea of its total income. Such schemes also bring more people to the theater since they attract individuals who would not otherwise visit the theater or go very rarely. These methods may be appropriate to amateur groups who can plan production dates well in advance. At the very least, discounts may be offered to theatergoers who buy tickets for two productions at the same time, and even if no discount is offered, tickets for the group's next performance should be available.

Discounts can also be offered as an inducement for groups such as schools, colleges and other organizations who could take a block of seats. Professional companies have successfully arranged educational evenings or weekends to coincide with productions, but this may be too ambitious for many amateur companies.

If possible, seats should be numbered and the box office supplied with plans so that early ticket buyers can be rewarded with the best seats. This also helps avoid a free-for-all before the curtain rises. In some cases, tickets are given to group members to sell in advance to friends, colleagues and neighbors. This can only be beneficial to sales but will not enhance the mental health of the box office manager. Tickets allocated in this way, or to agents, should be clearly recorded and signed for. Unsold tickets and money should be collected well before the production opens, possibly before any other sales are allowed.

Box office systems in professional theaters are often complicated, and tickets may be printed with three or four stubs. For amateur performances, where there is only a limited price range and just a few performances, life is much simpler. Perhaps the most important rule is to have only as many tickets as there are seats and to date and number all tickets in advance. Where possible, the ticket price should also be printed on the ticket, though this may be difficult where discounts are offered to parties, senior citizens or students. It is usually worthwhile having the tickets bound into a book so that they remain in order and cannot be lost by accident.

Organizing on the night The box office for a performance should be away from the door so that ticket holders can go straight to their seats without having to wait. The house manager must make sure that the audience can find their seats with no inconvenience and that they can remain there in comfort and safety. It may be simpler for many amateur groups to have seats available on a first come, first served basis rather than having to number each seat. However, when used, numbers should be marked on all seats and row letters should be clearly visible. Ushers should check tickets and guide people to their seats. They should not also have to distribute programs if other helpers are available to do this.

It is usual to sound bells at intervals before the start of the performance; three minutes before the start three bells sound, and two minutes before two bells sound. The house manager gives the go-ahead for the performance once he or she has received an all-clear from the stage manager. It is unreasonable to start if people are still waiting at the box office, but it is also unfair to the audience to delay for latecomers. The house lights should not be dimmed until the performance is definitely going to begin. If the group has a policy of not admitting latecomers until a suitable break in the performance, this

should be printed clearly on all the tickets.

Disabled members of the audience should be specially helped by making sure that they arrive in advance and are given seats which provide easy access to the aisles. Perhaps one usher should be responsible for them and ticket buyers should be informed that there will be special facilities through box office notices and information on posters.

Refreshments Using voluntary help as much as possible, it is always a good thing to provide refreshments, and a good way of making some extra money. Hot drinks and non-alcoholic drinks and snacks require little effort and are much appreciated. Avoid paper cups, which disintegrate when filled with hot beverages, and provide surfaces for empty glasses and cups. If there is a bar, whether it is run by the group or the owners of the theater or hall, a system that allows for drinks to be ordered in advance will ease the workload during intermissions and also increase sales.

LEGAL REQUIREMENTS

Fire and safety regulations Performing groups must always take special care to discover all their responsibilities. If a purpose-built theater is being used, or other premises are hired, it is reasonable to assume that most regulations concerning fire and safety will be automatically observed. But do not count on this – always check. Fire regulations are particularly important and premises may have to be visited by the fire department before an audience can be admitted. Certainly consult them before any production gets under way

Safety checks The owner of the premises or the fire department should advise which materials can be used on stage and on fire-proofing requirements. A safety curtain may be needed, and it must function properly. Smoking is often not allowed in auditoriums and notices stating this must be displayed. All electrical equipment is a potential fire hazard, so it must be well maintained and locked away when not in use.

In case of fire If a fire should break out, it must be possible for the audience to leave quickly, safely and without panic. Ushers should have a well rehearsed fire drill. Fire exits must be clearly marked and never obstructed. Seats must be fixed together and to the floor so that they do not fall over if pushed.

Insurance Equipment, buildings and people will require insurance. Again, this important legal consideration should be looked into carefully before a production starts.

Food and drink If a bar is to be run by the group, a licence must be obtained. When selling alcohol and tobacco, it is important to find out exactly what the legal requirements are. Catering may require health regulations to be met and this too should be sorted out early. Find out the necessary information from local authorities.

Performing rights Many plays, especially those written more recently, will not be available for non-professional groups. The owner of the performing rights on such a play may believe that amateur productions could prejudice future professional presentations. Check with the author's agent. Once a play has been released for amateurs, and up to 50 years after the author's death, a fee must be paid for each performance. Details are often given in the published script, but groups are responsible for ensuring that performing rights are not contravened, and this should always be carefully investigated before deciding on a play

1

2

3

CHAPTER NINE

CHOOSING THE PLAY

DRAMA THROUGH THE AGES

APPROACHES TO SHAKESPEARE

DISCOVERING UNUSUAL PLAYS

REVUES · IMPROVISATION

The repertoire of an amateur company is too often a chance medley of recent hits and standard classics. Some companies stick to a tried formula, whether it be Shakespeare, a safe diet of middlebrow comedy or works by committed modern dramatists. It is important to remember that the skills developed for a particular type of play can be transferred and used when a company produces new material.

Obviously choosing what to perform is conditioned by the size and available skills of a company and is determined by the preferences of the director and the group as a whole. But within these natural limitations, there is considerable room for innovation, and many opportunities for amateur groups to tackle interesting and unusual plays, particularly those with large casts which professionals might be reluctant to tackle.

There are times when what is happening in professional theater can be a direct inspiration for amateur companies. This is particularly important if a group is operating in a large town with a local professional theater company. The amateur group can complement the repertoire of the professional company by choosing to do plays from a similar period or filling in the gaps in the professional company's output. Direct competition is not a good idea, but a careful choice of plays can enhance your audience's enjoyment and increase your audience size. On a general level it is always wise to be on the lookout for anniveraries, particularly of local events, which might provide a theme for a season of plays. These might include, for instance, the births or deaths of local dramatists.

It may, however, be useful to look beyond what is being performed by others. People often assume that because an author or a particular play is not often performed that there must be a good reason in the poor quality of the work, but plays and authors often slip from notice for no good reason at all. For instance, much nineteenth century British drama was forgotten for many decades, but some excellent pieces are now being revived. They are no longer seen as vehicles for mindless audience participation, but as interesting plays in their own right. Authors such as Ibsen and Brecht have only a very limited number of their plays performed by either professionals or amateurs. The German dramatist Bertolt Brecht (1898–1956) wrote about 40 plays and the Norwegian Henrik Ibsen (1828–1906) wrote 26. Not all of them will be suitable for performance, but they provide the basis for a wider approach.

LIMITATIONS

Any company's choice of repertoire is conditioned by its own particular circumstances. Your theater may seem too small or the wrong shape for certain types of play. You may have too few or too many performers or a scarcity of stage staff which limits

Amateur companies can choose to perform anything from across the whole spectrum of theater. The humor and vitality of *Guys and Dolls* (**1**), based on Damon Runyon's witty gangster books, offer a challenge to an ambitious company with the singing, acting and dancing skills to tackle a Broadway musical. Leading actors wanting to come to grips with high drama will find John Webster's Renaissance tragedy *The Duchess of Malfi* (**2**) both demanding and rewarding. *The Woman* (**3**) is British dramatist Edward Bond's modern reworking of Ancient Greek themes, providing new perspectives on traditional stories and scope for a large cast.

the company technically. However, an apparent limitation can be turned into an advantage by making the company look again at its possible range from new and unfamiliar angles. Shakespeare, for example, used to be seen as a challenge to be faced only in a large theater with a large cast, but successful small-scale professional productions of Shakespeare have shown that his plays can work in a small space which brings the cast into close proximity with the audience. To do this, a good company is required in order to sustain the mood without any scenic distractions. However, only a good company should even try to tackle Shakespeare anyway.

The size of casts is often a problem, but a little ingenuity can usually be exercised to solve it. A common complaint is a surplus of actors of one sex. There is really no reason why male roles should not be converted to female roles or vice versa, as necessity demands. This applies particularly to minor roles such as servants or messengers, where the actual sex of the performer is of no importance. In some plays, casting one sex to play a role of the other sex can be a positive advantage. The seventeenth century version of Shakespeare's *Tempest* by John Dryden and William Davenant has an additional character, a young male lover whose role is written to be performed by a woman and it would lose much of its force if it were played by a man. On a rather different level, *The Lesson* by the modern French dramatist Eugene Ionesco (born 1912) works perfectly well if the male part of the professor is played by a woman. Hamlet has often been played by a woman, the French actress Sarah Bernhardt being the most famous female to play the part. There have been all male or all female productions, for instance the National Theatre of Great Britain has performed an all male *As You Like It*.

The most important point about transvestite casting is to use the opportunities it provides instead of treating it as an unwelcome necessity which has to be suffered rather than exploited. A telling theatrical point can be made through using an actor of one sex in a role written for the other.

CLASSICAL DRAMA

The chorus poses the major difficulty in staging classical Greek drama because it conditions every other factor in the production. If a full chorus is used, it has to go somewhere and this can be a major complication in a traditional theater, particularly if the chorus has to dance. Some directors have cut the chorus to one person which falsifies the original play but may well be the answer, especially if the production is in a confined space.

Any chorus of more than one person must be made up of performers who can handle unison work, whether singing or dancing. Ragged choruses have probably accounted for the majority of bad productions of Greek drama. Speaking in unison is very hard even for the most competent group of actors, and it is probably better to split lines amongst individual members rather than attempt a delivery in unison. If the chorus can be dealt with effectively, Greek plays are well suited to most types of theatrical space and they do not need to be done in the traditional togas and masks to achieve a satisfactory result on stage.

MEDIEVAL DRAMA

Medieval plays can be performed in a wide range of locations and styles. There are obvious affinities between medieval religious plays and churches which make them particularly appropriate as theatrical locations. The great challenge of medieval drama lies in its apparent lack of sophistication which can lead to rather patronizing productions. In fact, medieval plays often use highly sophisticated techniques to educate an audience in an entertaining and memorable way. These techniques are not the familiar ones created by the naturalistic dramatists of the late nineteenth century which still unconsciously condition so much thinking about drama. Medieval drama is much closer to Brecht's idea of an 'epic' theater, and it often performs well if approached from a similar viewpoint. Like Brecht's ideas, the purpose of medieval drama is overtly didactic, to educate the audience on questions of religion and morality, and the events depicted are illustrative of one of the great cultural forces in shaping the modern world.

Morality plays such as the Anglo-Dutch *Everyman* or *The Castle of Perseverance* present allegorical characters, representing qualities such as good and evil, in contests for the soul of humanity. Even in these highly serious plays comic effects have a major part. This is also true in medieval cycle plays such as the Wakefield *Second Shepherd's Play* with its burlesque nativity preceding Christ's nativity. The cycle plays relate to the church calendar and so offer the opportunity to detach one play for a special performance on a particular day in the church calendar. There is always a danger that a part detached from the whole will not achieve a major impact. Most of the individual plays from the cycles are very short but they can be readily combined to form a linked group. For instance, *Everyman*, *Adam and Eve*, and *Cain and Abel* could be performed under the provocative title of 'Sin'.

SHAKESPEARE AND RENAISSANCE DRAMA

Shakespeare is a major challenge for any company at any level because of the sheer brilliance of his writing and stagecraft, and because his plays are so well known through many media. Companies can be tempted to go for an outlandish interpretation simply to stamp their production as somehow different from everybody else's. But a new slant on a Shakespeare play is no simple matter. It must make sense at every level and not fit just one character or group of scenes. A new slant has to be capable of development throughout the whole play.

Choosing from the many editions of Shakespeare's plays is important and it is especially important that the whole company are using the same edition. Considerable confusion can arise, particularly in the early stages of rehearsal, if actors give each other cues or use speeches which are not in every edition being used. The best editions for production work are the readily available modern single volume ones with very little annotation on the page of text. Apart from being comparatively cheap, they encourage actors to concentrate on the play rather than the often informative but theatrically irrelevant notes that grace the pages of more scholarly editions. It is, of course, important that everyone understands what the text actually means, since it is unlikely that an audience will find any meaning in lines delivered by actors who do not themselves understand the words. The director should have a reliable, fully annotated edition for reference, so that any obscure points can be explained as the need arises.

Some words used by Shakespeare have changed their meaning, but still make half sense when used in the context of his plays. These need particular attention because they can be brushed over in rehearsal, but in a performance the result can be a blurred moment. If there are too many of these, the audience will gradually lose its way.

However, there are some words and phrases in Shakespeare which no longer mean anything except to specialist students of Renaissance literature. In general, plays should only be cut very sparingly because even a minor cut can destroy the rhythm and balance of a scene, an act or even the whole play. But a passage that is incomprehensible can do an equal amount of damage by turning an audience off. So, in some cases, it may well be better to lose a few lines rather than an audience. Purists will sometimes claim that every word and every line should be spoken but this ignores the practical demands of the theater. Lines are not destroyed by being cut, they are still available for future productions. But it is important not to cut any line that initially seems difficult to understand. It is often possible to find the meaning in rehearsal and eventually to communicate it to the audience.

Costumes can pose problems when producing Shakespeare because there are so many possibilities of how to tackle them. The question rests on interpretation, since the plays can be set in the period they depict, or in the period they were first performed or in another period in time which may point up some parallel with the events in the play. So *Hamlet* can be staged in some kind of early Danish or Viking costumes, in Elizabethan costumes, in contemporary costumes or some other appropriate period. Nineteenth century productions preferred to use the historical period in which the play was set but this posed problems with plays such as *A Midsummer's Night Dream* and *The Tempest*, since there is no legitimate historical period for these plays.

In deciding when to set your production, it is again important to check the interpretation against all the details of the text so that everything fits. A classic example of the difficulties which can arise comes in *Macbeth*. In Act 4, scene 3, Macduff learns of his wife's death. Malcolm says to him 'What, man! Ne'er pull your hat upon your brows; Give sorrow words'. This gives a clear indication of Macduff's actions – he pulls his hat over his face to express his sorrow and despair. This action is crucial, since Macduff says very little in this scene after he learns the news. His replies are tense, conveying a wealth of emotional power through his reticence and through action. But real problems can arise here if the production has been set in modern times. After all, modern men wear headgear much less often than Shakespeare's contemporaries did. It may be necessary in certain productions to suggest that this scene is taking place outdoors where the characters may more plausibly wear hats – many modern directors set the scene in some kind of camp. It may seem best to cut the line and substitute some similar action or set of actions to convey the same emotional impulse, but the line and its implications have to be looked at very carefully.

Other plays offer equally challenging choices of costume. For example, Malvolio's cross-gartering and yellow stockings in *Twelfth Night*, the women who appear disguised as men in many of the comedies, and the supernatural characters in *Macbeth* or *The Tempest*, all require careful consideration if the correct overall impression is to be created.

Modern stages can make it appear very difficult to

stage Shakespeare because some companies still believe that a specific locality has to be created by the use of scenery. The Elizabethan stage did not, in fact, rely on scenery to indicate where a scene was taking place. Scenery can be distracting, particularly if a company tries to use rather old fashioned stage practices by trying to reproduce classical Athens for *A Midsummer Night's Dream* or the Doge's palace for *Othello*. Such attempts can result in long waits for scene changes which can interrupt the flow of Shakespeare's carefully conceived dramatic structure, while also making the play unnecessarily long. Shakespeare always indicates where the action is taking place if the information is significant and he also clearly indicates if a particular piece of scenery is required, such as the balcony in *Romeo and Juliet*, the monument in *Antony and Cleopatra* or the grave trap in *Hamlet*. Too much emphasis on producing a naturalistic scenic background is likely to be counterproductive. It is not flats and canvases which create the woodland of *A Midsummer Night's Dream*, it is the verse. Prominent woodland scenery is more likely to compete with the verse than to complement it.

Shakespeare's plays require large casts and some doubling of actors may be both necessary and desirable. Otherwise the production might overflow from available dressing room space and out of available rehearsal rooms. It is very important to keep all members of the cast in touch with the production's progress and an assistant will be needed to coordinate the production.

Actors with small parts can often become disenchanted during long rehearsals where they have no more than a few lines at extended intervals. If this reaches the stage the attendant lords and extras who flesh out a scene can easily distract an audience by showing their lack of interest in the proceedings. If they are not interested, why should the audience be? It is advisable to split the cast into groups who can work together on individual scenes and then bring them together for more general rehearsals. In *A Midsummer Night's Dream*, for example, the fairies, the Athenian lovers and the mechanicals spend much of their time pursuing their own ends and they can certainly be rehearsed independently to useful effect.

THE RESTORATION AND EIGHTEENTH CENTURY

There is a tendency in dealing with plays from the late seventeenth and eighteenth centuries to think that all that matters is style. This is partly due to

Selecting by style The daunting prospect of choosing a play can be made easier by first deciding which style of theater the company should tackle next. Anton Chekhov's *The Cherry Orchard* (**1**) is typical of early twentieth century drama. Such tense and emotional plays of complex human relationships require great subtlety. The same is true of Jean Racine's seventeenth century drama, *Britannicus*. As with many period plays, it can be given a modern styling (**2**) through costumes and sets. The bold and zany world of the Cambridge University *Footlights* revue (**3**) has been popular for decades. Each year they present original comedy sketches.

Comedy of a very different kind is the rarely performed *The Prince of Hamburg* (**4**) by Heinrich von Kleist (1777–1811). Shakespeare's comedies, particularly those set mainly outside, are a good choice for open air performances. *Love's Labours Lost* takes place in a royal garden so Regents Park provided the perfect location for this production (**5**). George Bernard Shaw wrote with sharp humor and social comment to provide stimulating and entertaining modern theater. *The Philanderer* (**6**) is one of his most popular plays. He wrote over fifty, including many one act works and five full length plays which make up *Back to Methuselah*.

3

4

5

6

Hedda Gabler: two approaches One of the greatest female roles in the theater is provided by *Hedda Gabler*. Ibsen gave specific instructions for stage directions, settings and lighting in his script. His instructions reflect the inner vision of the play and are extremely effective. As a result most productions, including one in 1975 by the Royal Shakespeare Company starring Glenda Jackson (**left**), have followed them fairly closely. Charles Marowitz is known for his bold approach to famous plays. He adapted Ibsen's script for *Hedda*, at the Round House in London, 1980, with Jenny Agutter. He made explicit many elements in Ibsen's play which lie beneath the surface of the drama. Hedda's fascination with her father's pistol was expressed through a large cannon (**right**) on stage; an obvious phallic symbol.

terms such as 'comedy of manners' which are used to describe some of the plays. It suggests that if the outward appearance of manners is right then the production will be fine. Also, theater groups seldom venture outside the confines of well established comic classics of this period. But tragedies written in the Restoration period, from 1660 into the eighteenth century, can provide an interesting challenge for an ambitious group because there is no established convention for presenting them. Dryden's *All For Love*, Otway's *Venice Preserv'd* and Lillo's *London Merchant*, for example, are all worthwhile.

With the comedies, there are two well established models of how to perform them. One is highly artificial with the emphasis on the gloss of manners and appearance, and the alternative is equally to exaggerate the earthiness underlying the artifical manners. The problem with these plays is finding an approach which will give due weight to the wit without losing sight of the demands of the characters and plot. The best of these plays are certainly more than vehicles for racy asides and jokes so the company's task is to find the underlying structure of feeling which sustains them.

NINETEENTH CENTURY PLAYS

The nineteenth century is known for its melodramas which nowadays often tend to be sent up, with the audience hissing at the villain. In fact, there are many plays of this period which, despite their melodramatic tendencies, can be played straight with good results. A good example of this is *Streets of London* by the American-Irish dramatist Dion Boucicault (1822–1890). When produced recently by a good professional company this revealed that quality melodrama played with conviction can carry an audience without resorting to burlesque. *Streets of London* is also a good choice for amateur companies, since it exists in a number of versions according to the town in which it is played. The location can be changed to New York, for example.

As well as melodrama, there are some good farces and comedies of the period which might repay careful consideration. For instance, Boucicault's *London Assurance* was forgotten until the Royal Shakespeare Company revived it very successfully. There are many other nineteenth century British comedies, such as *Money* by Edward Bulwer-Lytton, and J. M. Morton's *Box and Cox*, or works by Americans such as Bronson Howard or William Dunlap which are likely candidates to join the comic works of Oscar Wilde and A. W. Pinero in the comedy repertoire of companies. With all nineteenth century drama before Ibsen, it is important not to apply the criteria which should be applied to Ibsen or Chekhov. Approach the plays on their own terms and discover their underlying truth rather than applying attitudes to them which belong to other forms and periods of drama.

The great dramatists of the late nineteenth century, such as Ibsen or Anton Chekhov, pose a different problem. The strength of their plays appears to lie in the discussions of major themes or

social questions, but it is important not to ignore the crucial way such dramatists use the resources of stage space. Ibsen's *Hedda Gabler* gains much of its power from Hedda's confinement to her home and the ways in which she tries to defend her space. Chekhov's *Three Sisters* also works through showing the gradual dispossession of the sisters from the house they own.

The stage directions in such plays are normally the author's so the sets, properties and actors they suggest have an important contribution to make to the overall impact of the production. What matters in the end, however, is finding the underlying emotional and intellectual truth which led to the results indicated by the stage directions and not to follow the directions merely because they are there.

ONE ACT PLAYS

Good one act plays have a lot to offer non-professional companies because they provide opportunities to use a large number of actors, directors and designers in one program. There have been many good one act plays written by eminent authors which are seldom revived professionally.

If you do decide to present a one act program as part of your repertoire, try to make it a coherent package by choosing a common theme for all the parts of it. For example, choose plays which deal with aspects of marriage. These could include *The Proposal*, a farce by Chekhov which deals with the tribulations of courtship, and *La Musica*, by the modern French playwright Marguerite Duras, which

is a serious modern play about divorce. These two plays could perhaps frame another play which deals with marriage from a serious or comic stand point.

This type of triple bill can involve three separate sets, groups of actors and directors if required, or a telling thematic point could be made by using, for example, the same actors to play the couple in all three plays.

Other linking factors for selecting a program could be plays written at the same time, say using Expressionist plays which are very short and form a highly coherent evening's entertainment. Good short plays from different periods can be found to provide a worthwhile package.

MUSICALS

There is no point in attempting to stage operas or musicals unless you have a full complement of good actor-singers for leads and chorus, good musicians, a choreographer, a rehearsal pianist and a musical director. Musicals are among the most difficult plays to stage because they make huge demands on every aspect of an organization. Confidence must be high in the abilities of everyone concerned before embarking on a musical because what might be minor blemishes in a straight play will be magnified in a musical.

Good rehearsal facilities and a piano are essential. Often time can be saved by scheduling two rehearsals at the same time, provided there is a choreographer who can go over dance steps while a director rehearses the leads. It is difficult to hold two

173

rehearsals with music if you have only one piano. Obviously, taped music can be used at certain times but this has to be carefully planned. Good planning and organization are the keys to any good production but opera and musicals require the very best if the end result is to be at all worthwhile. A lot of time needs to be taken to coordinate and link all the various elements of a production.

Some plays demand vocal performances from the majority of the cast but they do not demand good singing voices. These plays include the compilation about the First World War, *Oh What a Lovely War*, John Gay's *Beggar's Opera*, a major eighteenth century musical play, and Bertolt Brecht's *Threepenny Opera*, a twentieth century version of the same plot. They are, however, equally demanding in terms of time and organization as a straight musical. There is a danger that, because the final product is to appear deliberately rough, a company may not pay as much attention to the need for musical rehearsals.

The key is always coordination between departments so that the show gradually comes together as successive layers are added to the picture to produce the final result. A play that uses folk tunes or popular ballads requires just as much care as grand opera. You will not get an appearance of spontaneity and folk charm by under-rehearsal. There is another danger with musical plays, which is that the company will recognize the importance of getting the music right and concentrate on that, forgetting all the other elements that make a good production.

If you use any kind of sound system to boost weaker voices, it is absolutely vital that it is specifically designed to achieve a good coverage and range over the whole stage, and purpose built for the particular task you want it to carry out. There is nothing more disconcerting than the effect of microphones which make an actor sound as if he or she is approaching down a long corridor, reaching a central peak of audibility and then retreating down the corridor again. There are so many potential difficulties with using sound systems that you should be certain that the advantages outweigh the disadvantages by a considerable margin, and also that you have a well qualified sound engineer to cope with the difficulties that beset all sound systems.

You may be tempted to use a recorded music scene if there is a shortage of musicians to play for every performance. This could be disastrous since there can be no improvisation on a tape if something goes wrong on stage, and there can be no interplay between the musicians and the singers. Taped music may be useful in rehearsal, but it has no place in performance. Your audience is likely to feel they would be better off at home listening to the original cast recording.

REVUES AND CABARET

The quality of a revue or cabaret performance naturally depends on the quality of the material and the performers. Many of the considerations which apply to musicals also apply to revues and cabarets, but there is much more opportunity for individual rehearsals of individual numbers before bringing the whole show together. In general, shows with themes or recurrent elements work better than shows with no linking factors since they give a direction to the evening's entertainment.

IMPROVISED PLAYS

There are two distinct kinds of improvised plays, those that are improvised on the night of the performance and those created by a group through improvisation but fixed before the actual performance. The second kind will eventually exist in a fully scripted form and will be treated in performance just like a normal play.

The differences between the two kinds of improvisation are sometimes deliberately blurred so that some scenes may be improvised on the night while others are fully scripted. Even in shows which are fully improvised on the night it is usual for there to be a scenario which determines both the order and the rough content of scenes, and of course any specific lighting or sound cues need to be arranged in advance.

The fully improvised show needs a group who are very confident in one another's abilities because they have to cooperate on stage without the safety net of a fixed script, and often the show can become stuck in a groove as the group repeat well tried improvisations. If you have a really good group who want to work in front of an audience using improvisation, you can generate creative energy and excitement, but there is a real danger that the totally improvised show can be far too actor-oriented and may offer little entertainment to an audience.

Plays, which are created through improvisation and then scripted, work best if they are based on extreme situations. A tight domestic struggle or a complex historical epic can both be readily created from improvisation and research, then scripted.

The greatest danger with improvisation is that it depends heavily on the sustained inventiveness of the cast, and it can become hindered by dull formulae, presenting only stereotyped characters in hackneyed situations. Many improvised plays end with one such formula when apparently normal people suddenly indulge in some form of ritual murder. These pitfalls can be avoided if a company knows precisely what it wants to do and why improvisation is the way to achieve it.

MODERN VERSE DRAMA

Modern verse plays by such writers as the Americans T. S. Eliot and Maxwell Anderson or the British writer Christopher Fry pose a different challenge to those written, say, by Shakespeare. But the basic point about verse forms remains the same – the verse is there to help actors not to hinder them.

Traditionally, verse speaking stressed the musical qualities of the lines at the expense of the meaning. In modern times, however, the tendency is to stress meaning above music. However, both are important, and meaning and music should be indivisible in good verse lines. If the actor's stress and phrasing are correct and convey the meaning of the lines, the necessary music will emerge.

Some of the most effective modern verse dramas have been those which recreate a historical period such as Eliot's *Murder in the Cathedral* and Fry's *The Lady's Not For Burning*. In these plays the period setting served to legitimize the use of verse by suggesting parallels with verse plays from earlier centuries. Another type of modern verse play is about particular groups which are regarded as poetic, as in *Under Milk Wood* by the Welsh poet Dylan Thomas. The major problem with modern verse drama is relating the verse form to the reality of everyday experience, and perhaps the most successful modern poetic dramas are those which actually avoid traditional verse forms.

PLAYS FOR SPECIFIC OCCASIONS

It is always wise to be aware of local anniversaries and events that might provide a theme for a season of plays or one performance. If you have a local historical site or know of the birthday of a local author or prominent figure, it may be possible to create a specific performance to celebrate that place or person and even to perform the show in a place associated with their work.

If a show on a particular theme is to be created from scratch, as it often has to be, more time will be needed than if someone has the specialized information which can be used as a basis for the eventual show. Alternatively, the piece may have to be put together quickly because it is concerned with a current issue to which public attention should be drawn so widening discussion of the issue. In such cases, the result may well be less polished, but it will serve its purpose. In general, the dramatized documentary needs a considerable amount of work in order to assimilate the factual material into a viable theatrical form, and a succession of unadulterated facts is seldom very entertaining.

Shows intended for specific themes, spaces or events need to be more than mere extracts from an author's writings or from newspaper accounts of an event. However, as with all drama, careful attention to organization and detail will pay handsome dividends. There are a number of printed texts for successful fact-based shows which may indicate general avenues of approach. These include *In the Matter of J. Robert Oppenheimer* by the German playwright Heinar Kipphardt.

STREET THEATER

Street theater gives high public exposure to a company so it is often used for publicity, but it is a very entertaining theater form in its own right. The shows need to be short and easy to follow, if they are to make an impact on passers-by. Shows which use improvisation and a pantomime style create an easy rapport between performers and the public while allowing for the company to respond to the particular environment in which they are performing. It may be at a market or in a busy shopping center.

It is essential to check on local laws and to get proper permission before performing in the streets to avoid problems with local authorities. The crowds which gather around street performances can obstruct traffic and pedestrians, and they also provide opportunities for thieves. The police should always be informed about a proposed performance, and they may wish to be present. This can be helpful since they will dissuade members of the public from indulging in audience participation of an unwelcome kind.

Passers-by will often want to make small donations, but this could break local regulations concerning asking for money in the street. As with all performances outside a recognized theater or hall, close cooperation with civic authorities is necessary to ensure a successful venture.

OPEN AIR PERFORMANCES

The greatest natural hazard to performing outdoors is, of course, the weather. In any climate, open air performances are usually restricted to certain times of the year so be sure to plan such a venture only after checking local weather records.

Most open air shows will be inspired by a particular space, but, if a company simply wants to perform outdoors, they may find it difficult to find a suitable place. Public parks sometimes have arenas with paved auditoriums and supplies of chairs, but such places will be in great demand during summer months. The problem of a suitable space is always one of finding not only an acting area but also an audience area.

A natural amphitheater could be used but forward planning is essential for this because there are many restrictions on the use of open spaces for public performance for very good environmental and public health reasons. Using any outdoor location will involve contact with local authorities well in advance of the proposed performance.

Particular attention must be made to car parking facilities. It is not only important to have a large area available for this but to ensure that it will not become impassable if it rains, that a large influx of cars will not damage the area irreparably and that the police do not object.

Local residents will be affected by the performance so it is very important to have good relations with them and to cooperate with their needs. Give them plenty of warning of the proposed show.

One of the advantages of long-range planning is that you can check up on anything about the place which may affect a performance. Noises and distractions should be carefully considered. A regular flight from a local airport could destroy a dramatic effect completely, not only by drowning out the sound but also by creating a distracting contrast with the nature of the performance.

The sun can cause problems during a daylight performance. It is likely to shine either in the faces of the actors or the audience at some point. Check exactly where the sun will be as near as possible to the date and time of the performance, since even a few minutes difference can have a major effect on the sun's relative position and this could make the difference between success and failure. You can use the sun effectively as a stage effect if the circumstances are right. Sunset and dusk giving way to artificial lighting can stress the features of a natural landscape. Sunrise can also be used in this way, but you may find it difficult to attract either a cast or an audience at dawn!

Lighting and sound equipment can be damaged or stolen and needs to be even more carefully organized than usual. All equipment must be waterproofed, and this applies particularly to electrical connections. Special outdoor equipment can be

hired and is far safer and more reliable than homemade improvisations. Pay particular attention to the safety and reliability of your main power source.

If you intend charging for open air performances, you will need good security arrangements since open air theaters are difficult to police. This needs careful planning. You may also have to deal with stray animals and children. Extra house management staff will probably be needed than are used in an indoor venue. Toilet facilities and refreshments will be another complication in a temporary location, as will changing rooms for the cast and secure storage for costumes and props to be left in overnight. If you are operating close to your base, it may be wise to organize moving sets in and out each night if you have the helpers, and it is definitely worth doing this at weekends when open areas are particularly vulnerable.

Although there are many more hazards in open air performances than indoor ones, there are some great benefits. The contrast between natural scenery and a stage performance can be used to good theatrical effect and there is something magical about the change from twilight to artificial light on a warm summer's evening. Even real animals are less of a liability on stage in an open air performance.

ACTING EDITIONS

Amateur companies often use specially published editions of plays for their productions and there are dangers in relying on these acting editions. The majority include pictures of sets and property lists as well as stage directions which were used in the first professional production of the play. These details hinder rather than help if they are allowed to influence a new production unduly.

The conclusions one group of people arrive at in interpreting a play depend very much on particular circumstances. These include the type of theater they are performing in, the size of the stage, the designer and director's own views and the interaction between individual actors. An acting edition may show a photograph of the stage with a cross marked upstage left showing a specific move for an actor. This may represent a considerable amount of thought and effort on the part of the company that originally used that stage direction, but a company which tries to adopt it may find that the move is wrong because it does not represent the results of their own process of discovery in rehearsal.

Original lighting and property plots can be useful in providing a checklist for a new production, but the emotional value of a particular accessory or prop for one actor in one production can seldom be transferred to another actor in a subsequent production. For example, an actor may have a particular prop because it can help with characterization. However, slavishly searching for the same prop for another actor to use in another production is a complete waste of time because its value is emotional.

Acting editions should never determine what a company is going to do. They may be helpful by showing one set of solutions to the problems posed by a play, and they can be reassuring to an inexperienced director and cast. But they should never be allowed to short-circuit the creative process of grappling with a text's difficulties in order to understand it, and there is almost nothing worse than a production where characters move only as indicated in the text. Your rehearsal process can lead to a fresh set of actions which will be equally valid responses to the text and capture the same emotional power and range as the actions set out in an acting edition.

PERFORMING RIGHTS

Amateur companies are sometimes tempted to put on a production without paying the requisite performing rights. This is strictly illegal and highly unfair to the author since it reduces even further what is probably a small income from his or her writing. Putting on unauthorized performances is indulging in theft.

Performing rights' fees should be at the top of a production's budget and a company should not begin work on a play unless clearance has been obtained from the author's agent whose address will usually be found at the front of the published play. If a company cannot afford these fees it should stick to plays which are out of copyright. Laws concerning copyright are complicated but it should be straightforward to check if a particular play is out of copyright by contacting the publisher or agent, or by finding out when the play was written, when the author died and then checking what this information means in terms of copyright. Plays from the nineteenth century and earlier are generally out of copyright, but many translations of old plays are still in copyright if the translation is a recent one.

Paying fees can have useful side effects. Contact with an agent is one way of finding out if there are other potential productions of the author's work in your area, so removing the possibility of embarrassing clashes between productions of the same play. Contact with an agent can also lead to contact with the author who may be willing to allow changes in the script to point up local relevance by changing place names or even speech patterns. Most authors care about their work and continue to take an interest in it. They are often far more accessible for serious discussions about their work than is generally assumed.

RESEARCH

When considering a possible production, it is important to think about research and assess its potential advantages and disadvantages. With period plays or those with historical settings, the company should know as much as possible about the play and have a good idea of the historical and theatrical background. For example, knowledge of Restoration marriage patterns and the near impossibility of divorce can illuminate the underlying reality of plays from that period. On the other hand, however, the historical circumstances of composition and first performance should not determine the nature of your own production. The group's task is to make the play work now and too much historical knowledge can become a barrier to coming to grips with the actual play. Research can be very valuable in determining the nature and style of fashion accessories, for example. However, bear in mind that practicalities and limited budgets often mean that too much research may lead to frustration, since it may be impossible to act upon the research.

When producing period plays it is very useful to adopt some approximation of period dress quite early in the rehearsal period. Many actors find that the clothes they wear in period plays have a close relationship to their ability to get into a part. Dress in many earlier historical periods was often stiffer and more constricting than it tends to be today. There are many cases where a starched collar and collar stud can help an actor to understand the attitudes of a nineteenth century character, and where a long skirt and a corset will provide an actress with an insight into factors inhibiting women in earlier periods when they did not have the freedom of movement taken for granted by modern women wearing jeans.

However, the main factors to bear in mind when choosing a play for a professional or non-professional group are the resources at your disposal, both in terms of personnel and finance, and the theater or space in which the show is to be performed. The main temptation to avoid is developing a repertoire for a company which consists of an unadulterated diet of the same type of play. Never be afraid to try out a new challenge in the type of show you do.

FESTIVALS AND TOURING

PLANNING AND PREPARATIONS

PUBLICITY · COMPETITIONS

Two of theater's oldest traditions are festivals and touring. The classical drama of Ancient Greece originated in religious festivals, while in the Middle Ages strolling players were popular.

Festivals and touring present theater companies with almost identical problems. They both involve taking a show on the road and planning for any number of unknown factors. It is vital to work closely with the local organizers of a festival and to establish immediately who will be doing what. A common cause of disaster is when something which both sides thought the other was doing is not done. This usually arises from the matter never actually having been discussed.

Perhaps the most important aspect of a festival or a visit to an unfamiliar city with a play, is that it is a celebration. In performing a show your company is taking part in the celebration, but it is essential to go also to other shows, to explore the town and to enjoy the parties.

FINANCES AND ACCOMMODATION

Some festivals pay a fee and it is important to find out precisely what sort of fee it is. It could be a straight sum previously agreed, a percentage of box office, or a combination of the two. Having established the type of payment, the next step is to find out when the fee, and any expenses, will be paid and whether or not this will be in cash.

If a fee is paid, the company may be expected to do more than merely perform their show. In addition, festival managements sometimes expect companies to cooperate fully with their publicity effort and to be available for picture or photo calls, press conferences and interviews.

Transportation and accommodation may be part of a fee, and other expenses may also be included. It is important to establish precisely what a fee covers. Accommodation is often organized by the festival and if this is so, make sure that it is near the theater and that late food and drink will be available. Also discover if the company is to stay together or split up. If accommodation is not provided, find out the best places to stay within plenty of time, and, if there is to be a festival club, make sure your company are members.

PREPARATIONS FOR A TOUR OR FESTIVAL

Part of the attraction of touring or taking part in a festival is that, leaving the comfort of their own theater, a company can test their work in a market that does not know them and that has no previous loyalty to them. It is more important than ever, therefore, that the show is seen to its best advantage.

Festivals are often held in summer so that full advantage can be taken of outdoor locations for plays. Staging drama outside brings the festival into the community and so extends the audience, even to include passers-by. Two kinds of traditional drama are particularly suited to open air performance – classical Greek and medieval cycle plays. Individual plays from these periods are usually short so several can be performed to create a program of any length. This medieval play, *Noah*, was performed in a public park (**left**) in York, an ancient English city long associated with medieval drama.

Which production is performed must be very carefully considered with regard to the space or spaces it is to be performed in. Companies should find out as much as possible about the theaters to be used and should 'think the show through' in the new spaces.

When selecting a play to take on the road, consider if it is actually tourable. Big casts, awkward sets, complex musical arrangements and other factors will cause problems. Choose a play and prepare the production so that it is mobile and can be performed in unusual places. It is no fun having to dismantle a set because it will not fit on a stage or into a van for transportation. Similarly, you may find that an audience in a strange theater cannot see all the action of a play because of the way it has been directed and the seating arrangements.

It is best, of course, to visit an unknown theater or hall before performing there, but this is not always possible, and is particularly difficult when planning a tour of several theaters. However, it is possible to find out the details of spaces in advance. Photographs of both the inside and outside of theaters will be extremely useful in conjunction with precise measurements and detailed ground plans of the stage and auditorium plus a complete list of all technical and other facilities. The location is also important so that you know if you are in the middle of town or tucked away in a side street. Find out if there is adequate parking available in the area.

Well in advance, establish an agreement with the festival organizers or theater management to cover all areas of the production. Rehearsal periods, times for erecting the set and storage space available must all be agreed. Companies often have personal items stolen from strange dressing rooms, so make sure the security is adequate and that keys are provided.

Work out precisely the length of time in any day that you are allowed to be in the theater and exactly the extent of the premises which can be used by your company. There may be hidden expenses such as power for lights and heating, so find out about this.

The play or show you have selected may cause problems in certain places. Church halls, schools and even community centers may object to a show containing nudity or bad language. They are less likely to be worried about political content, but it is always worth checking because a mistake in this area may make your performance either unpleasant or curtailed.

No show can take place if a space does not have a license for public performances. It is unlikely that a company would be invited to perform somewhere illegally, but sometimes the organizers will not have checked the regulations carefully so it is best to either remind them of this or do it yourself.

Definitely make a point of establishing good relations with the staff, such as janitors, of any place as soon as you arrive. They can make your life very difficult if you do not.

PUBLICITY

Festivals are by their nature very competitive. Even if it is a festival which pays fees, many companies could be performing at the same time and will be in competition for audiences if not for financial survival. Touring places without regular theaters also involves hard publicity work in order to attract a respectably sized audience for a show. Good publicity is always vital and should not be the last item on a budget or a job given to inexperienced helpers.

At a festival or on tour, it is essential that members of a company are prepared to do far more than perform or undertake their usual tasks. A theater company away from home must be a resourceful unit ready to cope with any unforeseen problems. Publicity will require work from everyone involved.

Advance publicity If someone is able to visit a festival or tour hall in advance they can do a great deal of groundwork for the publicity while getting details of the theater and accommodation. It is most important to find out where your potential audience is likely to come from and then to aim your publicity at them. You will not be in a place long enough to educate a new public for the theater, so stick to those sections of the community with a proven interest in coming to a show. If there is no hard information available on this, take advice from festival organizers or companies which have visited a place before.

When discussing arrangements with festival or-

TOURING AND FESTIVALS TASK PLAN

Advance preparations: Contact the festival office, or the owners of the theaters to be visited on tour, as soon as possible • obtain detailed plans and information about the theater spaces to be visited and performed in, and check this information against the theater checklist • sort out finances taking into account all possible expenses and fees • organize transport for the crew, cast, set and props • work out any possible advance publicity • do a press release and distribute it • organize accommodation for all concerned • find out if rehearsal space will be needed and find it if necessary • if attending a festival, make sure the company has full use of all facilities • check arrangements for ticket sales

On arrival: make sure accommodation is adequate • make sure every item and person required has arrived safely • sort out arrangements for meals • work out publicity including possible street theater, stunts and leafleting • ensure company has access to theater at required times

THEATER
CHECKLIST

Whenever a company performs away from its home base the following details should always be checked at any theater, or other space, to be used: obtain plans, elevations and as many details as possible • ensure that the proposed set can be easily installed and erected • check that any electrical equipment has sufficient power outlets • check the sightlines from the audience area • check that lighting equipment can be erected and masked adequately • check what lighting equipment is available at the theater • make sure all fire, safety, health and any other regulations have been considered and cleared • work out arrangements for the box office, front of house, and refreshments for the audience and cast • ensure that rehearsal space is found if needed • check that there are adequate dressing rooms and make-up areas • find out what access the company has to the theater in advance of a performance and that there is time to set the stage • find out the names of any staff at the theater and establish good relations with them • double check financial arrangements such as rent

ganizers always find out what publicity they will be doing and whether your show is to be part of a program or large poster covering the whole event. You may have to supply information and pictures for this. They may also be organizing a poster specifically for each show and will definitely need material and approval for this. In some cases, individual companies may not be allowed to do their own publicity at all, or alternatively all publicity may be left to them.

Distributing and displaying posters should be organized in the same way as it is done at the company's usual space—using local businesses, stores, schools, libraries and so on. If your theater is in a busy street, find out if you can display publicity material outside, and if so prepare a large banner or poster and perhaps blow-ups of previous good reviews.

Consider advertising in newspapers, especially since smaller local publications offer reasonable rates. But also look into ways of getting free publicity from the media. Most papers publish a list of coming events and local radio stations will mention interesting activities between records, so contact both well in advance.

Getting a mention in a newspaper story is particularly important when touring or visiting a festival. Send out a short, carefully worded press release about two weeks before your appearance so that the local press know you are coming. Try to construct an angle for the press release that can be developed later. You must persuade the news editor that he or she has a potential story and not just a piece of publicity information. It does not matter if the angle has no connection with the show but do make sure

that the story will carry the time and place of the show prominently. Also find out who does theater reviews for local newspapers and make absolutely sure that he or she is in the front row for the performance.

Publicity on the day This is extremely important on a tour or at a festival. All company members should be out distributing posters in cafés, bars and any other likely and visible places. If you can get access to free tickets, they can be used in exchange for displaying a poster or some can be given to local organizations such as hospitals or colleges. Word of mouth is always the best form of publicity, so stimulate interest and discussion about the show in any way possible.

Handing leaflets to passers-by in the street could be illegal, so check on local regulations, but it may be worth risking if it is not strictly against the law, provided it is done in the immediate locality of the theater or hall and without causing any disturbance. If the police do appear, desist immediately and never break the law knowingly.

Street theater may be tolerated in certain places provided it does not cause an obstruction or a disturbance. Never accept money for street performances, because the publicity you will get from it will more than pay for the effort. Stunts are also worth doing on the streets if one can be thought up. Costume walks are great fun on a good day and in a busy street if the show has bright and unusual costumes. Combining a costume walk with some discreet leafleting and music can be extremely effective.

COMPETITIONS

Drama competitions have been a traditional part of dramatic activity in many countries since the Ancient Greeks. The exact format and rules of competitions vary considerably. Before deciding to enter a competition, check on the rules, regulations and eligibility. If the competition is taking place away from your home theater, follow the advice on participating in festivals about checking out the exact space for the performance. If the show is to be adjudicated, make sure that the adjudicator has a good seat, but do not be overzealous in trying to impress. Some competitions may award prizes. Find out in advance about the conventions for prize giving, whether speeches are expected and so on. If performances are simply commented on and graded, it is a good idea to establish whether a general discussion will take place with the judges after the performance. If so, try to have some useful questions prepared.

Open air performances

All the world is a stage provided an audience can be attracted and permission can be obtained to perform in a particular place. Streets and squares, parks and play areas, even fields and beaches, can be used for open air performances. It is essential to stand out and be heard, both to attract audiences and then to entertain them, so try and create a stage above the audience (1). Another good way to stand out is by using bright costumes and easily recognizable theatrical characters. Clowns are of course the most visually appealing, particularly for children (2). An open air performance in Edinburgh (3) during the city's International Festival, has completely transformed this square from its early morning tranquility (4). Bold banners and a lively, colorful band have attracted a large audience.

2

5

Festival publicity Getting noticed is essential at any festival since the limited audience has a wide choice. The famous Edinburgh 'Festival Fringe' attracts many companies and the society office (**5**) becomes a natural focal point for publicity activities. Throwaway posters, such as this simple sketch (**6**) can be handed out. Costume parades and placards are also effective.

6

GLOSSARY

Where terms are used in one country only, this is indicated by the abbreviations: US – United States; UK – United Kingdom; AUST – Australia.

Acting area – The area used by actors during the performance. It may include areas off the normal stage.

Ad lib A departure from the script, in order to cover an unexpected situation or hide a lapse of memory.

Anti-pros (US) Lights hung in front of the proscenium arch. The British equivalent is front-of-house (FOH) lights.

Apron In proscenium theaters, the part of the stage in front of the proscenium. Generally, a stage (or part of a stage) projecting out into the auditorium.

Arena theatre A theatre in which the audience sits on all sides of an acting area.

ASM Assistant stage manager.

Auditorium The audience area.

Auditorium lights See House lights.

Baby spot A small spotlight under 500 watts.

Backcloth, backdrop See Cloth

Backing unit Scenery placed behind a door, window or any opening, to limit the audience's view of the offstage area.

Backstage In proscenium theaters, the area behind the proscenium arch. The term also refers to such areas in non-proscenium theaters and to any part of the stage not in the acting area during a performance.

Bar cob A horizontal flown pipe or wooden bar for hanging scenery or lights.

Barndoor Adjustable device for limiting spill from a light and for shaping the beam.

Batten In general, a flown pipe or wooden bar on which lights or scenery are fastened. Also a length of wood along the top or bottom of a cloth, or used to join flats. In lighting, a horizontal or vertical group of flood lighting equipment hung overhead (UK). *See Border light (US)*

Beam light A light with no lens giving a parallel beam.

Beginners (UK) *See Places please*

Bifocal spot Spotlight with additional shutters to allow hard and soft edges.

Black light Ultra-violet light.

Blackout A total extinguishing of all lights, often at the end of a scene or act.

Board The control board for lights or sound.

Blocking The process of fixing the actors' movements during the performance, and a written description of those movements.

Book *See Promptbook*

Book flat (UK) A hinged flat, known as a 'two-fold' in the United States. To 'book' a flat means to close a book flat.

Boom A vertical lighting pipe.

Border A device for masking the lighting and flying areas from the view of the audience in a proscenium arch theater.

Border lights (US) Lighting battens or lengths of lights normally connected to three or four different circuits which are used for color mixing.

Box set Naturalistic interior set with three walls built from flats.

Brace *See Stage brace*

Brace cleat An attachment on a flat into which a stage brace can be hooked.

Breaking character When actors do or say something which is inconsistent with the character they are portraying.

Bridge A platform or catwalk giving access to lighting equipment, usually crossing the stage or auditorium.

Bring up To increase the intensity of the lights.

Build In lighting, to increase the intensity of the lights; in general, to construct a scene from its different elements.

Bump in/out (Aust) Australian term for get in/out or load in/out.

Call The main meaning of call is the message which informs actors and stage crew of the time left before the curtain. Call also refers to the notice given of rehearsal or other work session. It is also short for curtain call.

Center line An imaginary line from the back to front of the stage. In a proscenium theater, it runs through the exact center of the proscenium arch.

Channel A circuit in the lighting or sound system.

Check To decrease the intensity of a light.

Cinemoid A color medium or filter.

Circuit In lighting a complete route from the electrical supply to the light. If the route includes a dimmer it is normally referred to as a channel.

Clamp C- or G-clamps are normally attached to lights and are used to fasten them to the lighting pipes or battens.

Cleat A device usually made of metal or timber for tying ropes

etc. Cleats are normally found on the backs of flats or in the flys.

Cloth A large piece of scenic canvas which hangs vertically, usually across the stage area. A blackcloth indicates the rear of a scene, while a frontcloth is normally hung well downstage, often hiding a scene change .

Color frame Holder for the color medium or filter in front of a light.

Color medium The translucent filter material placed in front of lights to create a colored illumination. Color mediums can be made of glass or gelatine, but today are usually made from a plastic material such as cinemoid. *See Gel*

Color wheel A wheel attached to the front of a spotlight with openings for different color mediums. It is used for making color changes and can be motor driven or manually operated.

Come down When the show comes down, the performance is over.

Corner plate Triangle of plywood used to reinforce the corners of a flat.

Counterweights Mechanical weights which help to balance flown scenery.

Crash box Box used for creating sound effects.

Crossfade In lighting or sound, a change in which some channels are increased while, at the same time, others are decreased.

Cue A signal which indicates a change during a performance, whether for the actors, stage management, lighting, sound or other areas of activity.

Cue sheet A list showing the cues in correct order as they are to be carried out .

Cue-to-cue A type of technical rehearsal in which lines and action between cues are curtailed in order to work fully through the cues.

Curtain The drapery which hides the stage from the audience, usually in proscenium arch theaters.

Curtain down The end of the show.

Curtain line This is the final line of a scene or act which gives the cue for the curtain to come down. It also refers to the imaginary line across the stage which shows the position of the main curtain when closed.

Curtain up The beginning of the show.

Cut drop A cloth or drop which is cut into or edged to indicate decoration such as leaves or architectural features.

Cutting list In scenery and set construction, the list of wood required, together with the correct dimensions of the pieces.

Cyclorama Also known as a 'cyc', a cyclorama is a plain cloth which closes off the back of the stage. It is hung down to stage level, extending up and out to create an impression of great space.

Dead The marked position (height) of a piece of hung scenery. Also anything that is no longer of use.

Dim To lessen the intensity of the illumination on the stage.

Dimmer Electrical control which governs the amount of electrical current passed to a light, and thus the brightness of the beam emitted.

Dimmerboard Lighting control board.

Dim in To increase the intensity of a light.

Dip (UK) A small trap in the floor of the stage which allows access to electrical sockets.

Discovered at rise Usually refers to actors already on the stage when the curtain goes up.

Dock Also known as the 'scene dock', the storage area for scenery and flats. Ideally the dock should be high enough to accommodate scenery easily and

close to the stage to allow for easy movement of scenery.

Downstage The part of the stage nearest the audience, especially in proscenium arch theaters.

Dress See Dress rehearsal

Dressing See Set dressing

Dress parade Especially in the United States, the final check on the costumes before the first dress rehearsal. The cast parade each of their costumes in order before the director and costume designer, so any final adjustments can be made.

Dress rehearsal Also known simply as the 'dress', the dress rehearsal is the final rehearsal before the first performance. The actors are in costume and technical problems should have been sorted out before at the technical rehearsal.

Drop See Cloth

Dutchman (US) Thin material used to cover the crack between two flats.

Elevation A working drawing, usually drawn accurately and to scale, showing the side view of the set or the lighting arrangement.

Ellipsoidal The type of reflector used in many profile spots. Generally used in the United States to refer to a profile spot.

Exterior A setting depicting an outdoor scene.

False proscenium An inner frame which narrows down the area of the proscenium arch. It can help to hide lights or may be required by the design of the show.

Fit-up (UK) The initial installation in position on the stage of the scenery, lights and other equipment for a production.

Flash out A system to check whether the lights are functioning correctly by putting them on one at a time.

Flat A basic unit of scenery, a wooden frame usually covered with canvas and sometimes with plywood. Flats should be easily portable. They come in single, double and even triple units, and can have openings for doors windows and so on.

Flies The space above the stage in which scenery, lights and so on are hung invisible to the audience.

Floodlights Also called 'floods', lights which give a general, fixed spread of light.

Floorcloth A covering for the floor of the stage usually made from canvas.

Floor plan A scale drawing which shows the exact position of the openings, walls, windows and so on in a stage set.

Floor pocket (US) A small opening in the stage floor which allows access to electrical sockets.

Flown Flown scenery has been hoisted into the flies.

Fly To raise scenery above the level of the stage out of sight of the audience using lines or ropes, often counterweighted.

Fly floor Also called the fly gallery, a high platform which runs along the side of the stage from which the flying lines are operated.

Fly tower In a large theater, a high structure which contains the flies.

Focusing Adjusting a light to give a clear and well defined image. The term is used also to describe the whole process of adjusting and directing the beam of lights prior to the technical rehearsal.

FOH (UK) See Front-of-house

Follow spot A spotlight with a beam which can be directed to follow an actor around the stage.

Footlights A batten of floods mounted on the stage floor, generally obsolescent today, except for special uses.

Forestage In a proscenium theater, the area in front of the main curtain.

Foul To make lights or scenery hung in the flies become entangled.

Fourth wall The imaginary wall

which separates the audience from the stage in a proscenium theater.

French brace A non-adjustable brace attached to a flat. It can be folded flat for storage or to be moved.

Fresnel Type of spot, with a Fresnel lens, which gives an even field of light with soft edges.

Frontcloth, Front drop See Cloth

Frost A filter which diffuses the beam from a light.

Gauze (UK) See Scrim (US)

Gel Term applied to a color filter for a light. Originally made of gelatine, gels are now made of plastic.

Gel frame Holder for the gel in front of the light.

Get-in/out (UK) See Load-in/out (US)

Ghost A beam of light which inadvertently leaks from a light and falls where it is not wanted.

Gobo A device placed in the gate of a profile spot to shape the beam of light. Gobos can be used, for example, to create the effect of dappled woodland light.

Gopher The general dog's body who is sent to 'go for' things for the cast and crew.

Green room Room near the stage where cast and crew can relax.

Grid Arrangement of pipes or battens from which lights can be hung. A stage is also divided into a grid as a basis for lighting design.

Ground plan A drawing of the stage showing the exact position of lights, set and props for a production.

Groundrow In scenery, a piece of scenery which stands on the stage floor, usually showing earth rocks or similar. In lighting, a row of lights on the floor of the stage for lighting the bottom area of a cyclorama or cloth. This is usually masked by a scenic groundrow.

Grouping See Blocking

Half The 'half' is the cue given by the stage management half an hour (in practice 35 minutes) before curtain up.

Hand prop This refers to any prop handled by an actor, especially those, such as a pipe or walking stick, which the actor carries onto the stage.

Hanging Putting the sets of a play in position. *See Fit-up*

House The front and auditorium, rather than the stage and backstage areas, of a theater.

Houselights The lights which illuminate the auditorium for the audience before and after the play, as well as during intervals.

Inset A small scene set inside a larger one.

Interior A setting depicting an indoor scene.

Iris An adjustable circular shutter which can be used to vary the size of the beam in a profile spot.

Kill To kill is to turn off lights or sound effects. It can also mean to remove something from the set, such as a prop.

Ladder A ladder-shaped frame used for hanging side lights. It cannot usually be climbed.

Lamp In strict terms the source of light inside a lighting instrument. It is also used more loosely as an alternative term for the light itself.

Lantern A lighting instrument, particularly used in the United Kingdom.

Lash To bind together. The term refers particularly to joining flats together with a rope or lash line.

Left stage (US) The area on the

left of an actor standing facing the audience in the center stage.

Leg A long narrow strip of fabric, often colored black, used for masking.

Leko (US) Originally a brand name, but now the general term, for an ellipsoidal profile spot.

Levels The intensity or volume at which lights or sound effects are to be operated. The levels are usually expressed on a scale from one to ten. The term also refers to an area, or areas, of the stage raised above the main level of the stage by means of platforms, rostra steps or ramps.

Light A lighting instrument.

Lighting plot The exact description of each lighting change in a play, shown in sequence together with the necessary text or other cues.

Line drawings (US) Technically correct drawings, from which scenery and so on can be built.

Linnebach projector A projector used for projecting a picture from a gel or glass slide onto the set, often used to give a shadow effect.

Load in/out (US) The process of moving all a company's equipment into/out of a theater. This includes scenery, props, lights, costumes and so on. The British terms are get-in/out.

Lose To turn off lighting or sound or to remove an article from the set.

Luminaire A term used internationally for a lighting instrument. Its use is not restricted to special theatrical lighting.

Marking Indicating the position of scenery or props on the stage floor, usually with tape. Use different colors for different scenes to avoid confusion.

Marking out Indicating the outline of scenery, props and furniture on the stage floor during rehearsals. Tape is normally used for this.

Mask To hide, for example, lights or the backstage areas from the

audience. In lighting, a mask placed in front of a lamp can be used to shape the beam.

Masking Fabric, often black, or scenery, used to conceal equipment or backstage areas and to define the performance area.

Memory A memory board is an advanced type of lighting control system where the required levels for each light and each cue are stored electronically.

Mixer Desk for determining the balance, quantity and quality of electronically recorded or processed sound.

Offstage Backstage outside the performance area.

Onstage Inside the performance area.

OP, Opposite prompt In the United States this term, now generally obsolete, refers to stage left, while in Britain the term is normally applied to stage right.

Out front The areas of the theater in front of the curtain or acting area, including the auditorium, box office and so on.

Overture (UK) *See Places please*

PA system The public address or any sound amplification system.

Pan To move a lighting instrument from side to side. It can also refer to the movement of sound by crossfading from one loudspeaker to another.

Patch boarder panel A panel at which the circuits governed by individual lighting dimmers can be changed. Patching can greatly enhance the flexibility and scope of equipment with a limited range. It can also refer to a similar process in sound where leads are changed.

Perch A lighting position just behind the proscenium arch at one side of the stage. Older theaters may have special platforms for these.

Periactus A tall, prism-shaped piece of painted scenery which can be revolved to show various faces.

Pilots Lights which are of a low brightness, often blue, to give light to allow the actors and stage crew to work without actually illuminating the stage.

Pin hinge A hinge which is joined with a removable pin, often used to connect two pieces of scenery.

Pipe (US) Bar or batten from which lights are hung.

Places please Cue usually given by stage manager, and particularly in the United States, to tell the cast to take up their positions immediately before the show.

Platform A portable and often collapsible unit of staging which is used to increase the acting area or add to the levels of the stage.

Plot General term for the list required by each department of the stage crew showing in order the exact requirements for the production and, where appropriate, the cues. Thus there should be a lighting plot, sound plot, props plot and so on.

Practical This term describes something on stage which works or can be used, such as a window in the set which opens, or a desk lamp which actually lights up.

Preset To position props and furniture before they are needed. In lighting and sound, to preset is to set the levels required in advance of a cue.

Preset board A lighting board where one or more lighting changes can be prepared in advance without affecting the lights currently on.

Profile spot A spot with a beam which can be soft or hard. It can also project an outline or profile of a chosen shape.

Projector (US) A type of floodlight.

Prompt book The master copy of the play which includes all actors' moves, technical cues, action, plans and plots required for the production.

Prompter Person who helps actors by giving them the cue they have missed.

Properties, **Props** Any articles,

whether small or large, used on stage in a production which do not form part of the scenery, wardrobe, lighting or sound.

Props box/table Box or table offstage on which the props needed by the cast are kept. The cast should take their props as they are required and return them promptly when no longer needed.

Proscenium theater The proscenium is the wall dividing the auditorium from the stage. In the wall is the proscenium arch, and through this arch, or proscenium opening, the audience watches the play.

PS, Prompt side In the United States, this term, now generally obsolete, usually refers to stage left, while in Britain the term is applied to stage right. It literally means the side from which the stage manager runs the show.

Put together (US) A rehearsal when all the parts of the show are put together in correct sequence.

Pyrotechnics Any bangs, flashes or similar effects required by the production.

Rail Bottom or top batten in the frame of a flat.

Raking This refers to placing the stage, set or the auditorium seating, at an angle to improve sightlines for the audience. A raked stage is higher at the back than the front.

Read through A rehearsal, often the first, at which the whole script is read through.

Reflectors In lighting, the shiny surfaces in the back of the lighting instrument which help intensify the beam and give it direction.

Ring intercom A system of communication between different technical areas.

Risers The vertical part of a step.

Rostrum A platform, normally a collapsible, hinged frame with a removable top, which can be easily transported.

Royalty Fee paid to an author or composer for permission to perform their work.

Run Number of performances of one production.

Run through A rehearsal at which all the elements of the production are put together in their correct sequence.

Saturation rig An arrangement of lights in which the maximum number of spotlights is placed in every possible position.

Scatter The light outside the main beam of a spotlight which is lower in intensity.

Scene dock See Dock

Scrim (US) Finely woven fabric which can be translucent or opaque depending on how it is used.

Segue Originally a musical term for an immediate follow on, now used more generally for any immediate follow on.

Set To set is to get the stage ready for the coming scene by putting everything in its correct position. Also, the set or setting is all the scenery, furniture and props used to create a particular stage picture.

Set dressing The process of putting all settings, props and so on in their correct positions on stage. Also refers to props used to create atmosphere rather than those having a function.

Set of lines Set of ropes hanging from the grid, used for flying scenery.

Set piece A piece of scenery which stands alone.

Set props Props which are set on stage, as opposed to hand props.

Setting line Line normally parallel to the front of the stage, and just upstage of the curtain, from which the positions of the scenery are measured.

Set up To install the set and other requirements of a production.

Shutter In lighting, a device in front of a lamp which can alter or shape the beam of light.

Sightlines Lines indicating the limits of what an audience can see. The sightlines can be drawn on

plans or determined by someone in the auditorium. Side seats and pillars present particular problems for sightlines.

Spiking Marking the position of a set piece on the stage, usually with adhesive tape.

Special A light performing a particular function, such as a fire special or a window special.

Spill Unwanted light which is normally due to a poorly focused or shuttered instrument.

Spotlight A lighting instrument in which the angle and size of the beam can be controlled.

Spot line A line rigged from the grid to fly a piece of scenery.

Stage brace A support for scenery. The standard brace is adjustable and hooks into a cleat or screw eye on the flat. It is then weighted to the floor or secured by a special stage screw. See French brace

Stage call Meeting of cast and director before rehearsal or performance.

Stage directions Directions in the script about actions or arrangements on stage.

Stage screw Large tapering screw used to fix stage braces to the floor.

Stage wait Pause with no dialogue or action on stage, usually caused by a missed line or cue.

Stagger through A more realistic term for run through.

Stile The vertical batten in the frame of a flat.

Strike To clear the stage of scenery, props and so on, or to remove a specific article from the stage.

Strobe A strobe light is produced by a stroboscope which creates the impression of frozen action through a series of short, fast flashes of light. It is a spectacular device which can cause health problems and should be used with care.

Supernumerary, Super An extra or walk-on who says nothing.

Switchboard Board from which the lights are controlled.

Tab Any curtain, especially the front curtain. In the United States the term also refers to leg. See Leg

Talkback A system of two-way communication usually from the stage manager to the other stage crew.

Tallescope Aluminum vertical ladder with an adjustable base on wheels, used for erecting lights, reaching the grid and so on.

Teaser Originally, border of scenery behind the front curtain for masking the flies, now the term refers to any short drop used as masking.

Technical rehearsal, Tech A rehearsal at which all the technical elements are rehearsed and integrated into the production.

Theater-in-the-round A stage in which the audience sit on all sides of the stage.

Three-fold Three flats hinged together.

Throw The distance between the light and object being lit.

Thrust stage Type of stage which projects into the auditorium so the audience can sit on at least two sides.

Tilt The vertical movement of a light, as opposed to pan.

Toggle Crosspiece in a flat frame. Also called a toggle bar.

Top and tail To omit the dialogue between cues during a technical rehearsal. See Cue-to-cue

Tormentor Narrow curtain or flat used to mask the wings, usually at right angles to the proscenium.

Transformation A scene change where one scene appears to transform magically into the next. The effect is often created using gauzes or scrims and special lighting.

Trap A trap door opening into the below stage area which can be used for special effects.

Trim (US) To hang scenery or masking so that the lower edge is parallel to the floor.

187

Truck *See Wagon*

Two-fold Two flats hinged together. *See Book flat*

Upstage The stage area furthest from the audience. To upstage

someone is to move upstage of other actors thus forcing them to turn their backs to the audience.

Wagon A low platform with wheels or casters on which a piece of scenery can be moved.

Walk through A rehearsal in which the cast walk through their movements.

Wardrobe All the costumes and related articles required for a production. Also used for the staff responsible for costumes and where they are kept.

Wardrobe plot List, actor by actor and scene by scene, of

every single dress requirement.

Ways The channels in a lighting system.

Wings The area backstage to either side of the acting area, also curtains which mask these areas.

Working drawings Technical drawing made from the designer's drawings.

USEFUL ADDRESSES

UNITED STATES

Lighting and Control
Altman Stage Lighting Company
8 Guion Street,
Yonkers, NY 10701

American Stage Lighting Company,
1331 C North Avenue,
New Rochelle, NY 10804

A.V.E. Corp. (Projection),
250 West 54th Street,
New York, NY 10019

Berkey Colortran,
1015 Chestnut Street,
Burbank, Calif. 91502

Capitol Stage Lighting Company,
509 West 56th Street
New York, NY 10019

Electro Controls,
2975 South 2nd West Street,
Salt Lake City, Utah 84115

Electronics Diversified,
0625 S.W. Florida Street,
Portland, Oregon 97219

Four Star Stage Lighting,
585 Gerard Avenue,
New York, NY 10451

General Electric Company,
Lamp Department,
Nela Park,
Cleveland, Ohio 44112

R.L. Grosh & Sons,
4114 Sunset Boulevard,
Los Angeles, Calif. 90029

Hub Electric Inc.,
940 Industrial Drive,
Elmhurst, Ill. 60126

Rosco Laboratories (Color Media),
36 Bush Avenue,
Port Chester, NY 10573

Showco,
9011 Governor's Row,
Dallas, Texas 75247

Skirpan Lighting Control Corp.,
61-63 32nd Avenue,
Woodside, NY 11377

Strand Century Inc.,
5432 West 102nd Street,

Los Angeles, Calif. 90045

Strong Electric Corporation,
522 City Park Avenue,
PO Box 1003,
Toledo, Ohio 43601

Vanco Stage Lighting Inc.,
3240 Bronx Avenue,
New York, NY 10467

Hardware and Rigging
Peter Albrecht Corporation,
325 East Chicago Street,
Milwaukee, Wis. 53202

J.R. Clancy,
1010 West Belden Avenue,
Syracuse, NY 13204

Mutual Hardware Corporation,
5-45 49th Avenue,
Long Island City, NY 11101

Sound
Allied Radio,
100 North Western Avenue,
Chicago, Ill. 60612

EMC Corporation,
7000 Santa Monica Boulevard,
Hollywood, Calif. 90038

Showco,
9011 Govornor's Row,
Dallas, Texas 75247

General Theater Suppliers
Gothic Color Inc. (Painting Equipment),
727 Washington Street,
New York, NY 10014

Mole-Richardson Company (Effects),
937 North Sycamore Avenue,
Hollywood. Calif. 90038

Norcosto Inc.,
3203 North Highway 100,
Minneapolis, Minn. 55422

Oleson Company,
1535 Ivar Avenue,
Hollywood,. Calif. 90028

Stagecraft Industries,
1302 Northwest Kearney Street,
Portland, Oregon 97208

Theater Production Services,
59 4th Avenue, New York,
NY 10003

Tobins Lake Studios (Costumes etc.) 2650 Seven Mile Road,
South Lyon, Mich. 48178

Peter Wolf Associates Inc.,
3800 Parry Avenue,
Dallas, Texas 75226

UNITED KINGDOM

Lighting and Control
Berkey Colortran,
PO Box 5, Burrell Way,
Thetford, Norfolk IP24 3RB

CCT Theatre Lighting Ltd,
Windsor House, 26 Willow Lane,
Mitcham, Surrey CR4 4NA

Donmar Sales & Hire
Sales: 22 Shorts Gardens,
London WC2H 9AU
Hire: 39 Earlham Street,
London WC2H 9LD

David Hersey Assoc. Ltd,
15 Between Streets,
Cobham, Surrey KT11 1AA

Lee Filters Ltd (Color Media),
Central Way,
Walworth Industrial Estate,
Andover, Hants SP10 5AN

Rank Strand Electric,
PO Box 70,
Great West Road,
Brentford, Middx. TW8 9HR

Roscolab Ltd (Color Media),
69-71 Upper Ground,
London SE1 9PQ

Thorn Lighting Ltd,
Angel Road Works,
Edmonton, London N18 3AJ

Travelling Light,
177 Rookery Road,
Handsworth, Birmingham
B21 9QZ

Stage Equipment
Donmar Sales & Hire
Sales: 22 Shorts Gardens,
London WC2H 9AU
Hire: 39 Earlham Street,
London WC2H 9LD

Furse Theatre Equipment,
Traffic Street,
Nottingham NG2 1NF

Hall Stage Equipment,
Nona Works, Wynne Road,
Brixton, London SW9 0BE

Robert Luff Theatrical Hire,
36-38 Gautrey Road,
Nunhead, London SE15 2JQ

Northern Light,
134 St Vincent Street,
Glasgow, G2 5JU

Theatre Projects Services Ltd,
10 Long Acre,
London WC2E 9LN

Sound
Bristol Old Vic Tape Hire,
Theatre Royal,
King Street,
Bristol BS1 4ED

Rank Sound,
PO Box 51,
Great West Road,
Brentford, Middx TW8 9HR

Costumes, Props, Make-up
Bapty & Co. Ltd,
703 Harrow Road,
London NW10

Bermans & Nathans,
18 Irving Street, London WC2

Birmingham Repertory Theatre,
Hire Department,
Ozells Street, Birmingham

Brodie & Middleton (Paint etc.),
68 Drury Lane,
London WC2

Charles H. Fox,
25 Shelton Street,
London WC2H 9HX

C. & W. May,
9 Garrick Street,
London WC2

Russell & Chapple Ltd,
23 Monmouth Street,
London WC2H 9DE

S.B. Watts & Co. Ltd,
Princess House, 144 Princess Street,
Manchester M1 7EN

Robert White & Sons,
25 Shelton Street,
London WC2H 9HX

Page numbers in *italics* refer to the illustrations.

ACKNOWLEDGEMENTS

The photographs in this book are reproduced by kind permission of the following (bold numerals indicate page numbers):
2 National Theatre London , photo: Michael Mayhew; **6** Donald Cooper; **8** Citizens Theatre Glasgow, photo: John Vere Brown; **12** 1 Sonia Halliday, 2 Rank Strand, 3 Lincoln Center New York, photo: Ezra Stoller, 4 New Zealand High Commission, 5 Ace McCarron; **14-15** 3,4,5 Rank Strand; **20** 1,2 Nigel Luckhurst, 3 Ace McCarron; **21** 4,5,6 Simon de Courcy-Wheeler; **22-23** 1-12 Adrian Vaux; **26-27** 1,4,5 Donald Cooper, 2,6 Zoë Dominic, 3 George Oliver, 7 Citizens Theatre Glasgow, photo: John Vere Brown; **41** Zoë Dominic; **44** Zoë Dominic; **47** Nigel Luckhurst; **51** Revox; **52** Donald Cooper; **62-63** 1,5 Simon de Courcy-Wheeler, 2,3,4,6 Donald Cooper; **65** left Nigel Luckhurst, right Trevor R. Griffiths; **66** 1,4 Donald Cooper, 2,3 Zoë Dominic, 5 Simon de Courcy-Wheeler; **69** all Trevor R. Griffiths; **70-71** 1 Zoë Dominic, 2,3,4,5,6 Donald Cooper; **72** Citizens Theatre Glasgow, photo: John Vere Brown; **74-75** 1,2,3,6 Wimbledon College of Art, photo: Ronald Brown, 5 Zoë Dominic, 7,8 Royal Shakespeare Theatre Stratford, photo: Holte Photographics; **76** left Robert C. Ragsdale, right Alastair Moffat; **77** 1,4 Wimbledon College of Art, photo: Ronald Brown, 2 Ace McCarron, 3 Nigel Luckhurst; **80-81** 1,4 Angelo Hornak, 2 British Museum, 5 Victoria and Albert Museum, Crown copyright; **82-83** 2,3,4,5,6 Adrian Vaux; **86-87** 1-12 Wimbledon College of Art, photos: Ronald Brown; **88** 1 P. Nuttall, 2 Wimbledon College of Art, photo: Ronald Brown, 3 Donald Cooper; **90-91** 3,4,5,6,7 Donald Cooper; **92** Donald Cooper; **95** Rank Strand; **96** Rank Strand; **97** 2,3 Wimbledon College of Art, photos: Ronald Brown; **98** Rank Strand; **104** 1,4,5 Wimbledon College of Art, photo Ronald Brown; **107** 1 Rank Strand; **108** Wimbledon College of Art, photo: Alan Sherlock; **111** 2 Civica Raccolta della Stante Bertorelli, 4 The Bridgeman Art Library, by permission of the Marquess of Bath, 5,7,8 National Portrait Gallery London, 6 Victoria and Albert Museum, Crown copyright; **115** Albery Theatre, photo: John Haynes; **121** 1-4 Wimbledon College of Art, photos: Alan Sherlock; **122-123** 1-5 Wimbledon College of Art, photos: Alan Sherlock; **124-125** 1,3,4,5 Donald Cooper, 2 Royal Shakespeare Theatre Stratford, photo Holte Photographics, 6 Peter Smith; **126** 1-5 Donald Cooper; **130** below Nigel Luckhurst; **138** 1-7 Kenneth Lintott Collection; **152** center Nigel Luckhurst, below Ace McCarron; **153** 1 Simon de Courcy-Wheeler; **154** top Ace McCarron, center Trevor R. Griffiths; **166** 1-3 Donald Cooper; **170-171** 1 Zoë Dominic, 2,4,5 Donald Cooper, 3 Nigel Luckhurst, 6 National Theatre London; **172** Donald Cooper; **173** Donald Cooper; **178** Moira Clinch; **182-183** 1,2 Homer Sykes, 3,4,5 Alastair Moffat.

Filmset in Great Britain by Tradespools, Frome and Front Page Graphics, London
Colour origination by Hong Kong Graphic Arts, Hong Kong and Rodney Howe, London